Hospitality and Restaurant Marketing

PEARSON

Boston   Columbus   Indianapolis   New York   San Francisco   Upper Saddle River
Amsterdam   Cape Town   Dubai   London   Madrid   Milan   Munich   Paris   Montréal   Toronto
Delhi   Mexico City   São Paulo   Sydney   Hong Kong   Seoul   Singapore   Taipei   Tokyo

Pearson

Editorial Director: Vernon R. Anthony
Executive Acquisitions Editor: Alli Gentile
NRA Product Development: Randall Towns and
Todd Schlender
Senior Managing Editor: JoEllen Gohr
Associate Managing Editor: Alexandrina B. Wolf
Senior Operations Supervisor: Pat Tonneman
Senior Operations Specialist: Deidra Skahill
Cover photo: istockphoto

Cover design: Karen Steinberg, Element LLC
Director of Marketing: David Gesell
Senior Marketing Manager: Thomas Hayward
Marketing Coordinator: Les Roberts
Full-Service Project Management: Barbara Hawk and
Kevin J. Gray, Element LLC
Text and Cover Printer/Binder: LSC Communications
/Harrisonburg
Text Font: Minion Pro, Myriad Pro Semicondensed

Photography Credits

Front matter: i istockphoto/Thinkstock; vii (left) Suhendri Utet/Dreamstime; (right) Meryll/Dreamstime;
viii (top) Mtr/Dreamstime; (bottom) Stratum/Dreamstime; ix (bottom left) Aprescindere/Dreamtsime;
xv (bottom left) Petar Neychev/Dreamstime; 60 shutterstock; 150, 178 Comstock Images/Thinkstock; 19, 45, 73, 95,
149, 173, 233, 259, 294 Nikada/istockphoto

All other photographs owned or acquired by the National Restaurant Association Educational Foundation, NRAEF

11   18

ISBN-10:   0-13-218166-5
ISBN-13: 978-0-13-218166-2

ISBN-10:   0-13-305254-0
ISBN-13: 978-0-13-305254-1

Contents in Brief

Contents

About the National Restaurant Association and the National Restaurant Association Educational Foundation

Founded in 1919, the National Restaurant Association (NRA) is the leading business association for the restaurant and foodservice industry, which comprises 960,000 restaurant and foodservice outlets and a workforce of nearly 13 million employees. We represent the industry in Washington, DC, and advocate on its behalf. We operate the industry's largest trade show (NRA Show, restaurant.org/show); leading food safety training and certification program (ServSafe, servsafe.com); unique career-building high school program (the NRAEF's *ProStart*, prostart.restaurant.org); as well as the *Kids LiveWell* program (restaurant.org/kidslivewell) promoting healthful kids' menu options. For more information, visit www.restaurant.org and find us on Twitter *@WeRRestaurants*, *Facebook*, and *YouTube*.

With the first job experience of one in four U.S. adults occurring in a restaurant or foodservice operation, the industry is uniquely attractive among American industries for entry-level jobs, personal development and growth, employee and manager career paths, and ownership and wealth creation. That is why the National Restaurant Association Educational Foundation (nraef.org), the philanthropic foundation of the NRA, furthers the education of tomorrow's restaurant and foodservice industry professionals and plays a key role in promoting job and career opportunities in the industry by allocating millions of dollars a year toward industry scholarships and educational programs. The NRA works to ensure the most qualified and passionate people enter the industry so that we can better meet the needs of our members and the patrons and clients they serve.

What Is the ManageFirst Program?

The ManageFirst Program is a management training certificate program that exemplifies our commitment to developing materials by the industry, for the industry. The program's

EXAM TOPICS

ManageFirst Core Credential Topics

Hospitality and Restaurant Management
Controlling Foodservice Costs
Hospitality Human Resources Management and Supervision
ServSafe® Food Safety

ManageFirst Foundation Topics

Customer Service
Principles of Food and Beverage Management
Purchasing
Hospitality Accounting
Bar and Beverage Management
Nutrition
Hospitality and Restaurant Marketing
ServSafe Alcohol® Responsible Alcohol Service

most powerful strength is that it is based on a set of competencies defined by the restaurant and foodservice industry as critical for success. The program teaches the skills truly valued by industry professionals.

ManageFirst Program Components

The NRAEF ManageFirst Program includes a set of books, exams, instructor resources, certificates, a new credential, and support activities and services. By participating in the program, you are demonstrating your commitment to becoming a highly qualified professional either preparing to begin or to advance your career in the restaurant, hospitality, and foodservice industry.

These books cover the range of topics listed in the chart above. You will find the essential content for the topic as defined by industry, as well as learning activities, assessments, case studies, suggested field projects, professional profiles, and testimonials. The exam can be adminstered either online or in a paper-and-pencil format (see inside front cover for a listing of ISBNs), and it will be proctored. Upon successfully passing the exam, you will be furnished with a customized certificate by the NRAEF. The certificate is a lasting recognition of your accomplishment and a signal to the industry that you have mastered the competencies covered within the particular topic.

To earn the NRAEF's new credential, you will be required to pass four core exams and one foundation exam (to be chosen from the remaining program topics) and to document your work experience in the restaurant and foodservice industry. Earning the NRAEF credential is a significant accomplishment.

We applaud you as you either begin or advance your career in the restaurant, hospitality, and foodservice industry. Visit www.nraef.org to learn about additional career-building resources offered by the NRAEF, including scholarships for college students enrolled in relevant industry programs.

MANAGEFIRST PROGRAM ORDERING INFORMATION

Review copies or support materials

FACULTY FIELD SERVICES
Tel: 800.526.0485

Domestic orders and inquiries

PEARSON CUSTOMER SERVICE
Tel: 800.922.0579
http://www.pearsonhighered.com/

International orders and inquiries

U.S. EXPORT SALES OFFICE
Pearson Education International Customer Service Group
200 Old Tappan Road
Old Tappan, NJ 07675 USA
Tel: 201.767.5021
Fax: 201.767.5625

For corporate, government, and special sales (consultants, corporations, training centers, VARs, and corporate resellers) orders and inquires

PEARSON CORPORATE SALES
Tel: 317.428.3411
Fax: 317.428.3343
Email: managefirst@prenhall.com

For additional information regarding other Prentice Hall publications, instructor and student support materials, locating your sales representative, and much more, please visit *www.pearsonhighered.com/managefirst.*

Acknowledgements

The National Restaurant Association Educational Foundation is grateful for the significant contributions made to this book by the following individuals.

Mike Amos
Perkins & Marie Callender's Inc.

Steve Belt
Monical's Pizza

Heather Kane Haberer
Carrols Restaurant Group

Erika Hoover
Monical's Pizza Corp.

Jared Kulka
Red Robin Gourmet Burgers

Tony C. Merritt
Carrols Restaurant Group

H. George Neil
Buffalo Wild Wings

Marci Noguiera
Sodexo—Education Division

Ryan Nowicki
Dave & Busters

Pen Ann Lord Prichard
Wake Tech/NC Community College

Michael Santos
Micatrotto Restaurant Group

Heather Thitoff
Cameron Mitchell Restaurants

Features of the ManageFirst Books

We have designed the ManageFirst Books to enhance your ability to learn and retain important information that is critical to this restaurant and foodservice industry function. Here are the key features you will find within this book.

BEGINNING EACH BOOK

Real Manager

This is your opportunity to meet a professional who is curently working in the field associated with the book's topic. This person's story will help you gain instight into the resonsibilities related to his or her position, as well as the training and educational history linked to it. You will also see the daily and cumulative impact this position has on an operation, and receive advice from a person who has successfully met the challenges of being a manager.

BEGINNING EACH CHAPTER

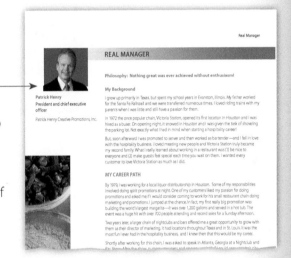

Inside This Chapter

Chapter content is organized under these major headings

Learning Objectives

Learning objectives identify what you should be able to do after completing each chapter. These objectives are linked to the required tasks a manager must be able to perform in relation to the function discussed in the book.

Case Study

Each chapter begins with a brief story about the kind of situations that a manager may encounter in the course of his or her work. The story is followed by one or two questions to prompt student discussions about the topics contained within the chapter.

Key Terms

These terms are important for throrough understanding of the chapter's content. They are highlighted throughout the chapter, where they are explicitly defined or their meaning is made clear within the paragraphs in which they appear.

THROUGHOUT EACH CHAPTER

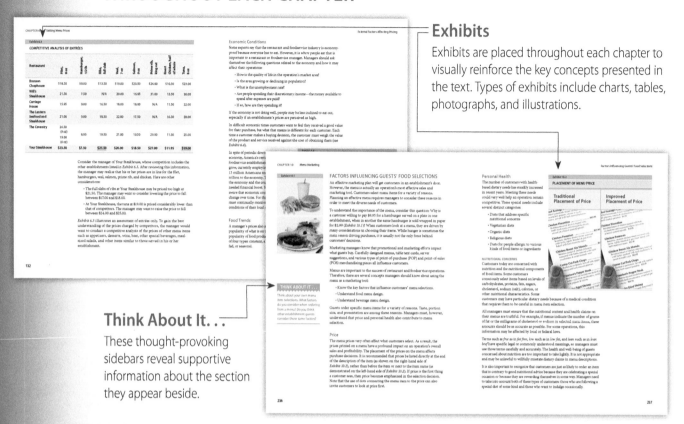

Exhibits

Exhibits are placed throughout each chapter to visually reinforce the key concepts presented in the text. Types of exhibits include charts, tables, photographs, and illustrations.

Think About It. . .

These thought-provoking sidebars reveal supportive information about the section they appear beside.

AT THE END OF EACH CHAPTER

Application Exercises and Review Your Learning

These multiple-choice or open- or close-ended questions or problems are designed to test your knowledge of the concepts presented in the chpater. These questions have been aligned with the objectives and should provide you with an opportunity to practice or apply the content that supports these objectives. If you have difficulty answering the Review Your Learning questions, you should review the content further.

AT THE END OF THE BOOK

Field Project

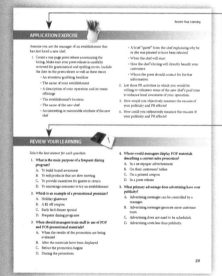

This real-world project gives hou the valuable opportunity to apply many of the concepts you will learn in a competency guide. You will interact ith industry practitioners, enhance your knowledge, and research, apply, analyze, evaluate, and report on your findings. It will provide you with an in-depth "reality check" of the policies and practices of this management function.

Patrick Henry

President and chief executive officer

Patrick Henry Creative Promotions, Inc.

REAL MANAGER

Philosophy: Nothing great was ever achieved without enthusiasm!

My Background

I grew up primarily in Texas, but spent my school years in Evanston, Illinois. My father worked for the Santa Fe Railroad and we were transferred numerous times. I loved riding trains with my parents when I was little and still have a passion for them.

In 1972 the once popular chain, Victoria Station, opened its first location in Houston and I was hired as a buser. On opening night, it snowed in Houston and I was given the task of shoveling the parking lot. Not exactly what I had in mind when starting a hospitality career!

But, soon afterward I was promoted to server and then worked as bartender—and I fell in love with the hospitality business. I loved meeting new people and Victoria Station truly became my second family. What I really learned about working in a restaurant was (1) be nice to everyone and (2) make guests feel special each time you wait on them. I wanted every customer to love Victoria Station as much as I did.

MY CAREER PATH

By 1979, I was working for a local liquor distributorship in Houston. Some of my responsibilities involved doing spirit promotions at night. One of my customers liked my passion for doing promotions and asked me if I would consider coming to work for his small restaurant chain doing marketing and promotions. I jumped at the chance. In fact, my first really big promotion was building the world's largest margarita—it was over 1,200 gallons and served in a hot tub. The event was a huge hit with over 700 people attending and record sales for a Sunday afternoon.

Two years later, a larger chain of nightclubs and bars offered me a great opportunity to grow with them as their director of marketing. It had locations throughout Texas and in St. Louis. It was the most fun I ever had in the hospitality business, and I knew then that this would be my career.

Shortly after working for this chain, I was asked to speak in Atlanta, Georgia at a Nightclub and Bar Show. After the show, numerous owners and operators asked if I could come to their city

and help them. That's when I decided I would start my own company. My first thought was to publish a monthly newsletter of promotional ideas and charge $295 a year for 11 issues. I thought that if an owner or operator got just two or three ideas from the newsletter each year, that would easily pay for the subscription. It was a challenge the first three years because I had only about 60 subscribers, but encouragement came from the numerous calls I received asking me to visit clients' locations to either speak to the staff or brainstorm with their team.

Before I knew it, I was being hired to work on promotions for various bars, clubs, and restaurants. I was working out of my house with only a couple of part-time people helping me. The business just kept growing because so many people were looking for promotional ideas to increase sales.

Today, Patrick Henry Creative Promotions, Inc. is a full-service food and beverage agency, specializing in beverage training, drink development, menu design, and the creation of revenue-generating promotional programming for national hotels, restaurants, and bars.

The company has created award-winning food and beverage programs for Interstate Hotels & Resorts, Hard Rock International, Ruby Tuesday, Hilton Hotels, Consolidated Restaurant Operations, Inc., Sherlock's Baker St. Pub & Grill, McCormick & Schmick's Seafood Restaurants, and Loews Hotels. Additional clients include TGI Friday's, BJ's, The Palm Restaurants, Columbia Sussex Corporation, Buffalo Wild Wings, Fleming's Prime Steakhouse & Wine Bar, The Cheesecake Factory, Smokey Bones Bar & Fire Grill, Quaker Steak & Lube, Omni Hotels & Resorts, and Auguste Escoffier School of Culinary Arts.

In addition, our company has been ranked as one of the "Best Companies to Work for in Texas" for six consecutive years by *Texas Monthly* magazine. We've also won numerous design awards, such as Summit Creative, ADDY, and Davey International.

Something I always think about: Giving back! Some of my proudest accomplishments have been in giving back to the community. Over the years, I have received the Enterprise Champion Award as a small business leader by the *Houston Business Journal*; **a Public Service Award for my involvement with the city of Houston's campaign to end domestic violence; and the "Every Day Hero" title by the Greater Houston Area Chapter of the American Red Cross for my community involvement.**

WHAT DOES THE FUTURE HOLD?

The future of our business is bright, and I expect that you'll see major expansion in the hotel and restaurant segment of our industry. I also predict that the beverage business will explode over the next 10 years. Finally, I believe that the food industry will become stronger and more competitive, with fresh new ideas and concepts, such as Mexican and burger.

MY ADVICE TO YOU

For students who are interested in working in the hospitality business, I suggest working in a hotel or restaurant to see exactly what happens on a daily basis. Try to learn every aspect of every department in the hospitality industry. Visit new concepts. Subscribe to hospitality publications, such as *Nation's Restaurant News.*

Be a good listener and be good to people both on the way up and on the way down. The success of our company is due to the fact that we care about our clients and we always make our decisions based on what is in their best interest. If you are respectful and good to people, you will be successful.

Remember: Without a doubt, I have been told over and over through the years that it is all about service and taking care of the customer. It all starts with service. Of course, food plays an important part, but it will always come down to service.

1

Introduction to Hospitality and Restaurant Marketing

INSIDE THIS CHAPTER

- Understanding the Marketing Function
- The Marketing Plan
- Marketing Plan Development and Implementation
- Evaluating Marketing Results

CHAPTER LEARNING OBJECTIVES

After completing this chapter, you should be able to:

- Explain why effective marketing is essential for success in the restaurant and foodservice business.

- Identify the characteristics of an effective marketing plan.

- Describe the major areas addressed in a marketing plan.

- State how managers assess the impact of a properly implemented marketing plan.

KEY TERMS

CASE STUDY

"I know our food will be great," said Jack. "And our service will be outstanding!"

"I really like the menu you put together for our new place," said Jana. "I'm very excited!"

Jack and Jana were talking about the soon-to-be-opened Mainsail Restaurant. The business was to open in the bay area shopping district. The bay is a bustling, popular place for shopping, business, strolling, and dining out. The view draws tourists and locals alike to the lovely waterfront. There, well-established restaurants with popular menus feature local seafood, area farm-raised beef, and organic chicken along with creative meatless options.

Jana was the owner of the Mainsail and she had hired Jack to be the new establishment's manager.

The menu that Jack and the establishment's chef Lisa developed for the new operation featured fresh seafood, grilled steaks and chicken, and a variety of creative pasta dishes.

"Jack, I know your staff will do a great job. But how can we make sure our future customers know about us? And that they stop in and give us a try the next time they decide to eat out in the bay?" asked Jana.

1. How can Jack and Jana best ensure their potential customers know about the Mainsail Restaurant's opening and what it will offer its guests?

2. What will likely happen if Jack and Jana are not able to quickly attract enough customers to make the Mainsail profitable?

Exhibit 1.1

UNDERSTANDING THE MARKETING FUNCTION

All restaurants and foodservice operations should be based on the foundation of excellent customer service. Without customers, the entire industry would not be successful. Managers in the restaurant and foodservice industry must be able to determine who their customers are, what their needs are, and what they can offer that the customers will value enough to buy (*Exhibit 1.1*). Then, when customers' preferences change, managers must detect the changes, interpret correctly how they could affect their operation, and form a plan to adjust to these changes. Having an understanding of marketing and its function in business is an important step in doing this.

In the restaurant and foodservice business, **marketing** is the formal process of telling and showing potential customers how their needs and wants will be met by a specific operation. Some managers confuse the concepts of marketing and selling. Marketing focuses on the needs and wants of customers. Selling is primarily an activity designed to convince others to pay for an operation's food, beverages, or services and thus increase the establishment's **revenue**, the sales achieved by an operation in a specified time period. Simply stated, marketing is customer-focused; selling is revenue-focused. The good news for restaurant and foodservice managers is that meeting the needs and wants of their customers will always result in many more opportunities to sell to those customers.

Selling products to customers is actually the end of a very long marketing process that begins with these types of marketing-related questions:

- Who are the operation's likely customers?
- What do those customers most want to buy?
- What will the operation sell?
- Where will the operation sell it?
- When will the operation sell it?
- How will the operation sell it?
- How much will the operation charge for it?
- How will the operation let its likely customers know about it?

Marketing professionals know that answering critical questions such as these are important actions that must be taken long before an operation actually begins to sell its food.

Skill in marketing starts with identifying what potential customers need and want. The establishment's **target market** is simply those potential customers whose specific needs and wants the organization will seek to meet.

It is important to recognize that not all guests want the same things from their dining experiences. Consider, for example, the needs of the following customers.

- A couple going out for a romantic dinner to celebrate their anniversary
- A worker stopping with coworkers for a one-hour lunch break
- A mother buying carryout pizza to feed her family at home
- A family with small children traveling by car on a cross-country vacation
- A patient in a hospital
- A college student living in a residence hall and eating all of his or her meals in the university dining hall
- Five friends having dinner and drinks while watching the "big" game on a sports bar's large screen TV

In each of these cases, the needs and wants of these customers likely will be very different.

One key function of the marketing process is the thoughtful targeting of customers. Doing this keeps these customers' very specific needs uppermost in a manager's plans.

There are many aspects to marketing. In fact, the area of marketing is so important that many large restaurants and foodservice companies employ professionals whose only job is the effective marketing of their businesses. For professional managers, marketing is one of many tasks that must be successfully mastered. This book was written to help managers do just that. The following topics are addressed in upcoming chapters:

- How the marketing process is applied in the restaurant and foodservice industry (chapter 2)
- How to understand the forces that impact the business environment in which managers work (chapter 3)
- How to identify customers' buying behaviors (chapter 4)
- How to prepare a marketing plan (chapter 5)
- How to set prices (chapter 6)
- How to use both traditional and nontraditional channels when marketing an operation (chapter 7)
- How advertising and sales are used in marketing (chapter 8)
- How promotions, publicity, and public relations are used in marketing (chapter 9)
- How to use a menu as a marketing tool (chapter 10)
- How to evaluate the marketing efforts of the establishment (chapter 11)

Manager's Memo

The best restaurant and foodservice managers know that putting guests' needs first makes it easier to sell to them. That's because when customers' needs are met, those customers are happy to buy.

Managers who continually assess how their actions will affect their customers are known to be "customer-centric" or "customer-focused." That is, they continually monitor their customers and focus their thoughts on their customers' needs when making decisions. It is important to recognize that nearly every decision made by managers has an effect on customers.

Decisions about what should be served on the menu, what food will be purchased to make the menu items, how the items are to be cooked and served, and even who is hired to cook and serve the items are all important ones that affect customers directly.

THINK ABOUT IT . . .

Consider the last time you went to a new establishment. How did you hear about it? What made you decide to give it a try?

The Manager's Role in Marketing

Many business experts believe that the primary role of any manager is to attract and keep customers. If too few customers are attracted, most businesses will not achieve the revenue levels they need to stay in business. When considered in this way, it is easy to see that restaurant and foodservice managers must always play a big part in the marketing efforts of their operations.

To be effective at marketing, managers must recognize that the menu items will have features and benefits for customers. In the restaurant and foodservice business, **features** are the characteristics of the actual menu items and services sold to guests. **Benefits** are the advantages or favorable results obtained from purchasing the feature.

To better understand the difference between features and benefits, consider a salesperson who sells cell phones. To be effective, he or she must understand that potential customers do not really want to buy a phone as much as they want to buy the benefits that come from being able to communicate easily. A feature is what the cellular business offers for sale, such as the cell phone itself. The benefits are what the customers gain, such as the ability to make calls, receive emails, surf the Net, and tweet!

Similarly, consider the traveling family who has almost reached their exciting beach vacation destination. This family stops at a highway interchange and buys lunch at an establishment offering drive-through window service. This family is certainly buying food and drinks (features). Just as important, however, they are purchasing convenience, speed-of-service, and the ability to quickly continue on their way to their vacation destination. These are benefits (what the customers actually get when they buy features) that are likely of great importance to this family.

Specific operations appeal to specific target markets. An important role of owners and managers, then, is to carefully identify the target markets of their establishment and to clearly and consistently communicate the features and the benefits to the identified target markets.

One of the best methods for understanding a target market is to develop a guest profile. A **guest profile** is a marketing tool that helps managers focus on the specific characteristics of guests they hope to attract to their operations. Guest profiles include detailed information about members of a target market. This includes demographic information about customers that allows them to be targets of a marketing message. **Demographic** information includes customers' age, gender, race, geographic location, or other personal characteristics.

Manager's Memo

In many cases, a restaurant or foodservice operation will be owned and managed by the same person. In other cases, owners hire professional managers who will run their operations for them. Regardless of the arrangement, it is essential that owners and managers work together to ensure the success of their operations.

Owners know the financial goals they have set for their businesses. Managers know how to satisfy guests. When owners and managers work closely together, financial goals are met and guests are pleased. That helps the business grow and ensures the long-term success of the operation.

Managers of different restaurant and foodservice establishments serve different target markets and often serve them differently. However, it is important to note that all customers share the same expectations:

- To be served safe food and beverages
- To be served in a clean environment
- To be served professionally
- To be treated with respect
- To receive good value for the money they spend

Value is the difference between what customers get when they buy a product or service and what they pay to get it. All customers desire good value. But good value is *not* the same as low price. In fact, when products or services are sold at prices so low it is not possible to deliver good quality, it is usually not possible to deliver good value.

For restaurant and foodservice managers, effective marketing means ensuring that good value is consistently delivered to existing guests and communicating that fact to their potential guests.

THE MARKETING PLAN

A **marketing plan** is a detailed listing of specific activities designed to reach the revenue goals of an operation. A marketing plan is like a road map for an operation's marketing efforts. It tells what and when marketing activities will be used to achieve revenue goals.

Developing a marketing plan is a formal process that involves answering the following questions:

- What marketing activity should be undertaken?
- Who will do it?
- When will it be done?
- How much money will be needed to implement the plan?
- How will the results of the plan be measured?

When managers plan, they want to affect the future. When creating a marketing plan, managers want to influence the way their current and future customers feel about their operations, how often customers will come to their operations, and what these guests will buy when they visit.

THINK ABOUT IT . . .

Consider a good establishment that does a poor job of marketing its value to customers.

Who is most responsible for making sure enough new and repeat customers will come to that establishment in the future?

A variety of approaches can be used to develop a marketing plan, and these will be addressed in chapter 5, but all effective marketing plans should include the following five features:

- Documentation
- Target goals
- Timeliness
- Marketing plan cost estimates
- Customer-focused goals

Documentation

It is important to recognize that a marketing plan should be a formal, written document. It simply is not possible for restaurant and foodservice managers and owners to do a good job planning what should be done, when it should be done, and who should do it without carefully recording the decisions made in response to these important questions.

Restaurant and foodservice managers and owners are very busy. They have to attend to many details. Unless marketing plans are committed to paper, and reviewed regularly, it would be easy for a manager to forget when an important marketing activity should be done, or even who should do it.

Target Goals

It is also important to understand that a marketing plan may have several parts, each of which addresses a strategic business segment. A strategic business segment is a specific revenue-generating source.

For example, an establishment that contains a dining room, a banquet room, and a lounge may consider each of those three areas to be a unique strategic business segment. Then special marketing activities may be undertaken to promote the banquet room only. Similarly, special marketing activities may be targeted at the establishment's lounge or dining-room customers.

One important job of restaurant and foodservice managers is to know their operations' individual strategic business segments and whether those segments can benefit from specific and targeted marketing activities. If they can, then the marketing plan should directly address those specific activities.

Timeliness

An effective marketing plan addresses a specific time period, such as a year or a month. If managers are to carefully monitor what activities should be undertaken, and when they are best done, it is essential that specific time periods for completion are identified. In some cases, the time period identified for completing an activity will be critically important to its effectiveness.

For example, assume an establishment has a large private banquet room in addition to its regular dining area (*Exhibit 1.2*). The establishment is located in a city with many large businesses that sponsor holiday-related social events in December. The manager wants to maximize banquet room revenue during this time by offering a special "Holiday Party" menu targeting area companies and offering packages that include drinks, appetizers, dinner, and dessert at one set price per person served.

Clearly, early December is too late to begin marketing these holiday parties. By that time, most corporate planners will have already made party arrangements. In this example, midsummer or early fall would likely be the best time to contact potential customers about booking the banquet room for holiday events.

Exhibit 1.2

Marketing Plan Cost Estimates

Any dollars committed to marketing activities are dollars that cannot be spent on other operational needs such as equipment, supplies, or staff. For that reason it is essential that the estimated costs of undertaking each marketing activity be thoroughly considered.

Some forms of marketing may be expensive, while others are not. In all cases, however, the costs of undertaking a marketing activity must be well known to restaurant and foodservice managers before they are undertaken. In some instances the costs of a specific marketing activity will not be known. Then it is important to secure a cost estimate before undertaking the activity.

To illustrate, assume a manager decides that it would be good to place an advertisement in a local magazine that is widely read by the establishment's target market. In this case it will be important for the manager to know the cost of placing an ad in the magazine prior to including that activity in a marketing plan.

The size of an establishment's marketing budget will often vary based on the revenue it currently achieves, its revenue goals, and a variety of other factors. In all cases, however, the costs of the individual activities to be included in the marketing plan must be known in advance if the manager is to stay within the operation's established marketing budget.

Customer-Focused Goals

Recall that marketing is a means of communicating with customers. For that reason it is essential that an establishment's customers are continually kept foremost in the mind of a marketing manager. The best managers know that each marketing activity undertaken should be chosen carefully and only after considering a number of factors:

- What message is to be communicated?
- How can the message best be sent?
- What is the customers' desired response?
- How can customer responses be evaluated?

Formal marketing plans help restaurant and foodservice operations in many ways. Despite that, some managers and owners fail to create effective marketing plans. Here are some of the reasons usually given:

- **Lack of time:** Some managers maintain they are simply too busy to take the time to plan their marketing activities.
- **Lack of budget:** Some managers feel their marketing budgets are too small to require the organized planning of their marketing activities.
- **Inability to measure effectiveness:** Some managers feel there is no way to measure the effectiveness of their marketing activities, so creating a formal marketing plan is a waste of time.
- **Lack of knowledge:** Some managers do not feel comfortable making the decisions needed to create an effective marketing plan.

Of course, if managers are to achieve their revenue goals, effective marketing is a must. Managers and owners who cannot *find* the time to plan simply must *make* the time. Similarly, a small marketing budget or even the challenges of assessing the effectiveness of marketing activities are poor reasons for neglecting the planning process. In fact, a small marketing budget makes the effective use of it even more critical.

Only the lack of knowledge is a good reason not to plan. This book seeks to inform managers about what they need to know about marketing, market planning, and how to evaluate the effectiveness of their own marketing efforts.

One of the first things managers should know about marketing activities is that they can be classified as either strategic or tactical. **Strategic marketing activities** are those that address an operation's basic business objectives. They tell managers what must be done. For example, which customers should the operation seek to attract? Which products should be sold? Which services should be offered? Answering these questions helps determine what the business is now and what it will be in the future.

Tactical marketing activities focus on how things are done. For example, if a specific target market has been strategically identified, the particular ways the business will seek to attract these guests are tactical decisions. Similarly, after the products to be sold have been determined (a strategic decision), the ways the products will be sold are tactical decisions.

MARKETING PLAN DEVELOPMENT AND IMPLEMENTATION

Chapter 5 of this book addresses how managers use their overall business plans as a guide to develop formal marketing plans. Development of a formal marketing plan requires managers to establish their marketing budgets based on forecasts of revenue, assign individuals to specific marketing tasks, identify targeted completion dates, and finally, assess the results of their marketing efforts.

The marketing plan is valuable not only because of the marketing-related decisions it records, but also because of the information the manager collects and the knowledge he or she acquires during the development process. That is, the exercise of preparing the plan is valuable in helping managers understand how their establishments operate in their marketplaces.

Preparing a marketing plan requires careful consideration of a variety of factors:

- Type of operation
- Market area
- Target markets
- Market trends
- Competition
- Marketing objectives

Type of Operation

Identifying whether an establishment is a destination restaurant or convenience restaurant is one way to describe the type of operation. For example, if the establishment is classified as a **convenience restaurant** it means that a customer usually eats at the facility because it is very easy for him or her to do so (*Exhibit 1.3*). An example of this would be restaurants at shopping malls. The customers' primary objective in going to malls is to shop, not to eat. However, if there is a restaurant close by, it will no doubt attract hungry shoppers. Convenience restaurant customers are usually concerned with convenience and speed of service.

Exhibit 1.3

The alternative to a convenience restaurant is a **destination restaurant**; one in which the visit is the primary reason to go there. Customers who are looking for a destination restaurant generally have higher expectations and will typically be willing to pay more if those expectations are met.

There are advantages to both convenience restaurants and destination restaurants. Each type helps its managers determine what their establishment is meant to be, the type of customers it will attract, and even the type of menu items it offers.

Market Area

Development of a formal marketing plan helps managers identify the geographic area their operations serve and the areas from which it attracts customers. The people in this geographic area may reside in the area, work in the area, be visiting the area, or be passing through it.

A formal marketing plan helps managers better understand existing and potential markets. Some factors to consider include the number of existing customers, why those customers are in the market area, a description of returning customers, and a description of new customers the establishment seeks to attract.

A market area's potential size can be estimated by studying the geography and the population of the areas surrounding an operation. Knowing about a market area's potential size can help managers establish realistic and measurable goals for the number of new and returning customers that can be served.

Target Markets

Recall that an establishment may serve more than one target market. Also, an operation may have different target markets for different meal periods. For example, an establishment might target commuters for breakfast, workers in local businesses for lunch, and families for dinner. Understanding which guest profile accurately describes the target market is one of its manager's most essential tasks.

Market Trends

It is important to assess trends in targeted markets. Market trends are long-term increases or decreases in some factor outside an establishment; for example, an increase or decrease in the following:

- Population
- The economy
- Competition
- Popularity of food items
- Popularity of beverage items
- Frequency with which customers dine out

Restaurant and foodservice managers should assess the impact of any market trend that can affect their establishments in the future. They can best do that by keeping up with current events and staying involved in their local communities.

It is also important to carefully distinguish a trend from a fad. A fad is a short-term increase, sometimes quite large, in the popularity of some product or service. In contrast, a trend is a long-term change.

Competition

Historically, competition was considered only to be other establishments offering similar menu items. Today, though, competition is everywhere. Realistically, competition occurs anytime a potential customer spends money on food at any place other than the specific establishment.

Exhibit 1.4

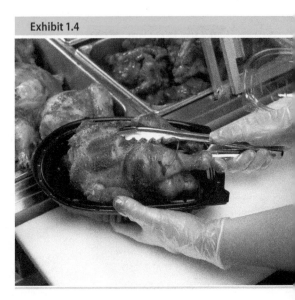

Other forms of competition now include grocery stores, gas stations, convenience stores, and other businesses in an area that provide convenience food such as pre-made salads, rotisserie chicken, and ready-to-serve desserts (*Exhibit 1.4*).

An operation's competitive advantage is something that makes the establishment different from and superior to its competition. Examples of competitive advantages include a convenient location, specialty food, personalized service, takeout service, delivery service, ambience, and entertainment.

Marketing Objectives

Identifiable objectives contained in a marketing plan may include the number of customers the operation seeks to attract, its total revenue goals, and measures of the average amount spent by guests during each visit.

Marketing objectives should be put in writing because written objectives enable managers to focus their energies on specific areas of their business. The marketing objectives should be reasonable (though not easy), measurable, and have a time frame established for achieving them. For example, a revenue-related marketing objective might be increasing breakfast sales by 10 percent in six months. Note that the objective is specific (*breakfast sales*), measurable (*a 10 percent increase*), and has an established time frame for completion (*six months*).

In summary, a formal marketing plan defines the operation, specifies its goals and objectives, and explains the business to others. A formal marketing plan can help managers do several things:

- Chart a path for the operation.
- Guide the operation to achieve its goals.
- Use resources wisely so they help managers reach their goals.
- Anticipate possible problems and roadblocks like changes in weather, increases or decreases in customer counts, and changes in customer preferences that affect sales.
- Plan ways to handle the problems and roadblocks.
- Prepare the operation for success.

RESTAURANT TECHNOLOGY

Advances in technology give tech-savvy restaurant and foodservice managers more choices than ever in communicating with guests.

By using instant message systems such as Twitter, managers can, in a matter of seconds, send marketing messages to extremely large numbers of their guests! The message may be that a last-minute special has been added to the day's menu, a wine is being offered at a special price, or any other information the manager feels may be of interest to guests.

MANAGER'S MATH

Assume that an establishment achieved $1,750 of revenue on Tuesday night when 150 guests were served.

What was the check average on Tuesday night?

(Answer: $11.67)

It is not a good idea for managers to try to keep the marketing plan "in their heads." That's because it is too easy for a mental plan to shift as the situation and feelings change. A written document, on the other hand, has several advantages:

- It does not change unless the manager wants it to.
- It does not change as a result of "forgetting" an important marketing task or deadline.
- It can be shown to others to gain their support and involvement.
- It can be referenced by others if need be.
- It makes managers accountable for executing it.
- It can be a solid basis for a follow-up evaluation of the operation.

An effective marketing plan should not merely sit on a shelf and collect dust. It should be implemented, shared, reviewed, and updated as situations change in a manager's operation.

If a manager has a plan, that manager is more likely to be successful. This is because he or she has already looked at all the elements of the operation, and has already thought through how to do things and when to do them. With a formal marketing plan, managers prepare their operations for success!

EVALUATING MARKETING RESULTS

Chapter 11 details the specific techniques managers use to evaluate the effectiveness of the marketing plans they implement. One way to think about assessing marketing plans is to evaluate the impact of its external and internal marketing activities. **External marketing activities** are those that involve sending messages to guests outside a restaurant or foodservice operation. Examples include radio and TV advertising. The goal of external marketing activities is to encourage more customers to come to an establishment.

Internal marketing activities are those designed to send messages to guests who are already physically present in an establishment. Examples include the use of the operation's servers to sell specialty items such as desserts and after-dinner drinks, as well as on-site signage designed to increase an operation's check average.

Check average is the average amount spent by each guest visiting an operation. The calculation for check average is as follows:

Total revenue ÷ Number of guests served = Check average

Managers interested in assessing external and internal marketing activities carefully measure any changes in the total number of customers served and the amount each served guest spends during a visit.

Customer-focused managers know, however, that a complete assessment of their marketing activities must include more than simply the number of served guests and revenue achieved. Rather, a full assessment of the marketing effort means carefully considering guests' overall dining experiences. To do so, managers can design and monitor several guest feedback systems. These can include surveys, comment cards, or simply a walk through the dining area and a conversation with guests to learn about their dining experience.

Regardless of the system used, it is important that managers evaluate their service levels as well as their customers' views about product quality. In most cases, operations seek to provide guests outstanding products *and* outstanding service. As a result, measuring overall marketing effectiveness means measuring the ability of the restaurant or foodservice establishment to do just that.

Once a marketing evaluation is completed, it is important to use the information obtained to identify how to improve the success of both the plan and the business. If, for example, an establishment falls short of an external or internal marketing goal, managers need to determine the cause and what needs to be done to correct the problem.

A marketing plan is a critical tool to determine exactly how to attract, please, and retain customers and achieve target profits. At the end of every marketing plan or section, the manager evaluates how well the team did so he or she can benefit from the mistakes and successes. The manager then can determine what he or she can do to better meet the operation's goals.

The remaining chapters of this book address the ways managers effectively market their businesses. Throughout the book, remember that a good marketing plan does the following:

- Makes the needs of targeted guests its primary focus
- Tells how an operation's products and services provide benefits that meet guest needs
- Includes measurable goals
- Can be implemented effectively
- Is cost-effective
- Can be evaluated after implementation
- Is continually improved

Establishing marketing goals and standards is essential for maintaining or increasing the profitability of operations. Evaluating activities included in the formal marketing plan to see which worked well and which did not will help the operation become more profitable.

Proper marketing plan evaluation minimizes future marketing mistakes. But, just as important, understanding marketing successes enables an operation to continually direct marketing resources toward the areas that will make the operation popular and financially successful.

SUMMARY

1. **Explain why effective marketing is essential for success in the restaurant and foodservice business.**

   Successful restaurant and foodservice operations must attract and retain enough customers to ensure they will stay in business. Operations can continue in business only if they consistently meet the needs of those customers. Marketing is the process that restaurant and foodservice operations use to communicate to their customers that their needs will be met each and every time they choose to visit. If the marketing of an operation is ineffective, too few customers will be attracted and too few will come back again. An effective marketing program communicates to customers that quality products and excellent service are to be expected and will be consistently delivered.

2. **Identify the characteristics of an effective marketing plan.**

   The best marketing plans are written and are targeted. They identify specific actions to be taken. The plans are time-sensitive, so activities are undertaken according to a set schedule. They include what is to be done and who should do it. Because marketing dollars are limited, cost estimates for each activity should be included in the plan. Finally, an effective plan is always shaped by management's view of how it will be seen from the point of view of the operation's guests.

3. **Describe the major areas addressed in a marketing plan.**

   A well-developed marketing plan requires managers to address a variety of important areas related to a business. These include the type of operation and the market area in which it operates. Additional areas addressed include an operation's target market and any buying changes or trends occurring within the target markets. Because the competitive environment in which a business operates is important, marketing plans address those businesses that are considered direct competitors. Finally, a well-developed marketing plan summarizes and addresses the marketing objectives established for a business. An effective marketing plan should be used extensively. Prior to implementation, it should be shared with those directly affected. Also, it should be modified as needed if the market environment changes in ways that directly affect the plan.

4. **State how managers assess the impact of a properly implemented marketing plan.**

   After a marketing plan has been successfully implemented, the effectiveness of its external and internal activities is evaluated by their ability to meet the plan's measurable objectives. These should include the operation's financial objectives and its guest service-related goals. If the goals have been met, the plan was successful. If the goals were not met, changes to the plan must be undertaken to improve its chance of future success.

APPLICATION EXERCISE

Lynn manages the employee cafeteria at Memorial Hospital. Each day she records her daily revenue and the number of customers she serves. Help Lynn calculate the check average she achieved each weekday last week by completing the following chart.

Weekday	Revenue	Number of Guests Served	Check Average
Monday	$1,500	175	
Tuesday	1,750	215	
Wednesday	1,250	160	
Thursday	1,200	200	
Friday	1,800	250	
Total			

1. What is Lynn's total revenue for the five days?
2. How many total guests did Lynn serve in the five days?
3. What is Lynn's check average for the five days?
4. What might be the impact of an effective marketing plan on the following:
   • The number of guests served
   • The amount each guest spends per visit

REVIEW YOUR LEARNING

Select the best answer for each question.

1. **What is the primary function of marketing?**
   A. Explaining and showing how a business meets its customers' needs
   B. Selling products and services at their maximum prices
   C. Advertising what a business has available for sale
   D. Selling new products to customers

2. **What marketing strategy would provide the most value to customers?**
   A. Quality products at very high prices
   B. Low-quality products at the lowest possible price
   C. Quality products at prices customers feel are fair
   D. Low-quality products at the highest possible prices

3. **What would tell managers the most about their targeted customers?**
   A. Services their competitors offer similar customers
   B. Features of all the products they sell
   C. Customers' guest profiles
   D. Type of customer comments posted online

4. **What is the purpose of segmenting guests by their demographic characteristics?**
   A. Increasing the number of features offered to guests
   B. Ensuring an operation appeals to every possible customer
   C. Allowing marketing messages to be highly targeted
   D. Decreasing costly features offered to guests

5. **What is an example of a customer demographic?**
   A. Weight
   B. Height
   C. Eye color
   D. Age

6. **What is the main purpose of external marketing activities?**
   A. Reduce marketing costs
   B. Increase the number of guests served
   C. Reduce the costs of providing guest features
   D. Increase an operation's overall check average

7. **What is the main purpose of internal marketing activities?**
   A. Expand a target market
   B. Reduce marketing costs
   C. Attract more customers to a business
   D. Influence the amount spent per guest

8. **A manager trains staff to encourage guest purchases of after-dinner specialty coffee drinks. What marketing activity is the manager using?**
   A. Market planning activity
   B. Target marketing activity
   C. External marketing activity
   D. Internal marketing activity

9. **What is an example of a measurable marketing objective?**
   A. Increase customer counts by 10% in 60 days
   B. Serve much better food in 90 days
   C. Improve overall service next week
   D. Increase word-of-mouth advertising

10. **An establishment served 50 guests one day and achieved $800.00 in revenue. What is the check average for that day?**
    A. $14.00
    B. $16.00
    C. $62.50
    D. $6.25

FIELD PROJECT

1. Consider your favorite local restaurant.

2. List five menu items, services, or physical *features* that you most like about it.

3. List the *benefit* you receive from each of the features you listed.

4. If you could suggest three ideas for better marketing this restaurant, what would they be?

2

The Marketing Process in Restaurants

INSIDE THIS CHAPTER

- Branding
- Marketing and Delivering Quality Products
- Marketing and Delivering Quality Service

CHAPTER LEARNING OBJECTIVES

After completing this chapter, you should be able to:

- Understand the importance of branding in the marketing process.

- Describe how marketing and delivering quality products is essential to the success of restaurant and foodservice operations.

- Explain how and why the delivery of quality service is essential to the success of restaurant and foodservice operations.

KEY TERMS

CASE STUDY

"I don't know, it just doesn't seem right," said Mike Brennan, the manager of the upscale Tamalitos Mexican restaurant. "It doesn't look right either."

"What do you mean? It looks great; it's just what you asked for," replied Emily, the sales representative for All-City Menu Design and Printing. Mike had hired All-City to help with the redesign and printing of his restaurant's menu.

"Well, it's plastic, and it's really big. Ours is printed and bound in leather jackets now. And the colors," said Mike, "these bright blues and greens and yellows. That doesn't seem to fit our décor."

1. Based on what you know, do you think an oversized and vividly colored plastic menu would fit well in the décor and ambience Mike has created in his restaurant?

2. How important do you think it is that an establishment's décor, menu, pricing, and even style of service mesh to send one unified marketing message to guests? What will likely happen if these components do not complement each other?

BRANDING

All restaurant and foodservice operations offer food to their guests, but all operations are not alike. For that reason establishments need to tell potential customers exactly who they are. This message of identity takes many forms, including the way an establishment looks on the outside, its décor, the items it serves on its menu, the prices it charges, and even the appearance of its staff. **Brand** is the single term owners and managers use to describe an establishment's distinguishing features. **Brand identifiers** are the name, logo, signage, employee uniforms, décor, pricing, service level, and other characteristics that, when taken together, make one restaurant or foodservice operation different from another.

Many of the most famous brand identifiers used in the restaurant and foodservice business are familiar to most readers. A **trademark** is a brand identifier that has been given special legal status so that only its owners can decide when and how it may be used. Brand identifiers can be very powerful. Consider the signs you have seen for restaurants at your local shopping center or along the highway. For millions of customers, these brand identifiers bring to mind specific images of the menu items sold, décor, and price.

A **brand name** is the specific brand identifier that contains the words, letters, or symbols that are used to identify a single establishment or a company consisting of many establishments. In the restaurant and foodservice industry, the best brand names have the following characteristics:

- Easy to remember
- Easy to pronounce
- Easy to spell
- Able to be translated into foreign languages
- Eligible as a trademark

Brand identifiers are especially important to chain restaurants. A **chain restaurant** is a group of restaurants, each of which utilizes the same brand identifiers. Because consistency is so important to the success of a chain restaurant or foodservice operation, it is not surprising that the owners of the individual operations in the chain want to maintain and standardize what the chain's brand will mean to customers. This is true whether the restaurants in the chain are owned by different individuals or the same company, or even if they are located in different parts of the world.

Experienced managers know that *every* restaurant or foodservice operation, whether part of a chain or an independent, sends an important message to its customers through the choice and use of its unique brand identifiers. To illustrate the importance of restaurant and foodservice brands, consider a customer taking a road trip. He is a long way from home and gets hungry. When he pulls off the highway, he finds himself driving in an area in which many establishments are located.

Some of the operations have brand names with which he is very familiar. Others do not. In many cases, his choice of where he decides to eat may be heavily influenced by the brands he recognizes. Market research confirms that many restaurant and foodservice guests are more comfortable frequenting establishments where they already know the brand. For that reason, it is important that managers carefully develop and maintain their brands.

It is important that managers make a distinction between *creating* a brand and *managing* that brand. When creating a brand, managers make specific messaging choices. For example, if an establishment is seeking to send the brand message that a casual service style will be offered to guests, staff uniforms would likely be chosen to reflect the casual environment being created. Then shorts and polo shirts with company logos may be good choices. If, however, an establishment's owner or manager wants to send the message that upscale dining and very high levels of service are to be offered, a more formal staff uniform (consisting, perhaps, of dark slacks, white shirts, and ties) may be more appropriate.

When managing a brand, care must be taken to ensure the standards originally intended by the brand are well maintained. In the example of the upscale establishment, if the manager does not require the white shirts worn by staff to be clean, neatly pressed, and tucked in, the message presented will not be an operation with high standards, but rather one with very low standards. It would be easy to see that, in this case, the image of the brand as originally *created* was not *managed* in an effective way. The result, in the minds of the establishment's guests, would be a mixed, rather than consistent, image of the brand.

It would be difficult to overestimate the value of a quality brand, but it is easy to see that it consists of much more than the physical components that make up its brand identifiers. A well-managed brand also includes the way its managers care for it, the manner in which employees believe in it, and even the ways in which guests embrace it.

When managers understand and are committed to a well-conceived brand, the results can be powerful and positive. That is because, in the minds of consumers, a quality brand offers the most value for the best price. Consumers know what they will get for their money and they know the value they will receive in return. A well-managed brand ensures standardization of product quality and consistent levels of service.

Brand Statements

An operation's **brand position statement** is a concise summary of the brand's values, competencies, company culture, and target market. A well-constructed brand position statement is of immense value for managers because it helps them determine the marketing strategy and tactics that will be developed in their formal marketing plans. In fact, nearly every marketing

Manager's Memo

Brand names in the restaurant and foodservice industry take a variety of forms. Some companies are named after the individual(s) responsible for initially developing the operations. McDonald's, for example, was named after the brothers who owned the first McDonald's restaurant in California. Wendy's was named after the daughter of company founder Dave Thomas. Other companies, such as Pizza Hut and Taco Bell, use their brand names to help tell guests what is on the menu. Still others, such as Texas Roadhouse, send the message that their food is made and served in the style of a particular geographic location.

Regardless of the reason for its choice, an establishment's brand name, logos, signage, and other brand identifiers must all work together to ensure customers know they will receive quality and consistency in food and service every time they visit.

decision made for a restaurant or foodservice operation should be evaluated on its ability to support and advance the operation's overall brand position statement.

A well-conceived brand position statement addresses four key areas: (1) target market, (2) brand placement, (3) solutions, and (4) reason to believe.

1. **Target market:** Recall that a target market is defined as the potential customers an establishment seeks to attract and serve. The attitudes, values, and demographic descriptions of the customers in the target market must always be an essential part of the brand position statement. While a manager may wish to serve several types of customers, the target group should always consist of those to whom the brand will appeal most and those who will become most loyal.

   A target market must include a sufficient number of potential customers for the operation to make a profit, but not so large it includes "everybody"! When that is the case, the target market is likely too big, and too unknown, to be communicated with directly in a personal way.

2. **Brand placement:** Brand placement refers to the category in which a restaurant or foodservice operation competes. To better understand this key area, consider hamburgers, the single most popular menu item in the United States. In some establishments, a hamburger may cost $1 or even less, be wrapped in plastic, and served in a bag. In other restaurants, the same menu item may be served on a china plate accompanied by fresh avocado, thick-sliced bacon, and alfalfa sprouts, and may sell for $15 or even more!

   Clearly, there is a target market for each hamburger product, and each service style, but they are not the same market. Brand placement seeks to identify key differences in the products or services offered by a restaurant or foodservice operation. Well-planned placement expresses to customers exactly what the establishment seeks to achieve and illustrates its strength compared to its direct competitors. Brand placement is a concerted effort on the part of the owners and managers to develop a loyal customer base and lessens the likelihood customers will be drawn to another brand.

3. **Solutions:** The solutions part of a brand position statement addresses precisely how the operation meets the desires of its target audience. It is called a *solutions* section because it seeks to inform customers about the ways their needs and wants can be successfully addressed by choosing the brand.

All establishments will satisfy the customers' hunger problem, but not all of them can meet the need for speedy service. Similarly, not all establishments can provide a romantic atmosphere or a unique cooking style. When those or other unique features are what guests want, then the operation with those features has supplied a solution to the customers' problems. When consumers truly feel a company has their best interests at heart and can solve real problems for them, that brand will win the loyalty of its target market.

4. **Reason to believe:** Loyal guests trust the companies to which they are loyal. It is sometimes very easy for an operation to make a promise to a consumer. For example, an establishment can easily *promise* great food and great service. But consumers quickly determine whether the promises are kept. Guests who become regular customers have a reason to believe the promises made to them.

When guests personally experience the ability of a restaurant or foodservice operation to deliver on its promises, the guests' belief in a brand position statement is strengthened. Their trust in the brand is elevated, and they know the brand will not disappoint them. Giving potential customers a reason to believe when they first select a brand is an important part of a brand position statement.

A reason to believe can include statements about quality such as "serving only the finest prime cuts of beef" or "all seafood fresh today"; operational statements such as "open 24 hours" or "speedy delivery"; or statements others have made about quality such as "Voted #1 pizza chain in the city."

In all cases, the reason to believe should provide convincing proof that the brand will stand behind, and consistently deliver, exactly what it has promised.

THINK ABOUT IT . . .

What would be required to make you switch from one brand-name product to another brand of that same product? What benefit does that brand-name product provide that you cannot find in its competitor's products?

Manager's Memo

Think about your favorite restaurant or foodservice brand. It can be part of a large chain or small chain or an independent operation. Practice creating a brand position statement by first reading the following sample and then creating one for your favorite establishment.

Vernon's Restaurant		*families*	*seeking casual meals*
(Establishment name)	offers	(Target market)	(Brand placement)

their greatest dining-out value		*of its low-priced 55-item kid-friendly menu.*
(Solution)	because	(Reason to believe)

Now you try!

(Establishment name)	offers	(Target market)	(Brand placement)

(Solution)	because	(Reason to believe)

Brand Management

When considering an establishment's brand it is helpful to understand the **4 Ps of marketing** because they are a well-known way to view the overall marketing process:

- Product
- Promotion
- Place
- Price

The 4 Ps of marketing are the four key ingredients that managers use to create their own recipes for marketing their operations. Some managers use more of one ingredient than another because that is their preference. Others find they simply have (or do not have) more of one key ingredient than another, and others vary the marketing mix recipe to best attract their target customers.

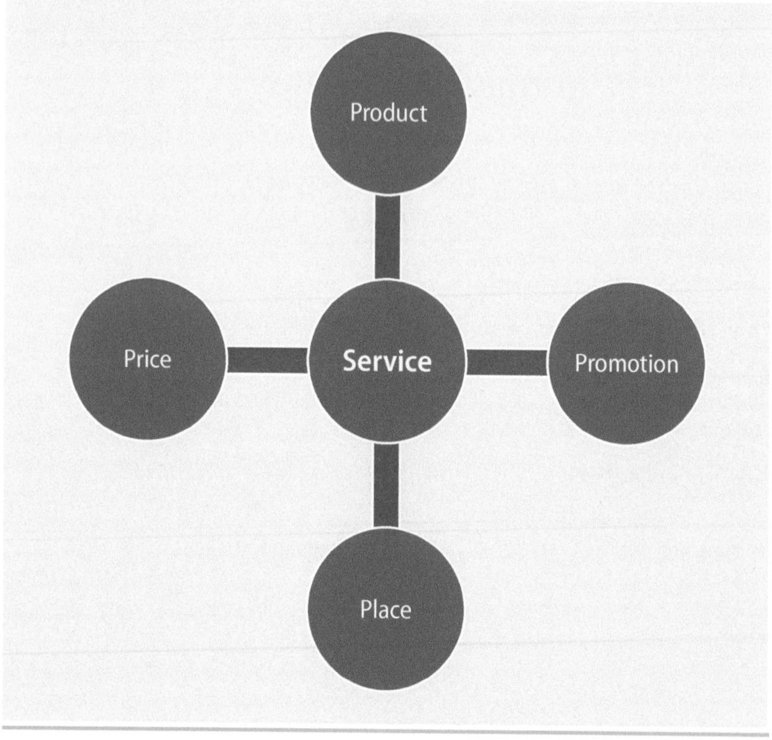

As shown in *Exhibit 2.1*, the restaurant and foodservice industry considers *service* as a fifth and critically important ingredient in the brand positioning and marketing recipe.

These key marketing ingredients are defined as follows:

Product: The product or feature sold by an operation to a customer

Promotion: The means of communication between an operation and a customer

Place: The location of the operation or the way the product is delivered

Price: What a customer gives up to obtain a product from an operation

Service: Actions or benefits provided to buyers of a product

The 4 Ps of marketing, and the ways they are mixed, are so important to brand positioning that each will be addressed in detail in this

Exhibit 2.1

THE FOUR Ps OF MARKETING + SERVICE = BRAND POSITIONING

chapter. The delivery of quality service is essential to success, and managers must consider how to address unique challenges and opportunities when marketing their establishment's services.

PRODUCT

In the restaurant and foodservice industry, products are the actual menu items purchased by customers. Recall from chapter 1 that establishments sell features that provide benefits to customers. As a result, the products can be assessed better by considering several aspects:

- Features such as the menu item itself, its portion size, and the method used to prepare the item

- Benefits such as speed, convenience, or ease of entering an establishment

- Quality such as a product's grade (e.g., beef and fruit), size (e.g., shrimp and lobster), or rarity (wines)

- Packaging such as suitable drive-through or takeout wrappings and containers

Managers and chefs expend a great deal of effort addressing product-related issues. This effort is important because it is focused on maintaining or improving the quality of the products sold. But it is also important to remember that "product" makes up only one part of an operation's overall brand statement.

PROMOTION

In the restaurant and foodservice industry, promotion is the means used to communicate to customers. In this book you will learn about several promotional tools managers use to ensure their customers receive, understand, and remember the messages sent to them. These tools include advertising, personal selling, and on-site merchandizing (chapter 8) as well as product promotions, publicity, and public relations (chapter 9).

Promotional activities can take place outside or inside establishments. A radio advertisement is an external promotional activity because it is a message sent to guests outside the establishment. A physical menu is a communication tool most often used to send a message to guests already inside the operation.

Today, other key marketing tools include email, the Internet, social media, telephone, and direct mail. In all cases promotional activities are designed to send a message, but they are also intended to develop a long-term relationship between an establishment and its customers.

THINK ABOUT IT . . .

Steak is an example of a product used to reinforce a wide variety of restaurant and foodservice brands, ranging from modestly priced to upscale operations. How many different steak quality levels are available in establishments near your home?

Positive relationships with customers are important because of these facts:

- Repeat customers spend more per visit than do new customers.

- Repeat customers refer their friends twice as often as noncustomers.

- It costs a lot more to get a new customer than it does to keep an existing customer.

Today, the Internet allows more operations to directly and cost-effectively communicate their brand message to their target markets.

PLACE

In restaurant and foodservice operations, place is the physical setting for selling or delivering products. Place is sometimes referred to as an establishment's

Exhibit 2.2

location. Location is considered so important by many in the restaurant and foodservice industry that the answer to the question "What are the three most important factors to consider when starting a restaurant or foodservice operation?" is usually "Location, location, location!"

Place, or location, is important but it consists of much more than a building and where that building is physically located. For most operations, place also includes the building's design, its exterior and interior lighting, its signage, furnishing, and décor. The look and feel of a building can go a long way in communicating the market positioning of an establishment (see *Exhibit 2.2*).

Depending on the specific operation, place can include any or all of these additional features:

- Ease to enter when driving or walking to it
- Parking areas
- Entrance areas
- Waiting areas
- Restrooms
- Interior lounges and bars
- Outdoor dining areas
- Visible kitchen areas

In chain restaurants, place can actually be considered multiple locations. For many companies, building or buying multiple establishments results in a number of advantages. First, the experience gained in the operation of one unit can be used to better manage other units. Second, the costs of sending a marketing message can be spread over several restaurants. Finally, satisfied customers who have eaten in one establishment are more likely to choose the same brand when they encounter it in another location.

In some cases, customers may not know the location of an establishment—for example, when guests buy pizza or other food and then have those menu selections delivered to their offices or homes. In such cases, customers are most likely to consider *place* to be one of the following:

- The delivery vehicle
- Delivery staff appearance
- Delivery staff uniforms
- Product packaging

This is so because those items will communicate, loud and clear, the operation's brand to guests as these customers receive their food deliveries.

PRICE

In the restaurant and foodservice industry, price is the amount of money given by guests in exchange for what they buy. While product, promotion, and place have always commanded a great deal of attention from managers, only recently have these professionals begun to truly appreciate the significance of price in the 4 Ps marketing mix.

Consumer Rationality. One way to better understand the power of pricing is to examine the concept of consumer rationality. **Consumer rationality** is the tendency of buyers to make their buying decisions based on their belief that the purchase will be of direct benefit to them.

To illustrate, imagine it is a warm day and a customer comes in to an establishment. In this situation the purchase of a refreshing cold beverage for $1 would likely seem to be a good purchase. If, however, the same refreshing beverage were selling for $100, the customer may not see its purchase as rational because what she would have to give up ($100) is not worth what she would get in return (the cold beverage and a feeling of being more comfortable).

To further consider this same example, assume now that the customer had been in a desert for several days with nothing to drink. In this case, paying $100 for a beverage that may save her life would likely be a very rational decision!

Consumer rationality makes the assumption that buyers consistently are reasonable about what is best for them. In most cases, buyers make their purchase decisions based on the sincerely held belief that it benefits them to buy. The important point for restaurant and foodservice managers to remember is that price can be perceived very differently by different buyers or even by the same buyer at different times. Each buyer's final decision will be based on the buyer's *current* perception of whether a purchase is, or is not, in his or her best interest.

WHAT'S THE FOOTPRINT?

Hybrid vehicles that operate primarily on electricity are an increasingly viable option for those operations that deliver food to their guests. Not only is the cost per mile falling rapidly with such vehicles, but also increasing numbers of customers are buying identical vehicles for themselves. Customers concerned about the environment may be attracted to operations that use eco-friendly vehicles.

In the future, it is very likely that such fuel-efficient vehicles, proudly displaying the logos and names of their establishments, will be an increasingly common sight!

MANAGER'S MATH

Assume that you own five establishments. You wish to run a radio ad on the upcoming weekend. The ad will cost a total of $4,000 if it runs for one day and $6,000 if it is run for two days.

1. How much will each establishment need to contribute if each pays an equal share of the cost for running the radio ad on one day?

2. How much will each establishment need to contribute if each pays an equal share of the cost for running the radio ad for two days?

(Answers: 1. $800; 2. $1,200)

For managers, the ability to understand consumer rationality is significant. Doing so involves knowing and effectively communicating to buyers exactly how they will directly benefit from a business transaction. In most cases, when buyers say they feel a price is "too high," the owner or manager must explain clearly why the price to be paid actually does represent a good value.

Customer Perception of Value. One helpful way to view the impact of price on a restaurant's market positioning and customer value perceptions is to remember that an establishment's brand seeks to communicate the value its customers will receive. One way this statement is communicated is by menu prices.

For example, the following common menu item listing states clearly the item to be sold and the price to be paid for it:

One pound Maine lobster $39.99

The buyer can easily see what will be received and what must be paid. When a seller states, "I will give you this, if you will give me that," buyers will make an assessment that the benefit received from the product (the lobster) minus the price paid for it ($39.99) will, or will not, result in adequate value *to them*.

From the perspective of an operation, value can be expressed in this formula:

$$\textbf{Benefit received} - \textbf{Price paid} = \textbf{Value received}$$

From the perspective of a customer, the formula would be restated as follows:

$$\textbf{Perceived benefit received} - \textbf{Price paid} = \textbf{Value perceived}$$

To illustrate how the concept of personal value actually works in the restaurant and foodservice industry, consider a customer who is used to paying $19.99 for a 16-ounce steak. A larger steak for the same price represents an *increase* in value. A smaller steak sold for the same price represents a *decrease* in value. Similarly, a reduction in price from $19.99 to $16.99 for a 16-ounce steak represents an *increase* in value.

Chapter 6 discusses how restaurant and foodservice managers establish menu prices. Marketing aspects of these pricing decisions are important. Consumers may decide not to go to an establishment because they feel the prices charged for its menu items are too high—or they may visit a restaurant primarily because its prices are low.

Price Points and Coupon Marketing. A restaurant or foodservice operation's **price point** is the position, or point, its prices hold on a scale of lower- to higher-priced menu offerings. In addition to the prices listed on its menu, an establishment's price point is affected by the number of coupons that managers issue and the size of the discounts granted to coupon holders. Traditionally, lower-priced operations most often offered coupons. Today, however, restaurants and foodservice operations at a variety of price points use printed or online coupons.

Using coupons is a marketing tactic that works well with customers who are on a budget or looking to save money. Coupons can also be an effective way to introduce a restaurant or foodservice operation to new customers, and to encourage current customers to try a new menu item or to return more frequently.

Coupons can be mailed directly to the homes of target customers, handed out at special events or printed in special event programs, distributed in newspapers, distributed in the establishment, or offered as downloads on a Web site. In all cases, coupons can have the effect of dramatically altering customers' views of the value they receive in a restaurant or foodservice operation.

A final aspect of price that should not be overlooked is that of how guests are allowed to pay for their meals. All operations accept cash payments, but those that also accept credit and debit cards make it easier and more convenient for customers to pay for their meals (see *Exhibit 2.3*). This is an area that is rapidly changing as technological advances in payment systems are increasingly applied in the restaurant and foodservice industry.

Exhibit 2.3

SERVICE

There is no question that product, promotion, place, and price are important in the restaurant and foodservice industry. Many professional managers would agree, however, that service quality is even *more* important.

It would be hard to overestimate the importance of service to a guest's overall dining experience. To see why, assume a guest visits an establishment. The food is wonderful; thus from a "product" perspective, the establishment has done an excellent job.

The customer visited the establishment because she saw an effective advertisement for it; thus from a "promotion" perspective, management performed very well.

When the customer arrives she finds the establishment is beautifully designed and decorated; thus from a "place" perspective, it is far above average.

Finally, the menu prices are such that the value the guest received for the amount she paid is very high; thus from a "price" perspective, she is extremely satisfied. In this example, the management team has performed flawlessly in managing the 4 Ps of the marketing mix.

Assume further, however, that during the same visit these situations occurred:

- The guest was treated very rudely on the phone when she called to make a dinner reservation.
- Upon arrival, the hostess was talking on her cell phone and thus she ignored the guest's presence for nearly 10 minutes.

OPEN FOR BUSINESS

RESTAURANT TECHNOLOGY

Not everyone carries around cash or a credit card, but increasingly people are carrying a cell phone that is connected to the Internet.

Technological advances in payment systems make it ever more likely that restaurant and foodservice guests will soon be able to pay their bills simply by punching the amount they owe into their cell phones. By doing so, they will be authorizing their banks to transfer the amount they owe directly to the bank accounts of the establishments they visit!

• The guest asked to be seated near the fireplace because several tables near it were vacant, but she was told that the server could not serve her there because it was not in the server's section.

• The server knew very little about the way the menu items were prepared, and thus could offer only minimal information to help the customer place her order.

• When the food arrived, the server could not remember who ordered which items.

• The guest waited nearly 20 minutes from the time she paid cash to the server until the time she received her change.

If all (or even some!) of these things had happened during your visit, do you think you (or other guests) would return to the establishment? In nearly all cases, the answer would likely be a resounding *no*!

In this example, poor service would have the power to offset all the excellent efforts previously spent on product, promotion, place, and price. For that reason experienced managers know that, in their business, product, promotion, place, and price are important in establishing a brand position, but service quality is even more important to long-term success.

Brand Identifiers

Recall that brand identifiers are the name, logo, signage, employee uniforms, décor, pricing, service level, and other characteristics that, when taken together, seek to differentiate one operation from another. Brand identifiers can exist within all of the 4 Ps of marketing and within the important area of service.

BRAND IDENTIFIERS: PRODUCT

The products or features sold by an establishment to its customers can be powerful brand identifiers if the products are unique or if their manner of cooking or service is distinctive.

For example, some establishments feature signature items. Signature items are those menu items that customers associate with a single establishment or chain of establishments. A signature item can be a drink, salad, appetizer, entrée, or dessert. The item may consist of recipe ingredients combined in a unique way, cooked in a specific manner, or served in a distinguishing style.

While it is not possible to trademark a menu item such as a hamburger or steak, it is possible to prepare these items in special ways, give them a special name, and trademark the name. When that is done effectively, guests may associate the entire operation with that brand identifier.

THINK ABOUT IT . . .

The method Brazilian-style steakhouses use to serve meats constitutes a strong product-related brand identifier. To see what it is, type "Brazilian Steakhouse" in your favorite Internet search engine.

1. What is unique about the way Brazilian-style steakhouses serve their products?

2. Why do you think customers can easily recognize this brand identifier?

3. What other restaurants offer other product-related brand identifiers?

BRAND IDENTIFIERS: PROMOTION

Promotion is the manner in which an operation communicates with its customers. This is often accomplished with unique logos, slogans, or phrases used in advertising and which customers can immediately recognize and associate with the restaurant or foodservice operation. Effective promotion-related brand identifiers can be very powerful. To prove it, see how many of these famous products or companies can be recognized simply by their well-known promotion-related brand identifiers (*then check the answers at bottom of the page*).

1. Breakfast of Champions®
2. Just Do It®
3. M'm! M'm! Good!®
4. Melts in Your Mouth, Not in Your Hands®
5. You're in Good Hands®

Repetition, catchy phrasing, and visual imagery can all contribute to an operation's effective use of promotion as a powerful brand identifier.

BRAND IDENTIFIERS: PLACE

Restaurant and foodservice operations exist in small and large towns, in urban and suburban areas, and in freestanding buildings or as tenants in larger spaces such as shopping malls or office buildings. With such great diversity it is not surprising that some operations can use their location, or the building in which they are housed, as a powerful brand identifier.

Recall that for most establishments, place includes the building's design, its exterior and interior lighting, signage, furnishing, and décor. Building design can be used as a brand identifier. For example, a building housing a seafood establishment near the seashore was built to resemble a sailing ship. In this case, the building is being used to give the guests a sense of being somewhere very different than a typical establishment.

Suppose the establishment's nautical theme is carried throughout the building with a décor that suggests the insides of a sailing ship and artwork that shows ships at sea. Perhaps the employees' uniforms suggest old-time sailor outfits. If so, the establishment will be using a variety of place-related items as a strong and unifying brand identifier.

Common place-related brand identifiers include the exterior signs used by restaurant and foodservice operations. When signage uses the establishment's logo or a trademarked symbol or phrase to describe the establishment, guests can readily get a strong sense of the brand position simply by seeing its sign.

(*Answers: 1. Wheaties; 2. Nike; 3. Campbell Soups; 4. M&Ms; 5. Allstate Insurance*)

THINK ABOUT IT . . .

Do any establishments you visit have a unique or memorable advertising *slogan* used to identify the brand ? How are the identifiers aligned with the establishment's brand positioning?

THINK ABOUT IT . . .

Do any well-known establishments have signage that you can immediately recognize? How do you think these place-related identifiers are effective in establishing the operation's brand position?

Fortunately, restaurant and foodservice employees can be trained to provide products and services meeting quality standards. All employees whose job influences the quality level of the guests' experiences (in other words, everyone!) should have access to specific, well-developed, and ongoing training programs. This type of training helps ensure consistent quality, reduces costs due to waste, and increases guest satisfaction.

Also, experienced managers know that a well-trained workforce is easier to manage than is a poorly-trained one. Most restaurant and foodservice employees truly do want to do a good job. As a result, managers who are committed to training will most often find their staff members committed to providing the quality products and service levels that will lead to their establishment's success.

To consistently market quality food and deliver on that promise, managers must ensure that employees have the proper training as well as the proper equipment and tools. For example, it is not possible for managers to develop and market a signature sandwich consisting of "thinly sliced smoked ham" if the equipment needed to create thin ham slices is not available. An improperly equipped kitchen simply cannot yield menu items of consistent quality.

Some managers responsible for the marketing of their products may feel their restaurant or foodservice operations do indeed provide their employees with the tools needed to effectively produce menu items of consistent quality. It is important, however, to recognize that the tools must also be provided at the right height, in the right location, and at the right time. If the proper tools and equipment are provided, but employees are not adequately trained in their use, consistent quality levels will be difficult to achieve. When well-trained employees have the proper tools, however, managers can effectively market and deliver quality in both food and beverage products.

MARKETING AND DELIVERING QUALITY SERVICE

Experienced managers know that the characteristics of their products are fairly easy to communicate to potential customers because these products' features are tangible. That is, the features of the products can be touched or held and, therefore, they can be easily evaluated. To illustrate, consider the following six typical products:

- 12-ounce sirloin steak
- 20-ounce draft beer
- Three flour tortillas
- ½ slab of ribs
- ¼ pound cheeseburger
- Chicken salad sandwich

In each of these cases, customers can order the menu item, assess it when it is delivered to them, and easily determine if they have actually received what they ordered.

The assessment of service levels, and particularly the assessment of high-quality service levels, is more difficult. To illustrate, consider the following six service characteristics most guests would like to experience when dining out:

- Friendly service
- Quick service
- Attentive service
- Responsive service
- Professional service
- Courteous service

In each of these cases, the characteristics that actually define these service conditions are intangible. The characteristics are intangible because they are *not* able to be seen, touched, or held before or after they are experienced. As a result, they cannot always be easily evaluated. In some cases, an identical service level can result in two very different assessments of that service. For example, two different guests may have very different views of what actually constitutes "friendly" or "quick" service. Because of its intangibility, some managers believe delivering quality service is more like delivering a theatrical performance than a product. Employees are actors on stage, with each seeking to give his or her best performance to their audience of guests!

Intangibility is indeed one challenge related to delivering quality service, but there are others. To effectively market quality service, restaurant and foodservice managers must understand the challenges they face when delivering it. Here are four unique challenges a manager who is dedicated to marketing and then delivering quality service will face:

- Intangibility
- Inseparability
- Consistency
- Capacity

Recall the difficulties involved in assessing intangible service levels. Consistency refers to the same level of service every time the guest visits the establishment. However, in the restaurant and foodservice industry, a guest's view of the service quality he or she has received depends, to a large degree, on the person delivering it. Thus, consistency in the delivery of service is much harder to achieve than consistency in the delivery of products.

To illustrate, consider a group of college students who are over 21 years of age. The group visits an establishment near campus that has large TV screens for viewing sports. If all the members of the group order bottles of a popular beer before their meal, the manager can be fairly certain there will be consistency in the product served.

However, the manager also knows that the attentiveness, skill level, appearance, dress, and attitude of the server will have an impact on this group's satisfaction level. In addition, the manager knows these same service characteristics can vary between servers and have a direct impact on the quality of the group's overall experience. It is for that reason managers responsible for marketing service in their operations should play an important role in the operation's training and service standardization efforts.

Inseparability refers to the tendency of restaurant and foodservice customers to connect the quality of service provided with the personal characteristics of the employee who provides it. Thus, a guest's view of service quality and his or her view of the individual employee providing the service are inseparable.

To illustrate, consider these two experiences at a restaurant or foodservice operation. In the first, a well-dressed and smiling member of the waitstaff takes the guest's order promptly. The order is quickly delivered 10 minutes later.

In the second visit, the guest's order is also taken promptly but this time by an employee dressed sloppily and in a dirty uniform. While taking the order, the employee never smiles and appears to be quite distracted with issues other than the guest's order. The order is also quickly delivered 10 minutes later.

Most guests will feel they received quality service during the first visit, but not during the second visit. Even though the order was delivered in the same time during each visit, the server forgot several key characteristics of quality service during the second visit:

- Making guests feel welcome
- Making guests feel special
- Making guests feel glad about their dining-out choice
- Dressing and grooming professionally
- Cheerfully addressing any service shortcomings and correcting them promptly

The inability to separate service quality from those who actually deliver it is important. It is one reason why many managers hire workers with positive attitudes and train them to do their jobs, rather than hire well-trained employees without a positive and customer-centric attitude toward guests.

Service capacity is an important service-related quality factor. Capacity refers to the different service-related situations and outcomes that exist when establishments are busy and when they are slow. To illustrate, consider a guest who arrives at an establishment on a very busy Saturday night. The guest places his name on a waiting list, waits in a comfortable lounge area and, in less than 10 minutes, is escorted to a table. In this example, the guest's view of the establishment's commitment to customer service would likely be very high.

Assume that on the next Saturday night the same guest arrives at an establishment that is nearly empty. He waits near the host stand for five minutes before a host finally arrives to escort him to the table. In this scenario, the guest is seated in five minutes. The wait time is only half of the wait time he experienced the prior Saturday. The guest's view of this establishment's commitment to attentive quality service, however, will most likely be *lower* than that of the establishment that took twice as long to seat him!

All establishments with a fixed number of seats face the service-related challenge of managing their seating capacity. In every restaurant or foodservice operation, unused seating capacity means the operation's managers must make decisions about scheduling the optimal number of service staff.

If too many service employees are scheduled to work when business is slow, labor costs may be too high to make the operation's desired profits. If too few service staff members are scheduled to work when the establishment is busy, however, the result may be poor levels of customer service.

In many establishments, one example of unused capacity is the time period between lunch and dinner. Service levels during this period must remain high despite the lowered number of guests likely to be served. To ensure service levels worthy of being marketed as "quality service," managers must staff properly during those time periods when the establishment is operating at, or near, its maximum capacity. It is important that managers realize poor staffing decisions most often result in poor customer service.

Despite the challenges associated with delivering quality service, managers know that service is as important and sometimes more important than product quality for ensuring an operation's long-term success. *Exhibit 2.5* summarizes the challenges identified in this chapter and some key methods for addressing them.

BY THE CUSTOMER/ FOR THE CUSTOMER

Maintaining product and service quality has always been important to restaurant and foodservice managers. Today, it is even more important. It is easy to see why.

Increasingly, guests use social media sites such as Facebook and Twitter to tell their friends and relatives about their dining experiences. While many of those posting express their satisfaction with the establishments they frequent, some customers do not.

The result is that even one negative experience can be shared with hundreds or thousands of other potential restaurant or foodservice customers. Word of mouth is powerful, so it is important that managers and their staffs strive daily to ensure consistent product quality and service is delivered to every guest, every time!

Exhibit 2.5

SERVICE CHALLENGES AND SOLUTIONS

Challenges	Solution
Intangibility	Establish, when possible, measurable service standards and communicate them to all affected employees.
Consistency	Enforce standards and ensure quality employee training to maximize reliable service delivery.
Inseparability	Hire for positive attitude; train to ensure adequate skill.
Capacity	Make thoughtful employee scheduling decisions that reflect the realities of both fluctuating volume levels and desired service levels.

Marketing Services

Experienced managers working in the restaurant and foodservice industry know that the number one complaint in establishments is not bad food, it is poor service. Poor service can begin even before guests enter an establishment. For example, poor service includes calls for reservations that are poorly handled or parking areas that are littered or poorly lighted. As a result, managers responsible for marketing their operations and for ensuring guests receive the quality service they have been promised must pay attention to every part of their guests' experience.

Successful managers recognize that the service, quality, and value marketing messages communicated to guests are delivered throughout a guest's visit. Managers must ensure the service-related messages are positive at all stages of the guest's experience:

- Arrival
- Greeting and seating
- Guest service
- Bill payment and departure

GUEST ARRIVAL

Many guests arrive by car. Those guests will form initial quality-related opinions about the establishment by observing its parking area and grounds. Parking areas should be kept litter-free and well lit. Landscaping should be kept trimmed and attractive. Exterior areas are so important that many restaurant and foodservice operations require their managers to inspect these on a daily basis.

When first entering an establishment, guests will make assumptions about it based on the cleanliness and attractiveness of its walkways, doors, windows, foyers, entrance, and waiting areas. Restrooms are another critical area many guests observe. In fact, some guests base their perceptions about the cleanliness and quality of an entire operation, at least in part, on the condition of these rooms. Restroom areas are so important that many restaurant and foodservice operations require them to be inspected on an hourly basis.

GUEST GREETING AND SEATING

Whether they are pulling up to a window to place a drive-through order or walking into the most elaborately furnished establishment in town, guests should be made to feel special and welcome when they arrive. A smiling and well-trained staff should greet the guests enthusiastically and sincerely. If guests cannot be served or seated immediately, they should be kept well informed about the estimated length of their wait, and the area for these waiting guests should be as comfortable and inviting as possible.

When guests are ultimately escorted to their seats, they should find tables and chairs that are clean and in good repair. Assistance for special-needs guests should be cheerfully given, no matter if the guests are young children needing child seats or individuals with disabilities needing wheelchair-accessible seating. By frequently spending time in their dining rooms during service periods, managers can easily observe how their guests are treated on arrival and seating. Managers should then ensure the experience is a positive one for all their guests, all the time.

GUEST SERVICE

The manner in which guests are served in the restaurant and foodservice industry varies tremendously. Some guests drive through and pick up their food. Others are treated to the most elegant of tableside cookery, with expectations of very high-quality and professional service. Still others are served at the front door of their homes by food delivery services.

Exhibit 2.6

In table-service establishments, guests should be presented with food menus or wine lists that are clean, easy to read, and informative. Guests should also have numerous personal interactions with well-trained and professional food and beverage servers (*Exhibit 2.6*). As orders are taken and menu items are delivered, all guests expect to be treated well and to be served in a professional manner.

It is an important part of the manager's job to ensure the right number of properly trained staff members are available to meet their guests' dining needs. When they do, their guests' overall dining experiences are enhanced and guest satisfaction levels will be high. If service-related problems or errors do occur, it is the manager's job to ensure these problems are corrected quickly, cheerfully, and to the full satisfaction of each affected guest.

Experienced restaurant and foodservice managers know that their guests' experience is not over until the guests have paid their bills and exited the establishment. To ensure this final portion of the dining experience is consistently positive, procedures must be put in place to ensure each guest's bill meets these criteria:

- Accurate
- Easy to read
- Presented at the proper time
- Processed promptly
- Processed correctly

Upon departure, each guest should be thanked for his or her business and invited to return.

If a restaurant or foodservice operation is to effectively market its services as well as its products, managers must carefully monitor service levels during guest arrival, greeting, seating, service, billing, and departure. When they do, quality levels can be easily monitored and maintained. The result is that excellent service can become a powerful part of the operation's overall marketing effort.

SUMMARY

1. **Understand the importance of branding in the marketing process.**

   In many cases, a customer's choice of where to eat may be heavily influenced by his or her familiarity with the establishment's brand name. Market research confirms that many restaurant and foodservice guests are more comfortable frequenting operations where they already know the brand identity. For that reason, it is important that managers carefully develop and maintain their brand images.

2. **Describe how marketing and delivering quality products is essential to the success of restaurant and foodservice operations.**

   Managers must establish the level of product quality expected by their target customers. They then must purchase the products that will meet this quality level. Regardless of the quality level chosen as appropriate by managers, their guests must receive good value for the prices they pay. Service levels must be high. When they are, guest satisfaction levels will be high, and those guests will return again and again. If an establishment does not deliver quality products that are consistent with guest expectations, most guests simply will not return.

3. **Explain how and why the delivery of quality service is essential to the success of restaurant and foodservice operations.**

   Managers help ensure their service levels are consistently high by regularly and very carefully reviewing what their guests encounter and experience when they arrive, are greeted and seated, are served, pay their bills, and depart. By controlling the guest experience at each of these critical service points, managers can recognize any need for additional staff training or procedures revision that must be implemented to meet the operation's quality service targets.

   Operations sell products but they deliver service. Even when an establishment's product quality is high, its facilities are attractive, and its prices are perceived to be fair, poor service quality most often will result in customers who will not come back or recommend the establishment to others. For that reason, a high level of professional service is needed in restaurant and foodservice operations of all types and at all price points.

APPLICATION EXERCISE

A business brand can be marketed via the 4 Ps and service:

- Product
- Promotion
- Place
- Price
- Service

Consider one of the most popular restaurants in your vicinity. Then answer the following questions:

- How does that establishment use *product* to help establish its brand?

- How does that establishment use *promotion* to help establish its brand?

- How does that establishment use *place* to help establish its brand?

- How does that establishment use *price* to help establish its brand?

- How does that establishment use *service* to help establish its brand?

What recommendations for improvement would you make for any of these areas?

REVIEW YOUR LEARNING

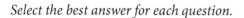

Select the best answer for each question.

1. **What is a trademark?**
   A. A special guest profile
   B. A brand position statement
   C. A brand identifier that has been given special legal status
   D. A customer demographic description that has great meaning

2. **What is a chain restaurant?**
   A. Operations in the same location
   B. Operations that use identical brand identifiers
   C. All those operations owned by the same company
   D. A group of operations owned by the same individual

3. **Which of the 4 Ps of marketing would be affected by a manager's decision to advertise in an online business directory?**
   A. Place
   B. Price
   C. Product
   D. Promotion

4. **What is the name for the process managers use to communicate their values and company culture to target markets?**
   A. Promotion
   B. Consistency
   C. Service quality outline
   D. Brand position statement

5. **Which of the 4 Ps of marketing would be affected by a manager's decision to add a new seafood item to the establishment's dinner menu?**
   A. Promotion
   B. Product
   C. Place
   D. Price

6. **What is a brand identifier related to the "product P" contained in the 4 Ps of marketing?**
   A. Logos
   B. Slogans
   C. Value pricing
   D. Signature items

7. **A server is competent but is not very friendly. The server's quality evaluations as submitted by customers are usually poor. Which service challenge must the server's manager explain to help the server improve his or her evaluation scores?**
   A. Inseparability
   B. Consistency
   C. Intangibility
   D. Capacity

8. **What is the name of the concept that states customers tend to behave in ways they perceive to be in their own best interest?**
   A. Inseparability
   B. Consistency
   C. Rationality
   D. Capacity

9. **An establishment's employee uniforms, name, décor, and logo are some of the items that form the operation's**
   A. brand name.
   B. trademarks.
   C. brand identifiers.
   D. customer service.

10. **What is the most common customer complaint in restaurant and foodservice operations?**
    A. Small portions
    B. High prices
    C. Poor service
    D. Poor food quality

FIELD PROJECT

1. Go to two or three establishments you have not previously visited. List five *intangible* service characteristics you like about them. (Intangible characteristics are those you are not able to see, touch, or hold before or after you experience them.)

2. List five *tangible* characteristics you like about the establishments. (Tangible characteristics are those you can see, touch, hear, or smell.)

3. Is it these operations' intangible or tangible characteristics that you like most about them?

   Which intangible characteristics do you feel most help establish these operations' brands?

   Which tangible characteristics do you feel most help establish these operations' brands?

3

Understanding the Market Environment

INSIDE THIS CHAPTER

- Sources of Market Environment Information
- Analyzing Current Market Conditions
- Identifying Target Markets

CHAPTER LEARNING OBJECTIVES

- Identify the key information sources restaurant and foodservice managers use to better understand their marketing environment.

- Explain the importance of the economic environment in understanding market conditions.

- Discuss the importance of the legal environment in assessing market conditions.

- Describe the importance of vendors in assessing market conditions.

- Explain the importance of competitors in assessing market conditions.

- Identify demographic factors used to define the target market.

- Identify psychographic factors used to define the target market.

KEY TERMS

CASE STUDY

"Well, what does it say, Darla?" asked Dan. "How much do they want?"

Darla, the manager at the Klondike Restaurant and Dan, the restaurant's bar manager, were talking about the contract they just received from the band called The Sea Cruisers.

Darla was at the computer reading the contract as she talked with Dan.

The Sea Cruisers were a '50s and '60s era band that Dan and Darla felt might help draw more guests to their restaurant's outdoor patio on Friday and Saturday nights.

"They want $1,000 per weekend. And we'd have to agree to a three-month contract," said Darla as she looked up. "So it's about a $12,000 commitment on our end."

"Well," said Dan, "we should sell more food and more drinks on the weekend if we have the band to help us draw more customers."

"I agree," said Darla, "but I think the real question is will we attract enough new customers to pay for the band and still make money?"

"Right," said Dan, "but how will we know unless we go ahead and give it a try?"

1. How can Dan and Darla predict the number of new customers who might be attracted to their proposed "live music" idea?

2. Why is it important to predict, as accurately as possible, the number of customers who might come to hear the band prior to signing a contract with it?

SOURCES OF MARKET ENVIRONMENT INFORMATION

A traveler reads about a destination and carefully studies a map before planning a trip. So too should restaurant and foodservice managers gather important marketing information before they develop their marketing plans.

The data that managers use to help form their plans must be accurate and up to date. Marketing information is simply the data, often in the form of facts or figures, used for making marketing-related decisions. Good information helps managers make strategic decisions that are wise. Decisions based on poor or incomplete data can cause a marketing plan—and an operation—to fail.

It is important to know that opinion is not the same as data. To better understand the difference between opinion and data, consider the following two statements that could be made by a manager:

1. "It seems like lots of new establishments have opened in our area recently."
2. "Five new establishments have opened within one mile of our restaurant in the past 18 months."

The first statement is an opinion. It may be accurate, but it provides no actual data that would be useful in analyzing the number of new competitors in the market area. The second statement contains factual information.

Managers who seek to develop a marketing plan must know a great deal of factual information about the market environment in which they will be operating. A **market environment** includes the economic, legal, vendor, and competitor conditions faced by a business.

To make good decisions about how to best operate in their market environments, restaurant and foodservice managers need sources of current, factual information. *Exhibit 3.1* illustrates how internal, secondary, and primary data collection and analysis lead to improved decision making.

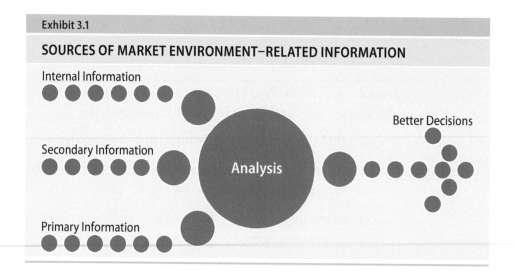

Exhibit 3.1

SOURCES OF MARKET ENVIRONMENT–RELATED INFORMATION

Internal Information

Secondary Information

Analysis

Primary Information

Better Decisions

Internal Information

Managers seeking to better understand their market environment may already have information that can help them. That is because businesses generate factual information every day as they collect and maintain internal data records. Internal information consists of factual records collected about actual sales, product usage, number of customers served, and other operating information.

If an operation is already open, its point of sale (POS) system can provide a wealth of factual internal data. That's because a **point-of-sale (POS) system** records an operation's sales, product usage, and other important information on a daily, by shift, hourly, or other basis. Companies planning new (unopened) operations may be able to use the internal information collected from their existing operations to provide valuable decision-making data.

Internal data can usually be obtained more quickly and at a lower cost than other types of information. If it has been properly collected, data obtained from internal information is also very accurate. It can help answer important marketing-related questions such as these:

- What is a good estimate of an operation's future daily sales?
- Are the operation's overall revenues increasing or decreasing?
- Is the number of guests served increasing or decreasing?
- What are the most popular menu items?
- What are the least popular menu items?
- When is the operation busiest?
- When is the operation least busy?
- How much does the average customer spend per visit?

If an establishment has not opened and does not have access to internal data, its managers will still have access to large amounts of both secondary and primary data.

Secondary Information

Secondary information is useful market-related data that already exist but were not generated internally by the operation. For example, professional trade associations such as the National Restaurant Association (NRA) as well as state restaurant associations frequently collect and publish current data and relevant information about the restaurant and foodservice industry.

In many cases, secondary information is free. This is the case, for example, when data collected by city, state, or federal governments are made available to citizens at no charge. There are several common sources of secondary data:

- U.S. Bureau of Labor Statistics
- U.S. Small Business Administration (SBA)
- U.S. Census Bureau
- State and local chambers of commerce
- Professional associations
- Private research firms
- Journals and periodicals

THINK ABOUT IT . . .

Have you ever made a decision that was based on information you thought was factual but later discovered was not factual? What was the result?

Accurate secondary information can be very helpful, but relying on secondary data for use in decision making can also present problems. For example, the information may not be current. In addition, the data may be inaccurate if questionable methods were used to gather the information.

Secondary data can provide a good starting point for collecting market environment–related information. When secondary sources cannot provide all of the information needed to make good decisions, managers often must generate their own primary information.

Primary Information

Primary information consists of data that are carefully collected to address a specific business need. The collection of primary information is initiated by the person or group that needs it for its own decision-making purposes. Primary information may be generated internally or obtained from an outside source.

For example, assume managers want to know the average time it takes customers to drive to their operations. The information would be valuable because, if known, the managers would have a better idea about where to place promotional advertising targeting current customers. Data of this type would need to be collected using well-designed market research. Market research is a process that seeks to obtain relevant and accurate information about particular groups of people or segments in a market.

When researching information to support future marketing activities, managers should be aware of market research options and resources. To ensure the data they find or produce are accurate and helpful, they must understand the marketing research process and how to apply it.

There are various types of marketing research that can be done, and there are a variety of areas that can be researched. Good marketing research serves several purposes:

- Identifies and defines market opportunities and problems
- Generates, refines, and helps evaluate marketing decisions

- Monitors changes in market performance
- Improves a manager's understanding of the marketing process

To ensure that primary research data are of high quality, the information should be collected through an organized process. A professional market research process involves several steps.

STEP 1: DEFINE THE MARKET RESEARCH PURPOSE

The first step in the market research process is for managers to identify what they want to learn from the research. They should define the problems they want to solve and then develop objectives for the research. At this stage, managers may have to collect data just to fully define the problem and the research objectives.

For example, a manager might review sales reports to identify day parts, days, or even seasons that he or she wants to research and improve. Once a problem has been identified, the manager can define what he or she wants to learn about it by developing objectives for research.

Depending on the problem, three main types of research objectives can be used:

- **Exploratory research** objectives focus on understanding more about a situation and defining it very clearly. The information collected through exploratory research is likely to be used as a foundation for additional research rather than decision making.
- **Descriptive research** objectives focus on revealing details about a market population. They address the questions of "Who, what, when, where, and how?"
- **Causal research** objectives focus on addressing the question "why?" This type of research looks for cause-and-effect relationships.

STEP 2: DEVELOP A RESEARCH PLAN

After a manager has determined what he or she wants to learn from the research, the manager can develop a plan for achieving the research objectives. The plan should describe the types of data needed.

Depending on the type of data needed, this step can be very involved. Internal information may be needed to help guide decision making. If, for example, sales of a particular menu item are declining, that internal data may be assessed as managers plan the research needed to discover why this is happening.

Secondary information provided from external sources may also be of value as managers research current and relevant information that may help them shed light on the marketing issues they seek to address. It may also help indicate additional internal information managers need to obtain to solve their problems.

A manager may use several methods to collect primary data:

- Questionnaires
- Surveys
- Face-to-face interviews
- Observation
- Telephone interviews
- Experiments

If a manager is using a method that involves some form of interaction with people, such as surveys or interviews, he or she also must determine the following:

- Sample: The people who represent the target market
- Sample unit: The smallest element being researched, such as a business, family, or individual
- Sample size: The number of sample units to be researched

Exhibit 3.2

STEP 3: COLLECT THE DATA

After the manager has a plan for achieving his or her objectives, it is time to begin collecting data. In this step, a manager implements the research plan. If the plan includes obtaining secondary data, this is the time to obtain it. For example, a manager might obtain government-supplied census or demographic data or hire a research firm to do it.

If collecting primary data, first develop the process, procedures, and methods needed for the research. If using telephone interviews, for instance, prepare the interview questions and a form for recording the information collected (*Exhibit 3.2*). This step also includes processing the data collected. For example, a manager may need to compile survey results by entering data into a database or spreadsheet.

STEP 4: ANALYZE THE DATA

Once a manager has collected and processed the data, it can be analyzed.

In this step, look at data in different ways and interpret the findings. For instance, assume a manager surveyed both current customers and random people in the market area. The manager would consider various measures for the customer group, the random group, and the entire group.

Also, within each group, break down the responses by target market segment such as gender or age. Doing this makes it possible to identify patterns based on segment, such as buying differences between men and women or among age groups.

The research is not complete until the findings are shared with others who have a stake in the operation. Reporting data is an important step because it enables others to review the data and make their own interpretations. It also provides a common knowledge base for making decisions.

The report may be formal or informal, but it is important to document all findings in a written report. Doing this produces a record of the manager's research, analysis, and interpretation in addition to listing his or her data sources.

Sources of Information

There are many sources of primary data available to most managers. They may purchase primary data from a secondary source or develop their own primary data internally. The data collected often depend on the size of their operations, the resources available to them, and the size of their market environment.

Managers in large restaurant or foodservice companies may have the resources to collect large amounts of data and may hold focus groups, which are small-group meetings designed to learn what people think of a new product, service, or idea. Additionally, they might hire a third-party company to collect specific data within a certain area through telephone interviews or surveys.

Some large organizations use a formal marketing information system to assist in their marketing efforts. A marketing information system (MkIS) is a combination of tools and procedures for collecting, analyzing, and distributing marketing information that is used for developing, implementing, and evaluating marketing activities.

The abbreviation MkIS is used to distinguish it from another common abbreviation, MIS, which usually means "management information system." Marketing information systems usually involve computers, databases, reports, and other information resources and can involve external resources.

Marketing research and MkISs are not just for large organizations. A smaller operation may also have many methods and resources available for collecting data and developing systems. However, that system may be smaller and less automated. For example, a small operation might use sales reports from a POS system and handwritten notes from customer interviews.

Managers in smaller operations also can gather data by purchasing data reports from third parties, distributing their own surveys and comment cards, and studying secondary data.

RESTAURANT TECHNOLOGY

The Internet is a powerful two-way communication device that can be used to provide customers with a way to give managers valuable feedback. Consider these examples:

1. A manager collects email addresses from customers and conducts a monthly survey that concludes by asking survey takers to return the email as *high priority* if they have any product- or service-related issues they want to discuss with the manager.

2. A manager regularly surveys customers about their dining experiences and offers a free appetizer coupon to any customer who completes the survey.

3. The manager of a large operation surveys customers annually to identify those holding special events in the future that could be hosted at the establishment.

The benefits of speed, low cost, accuracy, and convenience over traditional paper-based or telephone-based survey techniques ensure that online feedback systems in the restaurant and foodservice industry will continue to be widely used and accepted.

STATISTICAL RECORDS

Many research companies provide marketing data. Research information may be available to show how one item is selling against another, or consumer preferences for a location to determine its residents' age and estimates of their discretionary income. Discretionary income is the money left after a person has met all his or her expenses or debts.

SURVEYS

When an operation wants specific information about its customers, it can conduct its own research. A common research method used by restaurants and foodservice operations is to survey current customers. Sometimes, random people within the target market are also surveyed. Using surveys allows an operation to ask questions about its customers' true needs. For example, a survey might ask, "What would you like to see on the menu?" or "Rate your preference for the following items." To encourage customers to complete the surveys, operations often offer customers a free item or discount.

SUGGESTION BOXES AND CARDS

Another common way that operations collect their own data is by encouraging customers and employees to recommend new items, services, and other improvements through the use of a suggestion box. Suggestion cards may be left for the customers with their checks or on their tables to give them an opportunity to provide feedback. As with surveys, many operations provide a discounted or free item to encourage customers to complete and submit their suggestions.

When these methods are used, keep in mind that the information from suggestion boxes and cards may have a larger degree of error than other data sources. For example, a guest who had a bad day and then received substandard service might react more negatively than he or she would after having a good day. These types of influences can sometimes distort the results obtained during research.

Today, an increasingly large number of companies use the Internet when surveying customers. Some companies even have online suggestion boxes built into their own Web sites to make it easy to get feedback and new ideas for improvement.

INTERVIEWS

In some cases, managers might conduct interviews with selected or potential customers, or even randomly selected members of the general public. Doing this enables managers to have one-on-one discussions with customers about their needs and wants. During such interviews, questions can include asking about their favorite menu items, what they choose on the menu, and what style of establishment they typically frequent.

ANALYZING CURRENT MARKET CONDITIONS

Managers obtain information about their market environments from a variety of sources. It is important to know the kinds of market-related information they generally need.

A total market environment consists of external forces and people. These external forces can sometimes shape the market environment as much as, or even more than, the individuals in an operation's target market. The specific forces or conditions affecting an individual operation's market vary, but there are several sources that often apply to most establishments:

- The economic environment
- The legal environment
- The vendor environment
- The competitive environment

Because market environment directly affects managers' marketing decisions and because the components of these environments can change rapidly, managers need to understand and continuously monitor them.

The Economic Environment

The individuals in any operation's target market must have buying power. The economic environment consists of those factors that directly affect the purchasing power and the spending habits of those in a target market.

During the 1980s and early 1990s, the U.S. economy was extremely robust. The result was that many new establishments were built and the amount of food purchased away from home increased rapidly. Fueled in part by federal tax reductions, rising real estate values, and increased easy term borrowing, U.S. consumers spent a great deal, but they also incurred a lot of debt.

During this period, the baby boomers, generally recognized as those U.S. citizens born between 1946 and 1964, were entering their peak earning years. As a result large numbers of diners were willing and able to pay for frequent meals eaten out. This was so because, when economic times are good, restaurants are among the most favored places for spending discretionary income.

The recession that began in December of 2007 has caused Americans to be more careful with their spending. As a result, growth rates in overall restaurant and foodservice sales have slowed somewhat. The boom years of the 1980s and the more cautious years of the late 2000s are good examples of how the differences in the economy can directly affect overall spending for an establishment's products and services.

THINK ABOUT IT . . .

Internal information is produced by a business. Secondary information comes from external sources. Primary information addresses a specific business problem. Is the best way to obtain primary information from internal or secondary sources? Why?

THINK ABOUT IT . . .

When a local economy is not strong, the residents of the area may have fewer discretionary dollars to spend.

What can restaurants and foodservice establishments operating in economically depressed areas do to maintain their revenue levels in difficult economic times?

Managers should regularly monitor their local economies and those of their target markets. They also must recognize that the income levels of their target markets impact the amount guests have available to spend when dining out.

Lower- and middle-income consumers are not as wealthy as their upper-income counterparts. However, they do have enough money to purchase food away from home on a regular basis and dine out for special occasions, where their spending can be equal to that of upper-income consumers. In the United States, this market is large and traditionally has been very stable. Managers should continually monitor their local economies to ensure they are targeting those customers who have the ability to pay the prices charged in their operations.

The Legal Environment

A large number of local, state, and federal laws and regulations affect the operation of an establishment. Because the laws related to restaurant and foodservice operations change regularly, it is essential that managers monitor this important factor.

Managers have specific legal responsibilities to their guests, including the following:

- Responsibilities to all guests
- Responsibilities related to serving food
- Responsibilities related to serving alcoholic beverages

RESPONSIBILITIES TO ALL GUESTS

An establishment that does not satisfy its guests will not stay in business. Despite the importance of guests, there are specific legal challenges that arise any time guests are served. From a legal perspective, a **guest** is anyone using an establishment's services. This means guests include all diners, whether or not they are the person actually paying the bill for any purchases made in the establishment.

In all areas of the country, laws have been established that require restaurant and foodservice managers to treat all guests fairly. For example, federal law makes it illegal to deny service to anyone on the basis of race, color, religion, or national origin.

It is also a violation of federal law to admit a customer and then segregate him or her (for example, by restricting his or her seating only to predesignated sections of an establishment) based on those same characteristics. In addition, many towns and cities prohibit discriminatory practices such as those in privately owned and operated facilities such as country clubs and private city clubs.

Laws related to guest service may be made at the federal, state, or local level. In some cases these laws, such as laws prohibiting smoking or the sale of specific food items, may cause significant change in the way an establishment is managed and the services it can provide. As a result, managers and those who market an establishment's services must monitor the laws very closely.

RESPONSIBILITIES RELATED TO SERVING FOOD

Restaurant and foodservice managers have a legal obligation to sell only food that is wholesome, and to deliver it to guests in a way that is safe. This responsibility is required by law. As a result, an establishment is legally obligated to handle and serve the items it sells in a way that protects guests from foodborne illnesses or other harm.

To help owners and managers do that, local health departments conduct routine and mandatory inspections of kitchens and may offer training or certification classes for restaurant and foodservice employees. While operations can be held responsible for food-related illnesses they cause their guests, they can also help minimize this liability when they show reasonable care by providing food safety training to all of their employees who handle or serve food.

RESPONSIBILITIES RELATED TO SERVING ALCOHOLIC BEVERAGES

Throughout history, alcoholic beverages have been manufactured, served, and enjoyed in nearly every society, including the colonial Americas. However, in 1920, the U.S. Congress passed the Eighteenth Amendment to the Constitution that prohibited the manufacture, sale, and transport of all alcoholic beverages in the United States.

Not surprisingly, the law stopped only the legal manufacture and sale of alcoholic beverages. Many people still drank, but they drank illegally made, poor-tasting, and in many cases alcoholic beverage products that were actually dangerous to drink.

In 1933, Congress recognized the failure of Prohibition and repealed the Eighteenth Amendment, while allowing local states, counties, and towns to pass their own laws restricting or even prohibiting the sale and consumption of alcohol within their boundaries. As a result, a wide variety of alcohol-related laws exist in the United States and managers must know which apply to their own businesses. These laws can have a significant impact on an operation's alcohol-related marketing activities. In most locales specific alcoholic beverage–related laws address several important questions:

1. **Who may sell it:** In all states, a state-issued liquor license is required before a business will be permitted to sell alcohol.

2. **When it may be sold:** Most communities have laws that restrict the specific hours or, in some cases, the days on which alcohol may be sold.

3. **Where it may be sold:** In most states, businesses that serve alcohol are prohibited from operating close to schools or churches. In addition, the terms of a liquor license may restrict the sale of alcohol to limited and very clearly defined areas of an operation's building or its grounds.

4. **Who may serve it:** It is common for states to impose minimum age requirements for those who serve alcoholic beverages. The majority of states permit adults aged 18 or older to serve alcoholic beverages in an establishment, but these laws do vary.

5. **Who may buy it:** In the United States, guests must be 21 to purchase alcohol, but not all guests over 21 can be served legally. For example, establishments cannot sell alcohol to guests who meet any of the following criteria:

   a. Visibly intoxicated persons

   b. Those without proper identification

   c. Those suspected of buying alcohol for the purpose of giving it to a minor

6. **How it can be sold:** Most states and communities have laws that restrict how alcohol may be served. For example, many localities prohibit the service of more than one alcoholic beverage to a single guest at the same time. Others restrict the manner in which promotions, specials, or discounts on the selling price of alcohol may be offered to guests.

Laws related to alcohol service are an excellent example of the impact of the legal environment on restaurant and foodservice operations and explain why managers should monitor this important area carefully.

The Vendor Environment

Vendors are the people or organizations that sell the goods and services an establishment needs to operate (*Exhibit 3.3*). A typical establishment has vendors, also known as suppliers, for food, beverages, linen services, information technology (e.g., office computers and POS systems), security services, and other needs.

Monitoring changes in the vendor environment is important because restaurants and foodservice operations cannot effectively market products they cannot obtain. If, for example, an establishment heavily markets a specific menu item but then has trouble buying that item for resale to guests, the result will be unhappy customers and wasted marketing efforts.

In large communities, the number of vendors competing for business may also be large. In smaller communities the manager's choice of vendors may be limited. In all cases, marketing managers must be confident that their establishment has a dependable supply of all the items it will promote for sale to its target market.

Exhibit 3.3

As a result, the number and quality of available vendors in an establishment's market area must be carefully monitored. These factors directly impact the prices vendors can charge and operators must pay for their products and services.

The Competitive Environment

To be fully successful, a restaurant or foodservice operation must meet the needs of customers better than its competitors. Managers must understand who their competitors are and how much of a threat they pose to the success of the operation.

There are various ways to identify or categorize competitors. For example, competitors can be grouped based on the threat they pose to the market of an establishment. In such a case, an operation that opens 30 miles from another establishment would be a lower threat than a similar facility opening within one mile.

Another way to categorize competitors is by what an establishment considers to be its competition. These can include several types of establishments:

- **Establishments that sell similar products and services:** For example, a full-service, upscale restaurant would consider other full-service, upscale restaurants in their area to be their competitors. It would not likely consider a small, low-priced diner to be a direct competitor.

- **Other establishments that sell similar products but at different service levels:** For example, a restaurant that specializes in home-delivered pizza might also consider a restaurant that sold pizza in a traditional dining-room setting to be one of its competitors.

- **Establishments that sell food, regardless of the products they sell or the service level:** In this instance, the upscale, full-service restaurant would see the pizza delivery restaurant, the traditional table service pizza restaurant, and any other establishment that sells food such as grocery or convenience stores as competitors.

After managers have identified their competitors, they can begin to research them. They can visit these establishments, observe how they operate, and study their menus. Their goal should be to find out what these direct competitors offer target customers and to learn from them. When doing an assessment, managers should pay close attention to the following:

- Menu selections
- Pricing structure
- Décor
- Service levels
- Brand strength
- Chain affiliation (if applicable)

Most establishments have direct competitors so managers must be concerned about market size and market share.

Exhibit 3.4

MARKET SIZE

Market size refers to the number or value of units sold to an entire market in a given time period (normally a year). For example, in a town where 100,000 takeout pizzas are sold in one year, the market size of the takeout pizza business in that town would be 100,000 units.

If the average takeout pizza in the town sold for $10, then the market size for takeout pizza could also be expressed in monetary terms as $1,000,000:

100,000 takeout pizzas sold × $10 per pizza = $1,000,000

It is clear that if a manager operated a takeout pizza parlor in that town, it would be important for him or her to know about, and to continually monitor, the size of the local takeout pizza market.

Estimating the market size precisely in a very large market such as that shown in *Exhibit 3.4* can be challenging, but experienced managers know that a good estimate of market size must be obtained to calculate an establishment's market share.

MARKET SHARE

Market share is the number or value of units sold by a business during a given period and is expressed as a percentage of the total market size.

Like market size, market share can be expressed either as the share of units sold or share of revenue. For example, in the town whose market size for takeout pizza was 100,000 units and $1,000,000 per year in sales, an establishment sold 20,000 pizzas. That operation's market share would be 20 percent.

20,000 pizzas sold ÷ 100,000 market size units = 20% of market share units

Similarly, the takeout pizza revenue would have been $200,000.

20,000 pizzas sold × $10 per pizza selling price = $200,000

As a result, the market share expressed in terms of revenue would also be 20 percent.

$200,000 revenue achieved ÷ $1,000,000 market size revenue = 20% of market share revenue

If a market's size is known or can be closely estimated, an establishment can estimate its own market share based on its internal sales data.

It is also possible to estimate market share using externally published market size data, but care must be taken to ensure the source of the revenue data is credible.

OPEN FOR BUSINESS
MANAGER'S MATH

An establishment operates in a market whose size is estimated to be $8,000,000 annually based on sales made to 200,000 customers at a check average of $40 (see chapter 1).

Last year the operation achieved revenue of $1,200,000.

1. What percentage of market share did the establishment capture last year?

2. What number of customers did the operation likely serve last year?

(Answers: 1. 15%; 2. 30,000 customers)

IDENTIFYING TARGET MARKETS

Chapter 1 defined a target market as those customers whose specific needs and wants a business seeks to meet. To identify a target market, managers use a variety of strategies. These strategies primarily result from the decisions managers make about their target markets. These include which specific markets can be profitably targeted and why those potential customers should buy the operation's products and services.

No operation can be all things to all people. The most effective approach to marketing is to separate the entire group of potential customers into identifiable market segments and then directly address one or more of those segments. Managers select target markets to avoid doing mass marketing, and to focus instead on targeted marketing.

Mass marketing is the process of treating everyone in the market as having the same needs and wants. This can be good if what is to be sold truly appeals to everyone the same way. When it does, managers may be able to mass produce and distribute their marketing messages.

Most restaurant and foodservice establishments, however, should use a targeted marketing approach. Targeted marketing treats people as different from each other and seeks to make a focused appeal to the distinct portion of potential customers that make up the establishment's target market.

For example, if an establishment is located in a major city where there are large numbers of relatively wealthy people with a variety of tastes in dining, an operation targeting wealthy customers who like French food and formal service may make good sense. That same establishment, however, may make very little sense if it were located in a small, mid-priced shopping mall.

It is important to recognize that targeted marketing can focus on more than one target market. For example, the French establishment previously mentioned may wish to target wealthy businesspeople entertaining clients during the lunch period, but target couples seeking a romantic dinner during the evening.

Note that these two different target markets are similar in what they might purchase: French food and fine-dining service. They differ, however, in their reasons for wanting these things and perhaps in the frequency with which they will purchase them. These differences do not really matter in providing the products and services, but they do matter in promoting the products and services to these different target markets.

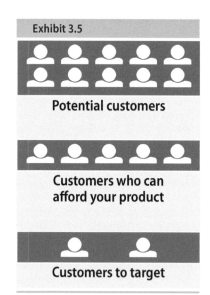

Exhibit 3.5

Potential customers

Customers who can afford your product

Customers to target

The process of selecting a target market can be thought of as a series of decisions that focus on markets with the most potential. To select a target market, establishment managers narrow the field of "potential customers" to a field of "customers to target" as shown in *Exhibit 3.5*. They can target customers by doing the following:

- Identifying all potential customers in an area. In the previous example, this would include all customers who like French food and formal dining services.

- Identifying all potential customers who are financially able to purchase their products and service. It is important to recognize that, in many cases, potential customers might be willing, but unable, to buy an establishment's products and service. This is not unique to the restaurant and foodservice business. Many drivers might be willing to buy, but unable to afford to buy, an expensive sports car. In this step, a manager would separate those potential customers who are willing and able to buy from those potential customers who are willing, but not able.

- Identifying the recognizable characteristics of their targeted customers. When selecting target markets, managers must consider two key factors: the potential profitability of the target market and their ability to address the customers' needs and wants.

In the French establishment example, a manager probably could not have targeted people who like French food and a formal dining service in a very small, isolated town because the number of potential customers in this market segment is too small to be profitable. Likewise, a manager would not want to select people who like French food and formal dining service as a target market if the establishment does not have the ability to prepare high-quality French cuisine and provide the fine-dining service levels these guests would expect.

In terms of the market segment's profitability, a segment would likely make a good target market if it meets several characteristics:

- Large enough

- Steady or growing in numbers, not declining

- Not filled with too many competitors

- Not blinded by loyalty to existing competitors

- Able to be attracted with the marketing budget available

- Profitable enough to pursue, given the costs the operation must incur and the revenues it can reasonably expect to obtain

In terms of an operation's capability, a customer segment will likely make a good target market for the establishment when it meets these criteria:

- The establishment has the capability to offer more value than competitors can offer (e.g., better food, better drink, or better service).

- Addressing this market fits well within the operation's image.

- The operation has the marketing budget needed to reach the segment with its marketing message.

- The operation has the financial and human resources needed to enter and survive in the market segment.

As part of analyzing a market environment, it is necessary to accurately identify target customers. Managers can obtain detailed information about their customers and then begin grouping them into categories, or **market segments**. Segmenting a market will provide a foundation for identifying the target market because it can help identify the people most likely to visit a specific operation. There are many ways to segment a market. One of the most common ways is to segment the market based on its demographics and psychographics.

Demographics

As addressed in chapter 1, marketing managers often segment their customers based on demographic variables such as these:

- Age
- Education
- Ethnicity
- Geography
- Home ownership
- Household size
- Income level
- Nationality
- Occupation
- Race
- Religion
- Sexual orientation
- Spending patterns
- Stage in family life cycle

THINK ABOUT IT . . .

Consider your most recent product purchase. Would you have purchased a high-priced version of that product if your bank account was unlimited? Are you part of the target market for the higher-priced product version?

Exhibit 3.6

TYPICAL GEOGRAPHIC CATEGORIES

Category	Typical Breakdown	Example
Region	• Northeast • Midwest • West • South	*Northeast:* Maine, Vermont, New Hampshire, Massachusetts, Rhode Island, Connecticut, New York, Pennsylvania, New Jersey, Delaware
City Size	• First tier • Second tier • Third tier • Fourth tier	*First tier cities:* New York, Los Angeles, Chicago, Houston *Second tier cities:* Atlanta, San Francisco, Washington, DC
Density	• Urban • Suburban • Small town • Rural	*Suburban (Chicago):* Naperville, Schaumburg, Wilmette, Lake Forest, Oak Park, Orland Park

Exhibit 3.6 shows examples of how one demographic, geography, can be even further segmented.

While geography may or may not be a critical demographic for all establishments, income and age are two demographic areas that are important to nearly all restaurant and foodservice operations. They are also good examples of how customers' demographics can help managers better understand their target customers.

AGE

Do most people eat the same thing as adults as they did when they were five years old? Although some adults may still enjoy some of the same types of food they ate as a child, it is likely that their culinary preferences and needs have changed over the years, and they will continue to change with age.

Managers should be familiar with this concept and how it can affect their business. Restaurant and foodservice managers need to understand the various population trends in aging and the needs of different age groups such as those shown in *Exhibit 3.7*.

For example, the number of retirees in the United States is expected to rise dramatically over the next 20 years, and businesses everywhere should take notice. In general, this trend is due to the aging of the baby boomer generation coupled with advancements in healthcare and improvements in the overall quality of life.

This demographic group is characterized by a large amount of free time and discretionary income. That allows them to visit establishments much more than people in the youth, young adult, and middle-age categories. This makes

Exhibit 3.7

TYPICAL AGE-LEVEL CATEGORIES

Category	Age
Child	0–9
Youth	10–19
Young adult	20–34
Early middle age	35–49
Late middle age	50–64
Retiree	65 and over

retirees a particularly desirable market for many restaurant and foodservice businesses (*Exhibit 3.8*).

Of course, retirees have unique needs that establishments must try to meet. Since health concerns are important to this group, specialized menu selections such as low-calorie, low-sodium, or low-fat items are an increasingly popular draw. In addition, portion sizes are often made smaller to suit this category. Even though many retirees may have large amounts of discretionary income, many also need or choose to be careful with their money, so they like establishments that offer low-cost, high-quality meals.

INCOME

Where customers choose to eat and how often they eat out is greatly affected by their income levels, especially their discretionary income. Consequently, markets are often segmented according to income level.

In addition to segmenting a market based on demographics, it can be useful to group people by other traits. While the various factors used to segment a market can be virtually limitless, segmenting customers by their psychographics, the way customers think and feel, are among the most popular approaches used by managers.

Psychographics

Unlike demographics, **psychographic** characteristics of a customer relate to that customer's personality, values, attitudes, interests, or lifestyle. In many cases, the psychographics of a target market are more important than its demographics. To illustrate, consider the manager operating the concession stand at a baseball stadium. In this case, the manager's target market are those who enjoy going to baseball games. This shared interest among the manager's customers would be more important for marketing purposes than would the game attendees' demographic factors such as age, race, or gender. In fact, many managers consider lifestyle-related psychographic factors to be of even more importance than demographics when defining a target market.

Lifestyle is one of those terms that most people understand but have a hard time defining. One useful definition states that **lifestyle** is the patterns in which people live and spend time and money. This definition is helpful because it sees guests in terms of how and what they buy. In other words, the definition predicts differences in consumer behavior. Behind the behaviors that encompass lifestyle, however, can lay a number of other complex factors related to consumers' personalities and values.

Psychographics are important to managers because they describe the human characteristics of restaurant and foodservice customers. These characteristics

Exhibit 3.8

WHAT'S THE FOOTPRINT?

Increasingly, customers are concerned about the impact they make on the environment. Some establishments have responded to this increased interest by making eco-friendliness a significant part of their marketing efforts.

Establishments may communicate to eco-friendly guests a variety of initiatives they have undertaken. Examples include using hybrid cars as delivery vehicles, recycling, and using the heat from their own ovens to warm their establishments.

As customers increase their own awareness of green practices, expect them also to pay increased attention to the green practices of the establishments they prefer to frequent. Restaurants and foodservice operations targeting these eco-minded customers would do well to point out that they too are eco-minded!

BY THE CUSTOMER/ FOR THE CUSTOMER

A relatively new customer psychographic is one that characterizes customers as "tech savvy." Restaurant and foodservice owners and managers who embrace new technologies in marketing their operations know there are powerful new tools for communicating with these tech-savvy customers. There are several popular social media sites used to communicate with customers:

- Facebook
- Twitter
- Yelp reviews

The number of tech-savvy consumers is growing, and tech-savvy managers should reach out to them in ways that guests appreciate and that fit into these guests' advanced technology lifestyles.

may have a direct bearing on guest responses to the following marketing-related activities:

- Pricing
- Promotions
- New product introductions
- Frequent diner and guest loyalty programs (see chapter 10)
- Proposed or actual changes in the products or services sold by the establishment

Psychographics are used primarily to help segment markets, but they have other purposes. For example, psychographics can be useful when managers try to determine a series of other marketing questions:

- What promotions should be emphasized?
- How would promotional efforts best be communicated to the target market (e.g., radio, TV, social media)?
- How will the target market likely respond to the promotion?

Psychographics are also important when managers design advertising and promotional materials. The words or phrases used, the graphic images displayed, and even the background music used should be selected with the preferences of a specific target market in mind. The result is promotional efforts that have more impact, produce more sales, and yield more profits.

In many cases, managers select the words actually used to describe the psychographic characteristics of their target markets. As they assess the demographics and the psychographics of their target audiences, marketing managers should remember that their goal is to cost-effectively communicate their operation's message to a defined target market. When they do this, they consistently keep their product and service promises, and their businesses will consistently grow and prosper.

Serving the Target Market

Once a manager has identified the target customer base, he or she will want to learn why these customers may want to visit the operation. Is the establishment their destination or merely a convenience? Managers should determine whether customers eat at their establishment because it is convenient for them or because dining at their establishment is the reason they go out. The results may determine, for example, whether managers speed up service or add entertainment for their customers. If customers come for both reasons, a manager will have to meet both types of these needs.

How far do customers have to travel to the establishment? Determining this will help determine how far the word about the establishment is reaching. This is illustrated in *Exhibit 3.9*.

If people come from a long way to visit an establishment, customer loyalty is being built. **Customer loyalty** is when customers make frequent, repeat visits to an operation, and it most often proves that marketing efforts are working.

Once key questions are answered, managers can find out if they are providing the right products and services to their target customers. Doing this also helps determine whether managers should consider increasing their customer base. To help determine future marketing directions of their establishment, managers should gather the information needed to answer the following questions:

Exhibit 3.9

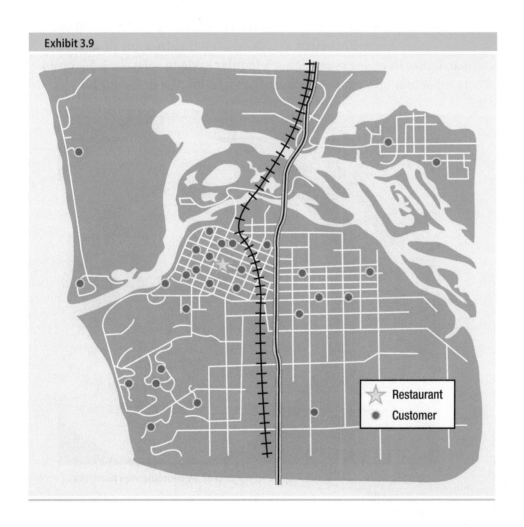

★ Restaurant
● Customer

Are customers returning? If not, managers must ask why, and then take actions to correct this problem.

How often do they return? If customers are returning to an establishment, the manager should determine if it is once a week, once a month, or some other time period. The ideal situation is for customers to come back night after night with friends, but that is not realistic. Depending on the establishment, perhaps a more realistic goal might be to have customers come back six times a year. The sooner they come back, the more managers will know that they are providing the right products and services at the right price.

Are they bringing friends? Are customers bringing friends or family to the establishment? If not, this may be an opportunity to increase customer traffic. If they are not bringing their friends, then managers must determine what to change.

What are they ordering? Determining this can be done through an assessment of the menu items the establishment sells most. This topic will be addressed in detail in chapter 11. Regularly scheduled menu evaluations can tell whether an operation has a drop-off in sales on a particular item, is experiencing a regular cycle in sales, or is involved in an actual upward or downward sales trend (see *Exhibit 3.10*).

Exhibit 3.10

Managers need to continually and very carefully monitor which of their menu items
sell best.

Is the manager receiving compliments from his or her guests? First of all, are they tipping well? Overall, customers will reward service staff for an enjoyable experience by giving compliments or tips. If the service staff is being tipped generously, then chances are the customers are enjoying themselves. If not, then managers must figure out why. It is part of every manager's job to find out what aspect of the service, food, or ambience is affecting this and to then make appropriate changes.

Are customers providing verbal or written compliments? Every operation should make it easy for its customers to give positive or negative feedback, because guest comments are a valuable source of information. Managers routinely use table cards, the backs of discount coupons, email surveys, questionnaires on Internet sites, or all of these methods to make it easy to gather feedback from their customers.

How did they find out about the establishment? Managers want their customers to give positive word-of-mouth publicity. If customers think highly enough of your operation to bring their friends, then customer loyalty is probably high. Table cards, the backs of discount coupons, email surveys, questionnaires on Web sites, or all of these methods can be used to determine how customers heard about an establishment.

In all cases, it is important for managers to know and understand their customers. The next chapter addresses more aspects of restaurant and foodservice customers, including what motivates them to buy and the different industry segments that have evolved to serve them and meet their needs.

SUMMARY

1. **Identify the key information sources restaurant and foodservice managers use to better understand their marketing environment.**

   Managers require factual information to make well-informed marketing decisions. Information used to make marketing-related decisions can come from a variety of sources. Internal information consists of data collected by the establishment and that are already in existence. Secondary information may be obtained from a variety of external sources, many of which distribute it at no charge. Primary information is data gathered for a specific decision-making purpose. To properly obtain it, managers may use an MkIS to generate factual information in ways that minimize cost and maximize accuracy.

2. **Explain the importance of the economic environment in understanding market conditions.**

   The goal of a marketing plan should be to obtain and retain customers. The ability of customers to purchase products and services is tied directly to the economic health of the city, state, or nation in which the establishment operates. For many customers, away-from-home food purchases are made from discretionary income. While a single establishment cannot change the economic climate of its operating area, marketers should monitor their local economies for trends that could have either positive or negative effects on their establishments.

3. **Discuss the importance of the legal environment in assessing market conditions.**

   There are local, state, and federal business laws that all restaurant and foodservice operations must follow. However, in many cases these laws vary in different areas of the country. Additionally, new legislation directly affecting restaurant and foodservice operations is enacted on a regular basis. To be most effective, marketing professionals must know about current laws affecting their establishment as well as any new laws or regulations that will be enacted in the future.

4. **Describe the importance of vendors in assessing market conditions.**

   It would be very difficult to operate a first-rate establishment without first-rate vendors. While the supply of needed products and services must be priced competitively, it is even more important that the supply be dependable. For that reason, it is important that managers continually monitor the number and quality of vendors available to service them.

5. **Explain the importance of competitors in assessing market conditions.**

   Within every establishment's market area a variety of competitors will likely seek to gain new customers. Of course, they will also try to retain their current ones. The restaurant and foodservice business is competitive. In most market areas, new establishments open and existing operations close. Also, the entire size of a market may expand or contract.

   Because this is true, the market size, the number of direct competitors, and the resulting market share are examples of information that must be carefully monitored.

6. **Identify demographic factors used to define the target market.**

   Demographic factors are among the most useful to managers as they seek to identify their target markets. Important demographic factors include age, education, ethnicity, geography, household size, income level, occupation, race, religion, spending patterns, sexual orientation, and stage in the family life cycle.

7. **Identify psychographic factors used to define the target market.**

   Psychographic factors include lifestyle, beliefs, attitudes, and other customer-defining characteristics. Psychographics are important because they describe the human characteristics of customers. These characteristics may have a direct bearing on their responses to marketing-related activities such as pricing, response to promotions, reaction to new product introductions, and reactions to proposed or actual changes in the products or services sold by the establishment.

APPLICATION EXERCISE

In many cases, a restaurant or foodservice operation will draw its customers from the nearby geographic area. Consider the area in which you now live. Search the Internet and consider your own views of the area to find answers to these market-related questions that could be of great interest to operation managers in that area.

1. What is the population of the area?

2. What is the average income of the area's residents?

3. What is the racial makeup of the area's residents?

4. What is average household size in the area?

5. Is the area population increasing or declining?

6. What are three key psychographic terms *you* would use to identify the area's residents?

Compile your findings into a well-written, one-page document that describes the members of your community in a way restaurant and foodservice managers would find helpful in identifying target markets.

REVIEW YOUR LEARNING

Select the best answer for each question.

1. **Which is an internal source of marketing environment–related data?**

   A. Statewide data detailing unemployment rates by county

   B. Federal Census Bureau records detailing population trends

   C. Saturday night sales records generated by an establishment's POS system

   D. City zoning records listing the number of establishments located in the city limits

2. **Which is a secondary source of marketing environment–related data?**

   A. An establishment's POS records of its monthly revenue

   B. An operation's POS records of its most popular menu items

   C. Information that will be obtained from an as yet unwritten guest survey

   D. Yearly establishment sales projections published by the National Restaurant Association

3. **Which is a primary source of marketing environment–related data?**

   A. An establishment's POS records of its most popular menu items

   B. Information that will be obtained from an as yet unwritten guest survey

   C. Yearly sales projections published by the National Restaurant Association

   D. City zoning records listing the number of establishments located in the city limits

4. **What is an example of a purchase made from a customer's discretionary income?**

   A. Rent payments

   B. Monthly student loan payments

   C. Payments for gas needed to commute to work

   D. The payment made for a birthday dinner eaten out with friends

5. **What event would have significant negative economic impact on an establishment's market conditions?**

   A. An additional wine vendor

   B. The opening of a new city parking lot

   C. The closing of a very large nearby manufacturing plant

   D. An increase in operation inspections by the local health department

6. **Which government action would affect the legal environment in which an establishment operates?**

   A. The decision to repave a key road leading into town

   B. Implementation of a local ordinance banning the use of trans fats in cooking certain food

   C. A decision to add more police patrols to downtown neighborhoods during the weekends

   D. The layoff of five teachers from a local elementary school

7. **Which activity would directly affect the vendor environment within which establishments operate?**

   A. The formation of a new off-site catering company

   B. A new produce supplier starting a business in the area

   C. A chain restaurant's decision to close an older and poorly performing store

   D. The city council's decision to extend the hours in which establishments are allowed to sell alcoholic beverages

8. **A small town has just announced that a major manufacturer will be building a plant nearby that will employ 2,000 new workers. When the plant is built and operating, what will be its likely impact?**

   A. The town's market size for restaurant meals will increase.

   B. The town's market size for restaurant meals will decrease.

   C. The market share for every restaurant in town will increase by the same amount.

   D. The market share for every restaurant in town will decrease by the same amount.

9. **Which internal promotion targets customers based on a specific demographic?**

   A. Two-for-one dinner specials on Tuesday nights

   B. Senior citizen's 10 percent discount on early bird meals purchased weekdays between 4 and 6 p.m.

   C. Buy one appetizer and get a second appetizer free on Fridays (only) between 4 and 7 p.m.

   D. Free lunchtime soft drink refills from 10:00 a.m. to 2:00 p.m. every day

10. **The manager of a pizza operation wants to develop an iPhone application for her takeout pizza business. Which characteristic would describe the customer she is targeting?**

    A. Male customers

    B. Female customers

    C. Tech-savvy customers

    D. Baby boomer customers

FIELD PROJECT

1. Visit your favorite local establishment. Spend some time observing its customers.

2. List five demographic customer characteristics you feel its target market possesses.

3. List five psychographic customer characteristics of its target market. Feel free to create your own psychographic categories based on your personal observation.

4. How would you describe the "type" of person who frequents this establishment?

5. What recommendations would you give this operation's manager about how best to market to the customers you observed?

4 Understanding Customer Behavior

CHAPTER LEARNING OBJECTIVES

After completing this chapter, you should be able to:

- List the steps involved in the purchasing decision process.

- Identify external and internal factors that influence buyer behavior.

- Describe the identifying characteristics of the four modern restaurant segments.

- Explain the differences between commercial and noncommercial foodservice operations.

KEY TERMS

CASE STUDY

"I thought the ads were great," Carole proclaimed. "And we spent a ton of money on them."

"I've seen a few new customers," said Stan. "But when I asked, they said they hadn't come because of our ads. They just saw our sign."

Carole and Stan are co-owners of the Easy Perch seafood house. After a good grand opening, the customer counts had leveled off. That's why Carole and Stan invested in a fairly expensive ad program emphasizing the quality of the restaurant's products and the variety of menu items offered.

"Well, those ads cost us a lot," replied Stan. "If they don't bring us new customers, why should we keep running them? And what else can we do to bring in customers?"

"I think what you're really asking is, how do customers decide where to eat?" said Stan. "And how can we make sure it's with us?"

1. What could be some reasons for the flattening customer counts at the Easy Perch?

2. Why is it important for Carole and Stan to know how their target customers choose a restaurant?

WHY CUSTOMERS BUY

Because restaurant and foodservice establishments sell both services and products, sometimes it can be a challenge for managers to determine why consumers choose one establishment over another. Some guests may come to an establishment primarily for its products, while others may come because of the service or convenience it provides. Still others come for multiple reasons. As a result, one of the most difficult aspects of a manager's job is that of understanding why and how customers make purchasing decisions.

The study of why customers buy and how they make their purchasing decisions is based on two basic principles. The first is that consumers are rationale. Chapter 2 stated that consumer rationality is the tendency of consumers to make their buying decisions based on their beliefs that their purchases will be of direct benefit to them. As a result, buying behavior can be predicted.

The second principle is that restaurant and foodservice managers can influence buying behavior through their knowledge of the customer and by the products and services the establishment offers as a result. For example, a manager knows that a new beverage product is becoming increasingly popular with a specific population segment. This manager also recognizes that this population segment includes many individuals in his or her target market. In this case, adding the new beverage item to the operation's menu, and promoting the fact that it has been added, may influence customers' buying behavior.

The manager took these specific actions in the example:

- Recognized a change in target market behavior
- Assessed the potential impact of the change
- Made adjustments to product offerings in response to changes in target market preferences

As this example demonstrates, managers must understand how their customers make buying decisions. They must also be aware of the external and internal forces that affect buyer behavior. Armed with this information, managers can make decisions that are consistently in the best interests of their guests and of their own establishments.

Understanding the Customers' Decision-Making Process

The reasons behind purchasing decisions are complex, but it is critical that restaurant and foodservice managers understand this behavior. When faced with a purchasing decision, most consumers follow a predictable process. *Exhibit 4.1* illustrates the five steps associated with the purchasing decision process.

Exhibit 4.1

THE PURCHASING DECISION PROCESS

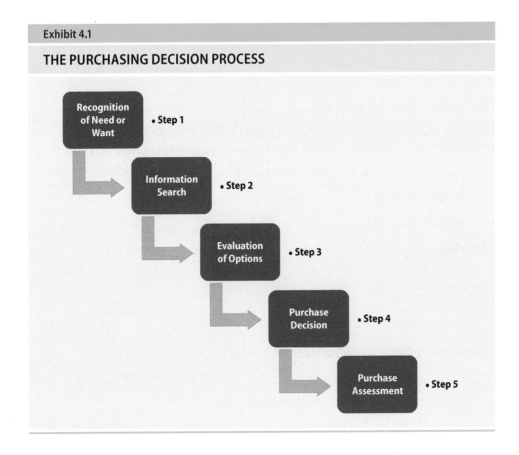

STEP 1: RECOGNITION OF NEED OR WANT

In this initial step, a buyer recognizes the need or want to make a purchase. A **need** is an emotional or physical requirement that occurs when a person is deprived of something. For example, a person deprived of food will develop a need to eat. Closely related to needs are wants.

A **want** is a desire that is shaped by a person's culture and personality. For example, an American college student might want to eat pizza, whereas a Peruvian college student might want to eat ceviché. Wants are affected by external and internal factors. People need to eat daily to live; however, they *want* to eat in a restaurant but they do not *need* to eat in a restaurant. In the restaurant and foodservice industry, customers may have a need to satisfy their hunger, but just as likely, they may have a want to join their friends at an establishment, whether they are hungry or not.

STEP 2: INFORMATION SEARCH

A potential customer with a recognized need or want may seek additional information. The amount of information a potential buyer seeks may vary depending on the situation. A spur of the moment decision to buy a dessert after a meal may require only a quick look at the menu options. Determining where to celebrate a 25th wedding anniversary, however, may call for a good deal of research into appropriate alternatives.

STEP 3: EVALUATION OF OPTIONS

Once the available options have been identified, consumers consider all of the attributes they will acquire when making their purchases. These attributes may be factors for a person purchasing a typical consumer product:

- Product quality
- Models available
- Price
- Warranty
- Delivery
- Perceived status

The following factors may influence a person making a dining choice:

- Location
- Price
- Menu variety
- Food quality
- Service quality
- Décor

As illustrated in these two examples, consumers typically see a purchase as buying a bundle of attributes. Rarely does a single attribute drive the purchase of a product or service.

STEP 4: PURCHASE DECISION

In this step, the actual purchase decision is made. Note, however, that the purchase decision may not be based solely on the buyer's individual preferences. For example, a mother may choose an establishment with a menu that appeals to her children, or a husband may choose one that serves his wife's favorite cuisine. In both of these examples, the decision maker's concern for another person, rather than his or her own preference, prompts the final purchase decision.

STEP 5: PURCHASE ASSESSMENT

Buyers always consider the wisdom of their purchases after they have made them. If the food and service match the customers' expectations, they will be pleased with their purchase, their satisfaction levels will be high, and the chance of those customers returning increases. If the products or services are poor, customers' expectations will not be met and it will be very difficult for any marketing efforts to make them repeat customers. This is one reason managers must ensure they and their staff do all they can to correct service errors before customers leave the operation.

Unhappy customers may express their displeasure in a variety of ways. They may return a food item or complain to their server or ask to see a manager. They may even demand to have the cost of an unsatisfactory item removed from their bill. Managers must be ready to handle each of these expressions of dissatisfaction in a manner that is fair to both the guest and the establishment.

In the worst-case scenario, unhappy customers will say nothing. They will simply leave, never to return again. But they will tell others about their poor experience! Managers and their staff can mitigate this experience by checking on customers during meal service to ensure that the products and service meet expectations and to correct any problems that arise *before* the customers leave the establishment.

All customers go through the process outlined in *Exhibit 4.1* every time they make a purchasing decision. However, external and internal factors may also influence these decisions.

External Influences on Buying Behavior

When consumers make purchase decisions, they are affected by both external and internal influences. These factors have a powerful impact on the decisions buyers make, so understanding these influences is key to better understanding consumer behavior. The following are among the most important external factors directly affecting consumer purchasing decisions:

- Income
- Background
- Peer group affiliation
- Household status

INCOME

A buyer's income level is one of the most influential factors affecting purchasing decisions. Before most consumers decide to spend their money they must have (1) the desire to buy and (2) the ability to buy.

To illustrate how income influences a buying decision, assume that a consumer is considering buying a new automobile. Basic models start at around $15,000, while stylish sports cars can cost $100,000 or more. Many car buyers have the *desire* to buy the expensive sports car. However, only a few buyers have incomes that provide them the *ability* to buy it.

THINK ABOUT IT . . .

Have you ever had a less-than-positive experience at an establishment? Did you later tell others about your poor experience? What can managers and their service staffs do to help avoid situations such as this?

Manager's Memo

Understanding the interplay between a customer's desire to buy and his or her buying decision is important for managers. Sometimes a decrease in menu price will increase a customer's desire to buy. For example, when an establishment offers half-price appetizers, it uses reduced price to drive customers' buying decisions.

In other cases, managers use suggestive selling to increase customers' desire to buy. Suggestive selling is the recommendation of additional items to customers already making purchases.

Effective suggestive selling techniques include a variety of actions:

- Recommending appetizers to guests purchasing entrees
- Offering wine or beer choices that complement a guest's entrée choice
- Offering a larger size of a selected item at a modestly increased price
- Recommending a featured dessert

When implemented effectively, suggestive selling is a powerful way to increase sales and guest satisfaction while charging prices that are fair to customers and fair to the business.

Likewise, in the restaurant and foodservice industry, many customers have the desire to eat in the high-end establishments that serve expensive food and wine. Many, however, do not have the income required to do so on a regular basis. For these customers, income limitations heavily influence their buying decisions.

It is important that restaurant or foodservice managers recognize that their target market must have both the desire and the ability to buy the items the establishment sells. Effective marketing can create in consumers a strong desire to buy. These consumers' willingness to buy, however, must be matched with their ability to buy or the marketing efforts will not result in increased customers.

Restaurant and foodservice managers must be aware of the socioeconomic status of their target market. **Socioeconomic status** is the financial position of a consumer or group of consumers relative to other consumers. Chapter 3 stated that consumers can be grouped into upper-income, middle-income, lower-middle-income, and lower-income categories. Restaurant and foodservice managers ensure that their product quality and pricing structure appeal to target markets' socioeconomic group or groups, so that their customers have both the desire and ability to buy.

BACKGROUND

A customer's religious, ethnic, and cultural background all heavily influence buying decisions. As an example, consider an individual whose religion prohibits the eating of certain food. Consuming the prohibited food violates that person's religious views. In addition, the act may have a negative social impact on that individual's relationship with friends and family. It is unlikely that a restaurant or foodservice manager, regardless of the marketing effort undertaken, could persuade such a customer to order and eat the prohibited food.

The ways in which persons with similar backgrounds make purchasing decisions are also related. Establishments may wish to cater to certain backgrounds. For example, a manager whose target market consists primarily of Americans might decide to market its menu items and services differently than would a manager whose establishment primarily targets a European clientele. Here are other examples of catering to specific backgrounds:

- Advertise Easter Brunch in a heavily Christian market area.

- Promote specials offered on Cinco de Mayo day in market areas that include large numbers of Mexican Americans.

- Carefully identify menu items that are halal or kosher, allowed under Islamic or Jewish dietary laws, in areas with significant Muslim or Jewish customers.

As demonstrated in the previous examples, managers must understand the backgrounds of their target customers. Doing so will allow these managers to create marketing programs tailored to these specific backgrounds.

PEER GROUP AFFILIATION

A peer group is a social group consisting of people with similar characteristics such as interests, age, education, or socioeconomics status. For peer group members, acceptance by others in the group can be of critical importance. Members of peer groups often make purchase decisions based on how others in the group will perceive that purchase.

When a person makes a purchase, including those made at restaurant and foodservice establishments, they subconsciously seek to fit into their peer group's perceptions of proper behavior. If dining at a particular establishment is considered the "in" thing to do, some individuals will make the choice because of status. This phenomenon helps explain why establishments operated by celebrity chefs are so popular. Dining at these establishments can help people "prove" they are aware of the newest and trendiest operations. Savvy operation managers recognize that opinion shapers such as food critics, celebrities, and other well-known individuals can have a powerful impact on the behavior of others.

HOUSEHOLD STATUS

A household is defined as all of the people who occupy the same dwelling. For example, a husband and wife living in the same house with their three children would represent one household. Similarly, a single college student living alone in an apartment near campus represents one household.

There are more than 112 million households in the United States. In some cases, only one member of the household earns income. In others, there may be several income earners. Households may have a single head (head of household) or several who share leadership in different areas. For restaurant and foodservice managers, understanding the household makeup of target customers is important because households tend to buy as a group and because individual members of a household can influence the purchasing decisions of the other members.

Households of one or two persons, for example, may not desire the services offered by family-oriented establishments as much as would households with families consisting of five or more persons.

MANAGER'S MATH

An operation achieved $2 million in revenue last year. The manager is convinced that a suggestive selling program could have a very positive impact on her sales for next year.

1. By how much would her *annual* revenue increase if she implemented the suggestive selling program and it generated a 1% increase in sales?

2. By how much would her *annual* revenue increase if she implemented the suggestive selling program and it generated a 10% increase in sales?

(Answers: 1. $20,000; 2. $200,000)

BY THE CUSTOMER/ FOR THE CUSTOMER

Social media sites are popular in part because going out for dinner and receiving so-so food and service can be a big disappointment. To avoid unmet expectations, increasing numbers of customers use Internet-based consumer and critic review sites to help them choose where they eat. Restaurant and foodservice managers responsible for marketing their operation must regularly monitor these sites. The most popular review sites can change rapidly, so it is essential that restaurant managers carefully follow the sites currently most attractive to their own target markets.

Exhibit 4.2

Several key changes to household makeup may have an impact on the restaurant and foodservice industry:

- In the past, the majority of households in the United States were married couples. Not today. The 2010 census documented the fact that for the first time in American history, married couples are a minority in the United States because the number of people living alone is growing rapidly. Smaller household sizes affect the packaging and portion sizes of entrées offered to guests.

- The ethnic makeup of households is changing rapidly. In the two largest states in the United States—California and Texas—no race or ethnicity makes up a majority (more than 50 percent) of the population. In the 10 largest U.S. cities, no single ethnic group constitutes a majority. As a result, the popularity of ethnic food is increasing.

- Average household age is increasing. Average life spans of Americans continue to increase. As a result, there are increased numbers of multigenerational households. Older people (aged 60 and over) living with their children or grandchildren have a bigger impact than ever before on what those in younger generations are buying (*Exhibit 4.2*). In addition, the preferred dining times of older customers are typically earlier in the day than those of younger customers.

- Difficult economic times have created more households in which older children (21 years and older) are returning home to live with their parents.

An awareness of the changing nature of the household is critical for restaurant and foodservice managers. Understanding these changes, as well as understanding the other external factors influencing buying decisions, allows managers to more effectively market their products and services to their target consumers.

Internal Influences on Buying Behavior

Factors such as income level, background, peer group affiliation, and household status exert external pressures on individual buying decisions. However, internal factors also influence individual choice. Most notably, factors such as age, gender, and lifestyle influence customers' purchases. Managers aware of these factors can tailor their marketing efforts to address these influences.

AGE

As discussed in chapter 2, food and beverage purchases change as people age. Consumers in their 20s and 30s are more easily attracted to high-energy establishments that may be loud, busy, and crowded with others like themselves. Parents of small children look for operations considered kid-friendly, while middle-aged and older diners tend to put more emphasis on cleanliness, atmosphere, location, and the ability to be seated upon arrival. It is the job of managers to understand the age of their target markets and to create menus, service procedures, and operational policies that cater specifically to those age groups.

GENDER

Establishment managers regularly make generalizations about their target markets to more efficiently develop their marketing plans and focus their marketing efforts. Yet, in a society that values equality between men and women, using gender as a means of differentiating customers can be tricky. Some consumer behavior researchers state that men and women seek exactly the same things when making a buying decision: value, fair price, and quality. Other researchers state that there are real differences in what motivates men and women to make their buying decisions and these differences should be addressed in marketing efforts.

Most managers would agree that targeting gender in a promotional effort is not inherently problematic. Managers need to have a sense of their target audiences' demographics to be successful in communicating to them. If the target audience for a product or service is primarily of a specific gender, communicate to that audience in appropriate ways. Take care to avoid overgeneralizations that could be perceived as discriminating. The appropriateness of gender-based marketing initiatives should be based on common sense and sensible research. Carefully gathering internal and external data concerning the preferences of target customers based on gender makes good sense if the information is used properly.

LIFESTYLE

Consumers who are the same age, the same gender, and who come from the same socioeconomic and cultural background may nonetheless live very different lifestyles. A lifestyle is the way a person lives his or her life. Lifestyle is expressed in terms of the activities people engage in, their interests, and their opinions.

External factors including income, background, peer group affiliation, and household status, as well as internal factors such as age and gender can have a direct impact on a person's lifestyle. In fact, it is how all of those factors and others are blended by an individual's unique personality that results in a chosen lifestyle. From that perspective, it can be said that a person's lifestyle paints a total picture of that individual.

THINK ABOUT IT . . .

Do your friends of the opposite gender order the same menu items as you do? What other menu choice differences do you notice when dining out with friends of the opposite gender?

OPEN FOR BUSINESS

WHAT'S THE FOOTPRINT?

A lifestyle-based group of consumers rapidly increasing in size is the one that contains environmentally conscious individuals. In some cases, the actions of this group's members can take the form of routinely recycling at home. In other cases, they can take the form of customers who choose establishments based on their perceptions of the operation's eco-friendliness.

Restaurant and foodservice managers in all segments would do well to continually monitor the growth of this group and to educate the public about the many good things their establishments are doing to help protect the environment. Recycling, conserving energy, and purchasing environmentally friendly equipment and supplies are among the actions most operations can proudly point to as they communicate their value message to this increasingly important lifestyle group.

Exhibit 4.3

INFLUENCES ON LIFESTYLE CHOICE

Activities	Interests	Opinions
Work	Family	Politics
Sports	Home	Education
Social gatherings	Fashion	Social issues
Vacation	Food	Economics
Hobbies	Recreation	Culture
Fitness		

Those who study lifestyles of individuals have identified activities, interests, and opinions that are often used to define various lifestyles. *Exhibit 4.3* lists 15 of the most well-recognized influences on lifestyle choice.

Marketers use lifestyle as a means of grouping consumers who spend their time and money on similar interests. Lifestyle can include things like an interest in golfing, fitness, cooking, the environment, biking, bowling, attending concerts or car races, owning pets, politics, or watching sports on TV. When restaurant and foodservice managers use information about identifiable groups, they can often effectively target those groups in their establishment's promotional efforts.

MODERN RESTAURANT MARKET SEGMENTS AND TARGET MARKETS

The restaurant and foodservice business is part of the service industry. The service industry is made up of companies that primarily earn revenue by providing products and intangible services. Other service industry segments include lodging, retail, transportation, and distribution. All types of restaurant and foodservice operations are part of the service industry, regardless of their size or type of products they offer.

Restaurant and foodservice operations are similar in that they generate most of their revenue from the sale of food and beverage products. Professionals in the industry use a variety of ways to group restaurant and foodservice operations. For example, operations could be classified as being either large or small in size. Other classification systems could be based on the type of menu items offered (e.g., subs, wraps, barbeque, Italian, Chinese, or Mexican) or whether the food served is typically eaten in a designated dining area or is taken away from the establishment to be eaten elsewhere. Alternatively, pricing could be used to classify various operations. Different types of operations will have different marketing strategies appropriate to their unique needs and target markets.

While it is easy to see that there could be many different ways to classify restaurants, the most popular way is to place each operation into one of the following four commonly recognized restaurant and foodservice industry segments, based on the service and price levels its individual operations provide to guests:

- Quick service
- Fast casual
- Casual
- Fine dining

Quick-Service Restaurants

The quick-service restaurant (QSR) segment is one of the largest and most visible of all restaurant and foodservice groups. QSRs are characterized by their limited menus, fast service, and modest prices. QSRs are extremely popular with customers who are in a hurry and those on a budget. The menu items served in quick-service operations are limited by what people like to eat, how quickly the menu items can be prepared, the prices people expect to pay, and the time people are willing to spend eating, as well as the costs of food, equipment, and labor. In most cases, QSRs serve simple food items with simple preparation requirements and because they do, menu prices can be kept as low as possible. Whereas hamburgers represent the single most popular QSR restaurant type in the United States, a large group of QSRs are very successful featuring different menu items. Examples include establishments that offer hot dogs, sandwiches, fried chicken, gyros, and fried seafood.

QSRs typically provide an indoor dining area for their customers. Many QSRs, however, sell as much or more of their food to drive-through customers as they do to those eating in their establishments (*Exhibit 4.4*). Drive-through customers are those who place and receive their take-away food orders without leaving their cars. Increasingly, portable food carts and food trucks are used to make quick food service items available wherever large numbers of customers congregate.

Exhibit 4.4

The services offered in QSRs are limited and, of course, quick; this speed of service is one of their primary competitive points of difference. As a result, the service is very limited in nature and the customers often provide parts of it for themselves. In a QSR the menu is usually posted on the wall or a signboard. Customers may order at one end of a counter and pick up their food at the other end. The food typically is served in paper or plastic containers. Customers also usually pick up their own utensils and condiments from a central station and then take everything to a table they find for themselves. When they have finished eating, it is very common

used dishes and utensils and takes them away. When the meal is finished, the server presents the bill to the table and collects payment.

All these services cost quite a lot in comparison to the more limited services provided at QSRs and fast-casual operations. Also, the quality of these services and the compensation of employees who provide these services vary markedly over this category of operation, but they are distinctly more costly to provide than those of QSRs and fast-casual operations. As a result, menu prices in casual restaurants are typically higher than in earlier mentioned segments.

Fine-Dining Restaurants

Exhibit 4.7

Fine-dining restaurants offer guests the highest-quality food and full table service. Fine-dining operations are the type that comes to mind for many hospitality professionals when they think about owning or managing the very best of establishments (*Exhibit 4.7*).

Like the other segments addressed in this chapter, there is no universally accepted definition for fine dining. However, most industry professionals would likely agree that fine-dining restaurants differ from other segments in three critical areas:

- Product offerings
- Service levels
- Ambience

PRODUCT OFFERINGS

The type of cuisine offered in fine-dining restaurants varies greatly; however, in all cases these operations serve masterfully prepared food of extremely high quality. Many fine-dining restaurants are either chef-owned or employ a talented chef who develops the operation's menu. Chefs may creatively vary menus seasonally to take advantage of locally produced fresh ingredients, and the chef's extensive skills are often a point of competitive difference.

The actual number of menu items offered in a fine-dining restaurant may be large or rather limited; however, each item must be outstanding. In most cases, fine-dining restaurants also offer their guests extensive and high-quality beer, wine, and spirits menus to complement the food they serve. In short, fine-dining restaurants of all types offer the best in ingredients, food quality, and preparation methods.

SERVICE LEVELS

Fine-dining establishments provide their guests with exceptionally high levels of personal service. All restaurant and food service operations must seek to provide good guest service; however, in most cases a fine-dining restaurant's well-trained staff would also likely do these tasks:

- Escort guests to the table

- Explain complex menu items in detail

- Recommend appropriate beverages to accompany menu selections

- Clean the guest's table between courses

- Replace cloth napkins and serviceware between courses

In the restaurant and foodservice industry, there are several different styles of table service that date back for generations. These table styles are typically found only in casual and fine-dining establishments. Each style demands different preparation and presentation procedures. The more labor-intensive the style of service, the more costly it is for the owner to provide. Four styles of table service commonly used in establishments in the United States are described in *Exhibit 4.8.*

Exhibit 4.8

STYLES OF TABLE SERVICE

American-style service: The food is placed onto a plate for each diner and then brought out to the customer. The plates are distributed to the proper diners. This is the most common form of table service in the United States.

English-style service: Also known as familystyle dining, this type of service is the simplest and least expensive. The food is brought to the tables on platters and serving bowls. The host of the table then serves the meal on the plates for the other diners, or the dishes are passed around the table so diners can serve themselves.

French-style service: While this is the most elegant of the styles of service, it is also the most expensive. The food is placed into serving dishes and then brought out on a cart. It is then served onto the diners' plates at the table. The food is kept hot by a warming unit in each cart. This type of service is expensive to implement because of the expensive carts and the additional skills required of the servers

Russian-style service: Each diner's hot food is placed onto hot plates and cold food onto cold plates. All the diners' plates are brought to the table on a cart where they are distributed to the diners. A small investment is required by the restaurant owner for the expense of the carts.

THINK ABOUT IT . . .

Where might you eat if you have only $10 to spend? Where might you eat if you have $80 to spend? What differences might you expect to find at each establishment?

To decide which service style is best for them, fine-dining managers take many factors into account:

- Target markets they choose and how well their operations can meet those markets' needs

- Size, décor, and cost of their facility, its equipment, and its furnishings

- The number and types of employees required, the skills they must have, and the amount of compensation they are paid

- Availability and cost of required food and nonfood supplies

In most cases, the more service provided, the more investment required, and the more ongoing expenses incurred. As a result, higher prices must be charged for the meals.

Finally, in addition to waitstaff, some fine-dining establishments employ sommeliers, service staff members who assist customers in selecting wines to go with their menu choices. Additional service staff positions that may be found in fine-dining restaurants also include parking valets, coatroom attendants, and restroom attendants.

AMBIENCE

Some of the most beautifully designed interiors in the world are found in fine-dining establishments. The walls, flooring, and artwork reflect the operation's upscale ambience. Even the staff's uniforms and the china, glassware, and other tabletop items are carefully chosen to complement the ambience. In all cases, the job of the manager is to create a luxurious environment that is as memorable as the food and beverages served.

Noncommercial Foodservice Operations

Some foodservice operations are not typically considered to be restaurants. Although there are no legally mandated ways to segment foodservice operations, one very popular method used by industry professionals to categorize meals served away from home is to consider whether the food is served in a commercial or a noncommercial setting, as demonstrated in *Exhibit 4.9*.

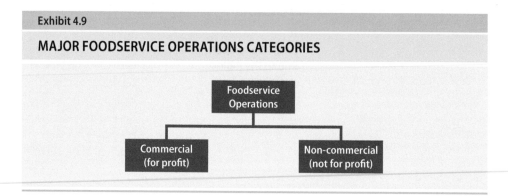

Exhibit 4.9

MAJOR FOODSERVICE OPERATIONS CATEGORIES

Commercial foodservice operations such as the restaurants addressed earlier in this chapter are typically open to the general public. These operations most often seek to make a profit by providing food and beverages to as wide an audience of customers as possible.

Noncommercial foodservice operations are not typically open to the general public. The goal of these units is to provide cost-effective meals for a specially targeted audience. This segment is also commonly referred to as not-for-profit (or nonprofit) or institutional foodservice.

Exhibit 4.10 lists some examples of foodservice operations that are commonly classified as either commercial (for-profit) or noncommercial (not-for-profit). When defined as a location serving food to those away from home, it is easy to see that professional foodservice managers will be found in both types of settings. It is also true, however, that most foodservice professionals use the term *restaurant* to indicate those profit-seeking businesses open to the general public.

In some cases, the line between commercial and noncommercial foodservice operations is not clear. For example, a coffee shop located in the student union of a college campus or a cafeteria located in a large hospital may indeed be open to the general public. The college and the hospital may even seek to operate these facilities profitably. In these

Exhibit 4.10

EXAMPLES OF COMMERCIAL AND NONCOMMERCIAL FOODSERVICE OPERATIONS

Commercial Foodservice Operations	Noncommercial Foodservice Operations
Restaurants	Employee cafeterias (includes offices and factories)
Bars and pubs	
Hotel and motel restaurants	Schools
Public country clubs	Religious institutions
Casinos	Private country clubs
Amusement parks and recreation facilities	Colleges and universities
Stadiums and sports arenas	Military bases
Vending	Hospitals, nursing homes, and retirement centers
Retail (e.g., food trucks, food carts, farmer's markets, and grocery stores)	Transportation (airlines, cruise ships, and trains)
	Correctional facilities

examples, two noncommercial entities (a college and a hospital) have elected to operate a commercial foodservice operation for the benefit of those they are serving.

Regardless of the segment they work in, or whether their operations are considered to be commercial or noncommercial, in all settings professional restaurant and foodservice managers use the same techniques and principles to create their marketing plans and successfully operate their businesses.

SUMMARY

1. **List the steps involved in the purchasing decision process.**

   Knowing the process consumers use to make a purchase decision is important so that managers can predict consumer behavior and influence that behavior. Before making a purchase, consumers must have an identifiable need or want. Customers seek information and evaluate the available options before making a purchasing decision. After a decision has been made, consumers evaluate the value received from that purchase.

2. **Identify external and internal factors that influence buyer behavior.**

   A number of external and internal factors impact buying behavior. External factors include income, background, peer group affiliation, and household status. Internal factors found to influence buyer behavior include age, gender, and lifestyle.

3. **Describe the identifying characteristics of the four modern restaurant segments.**

   The restaurant and foodservice industry is a service industry that can be divided into four major segments: QSRs, fast-casual, casual, and fine-dining establishments. QSRs generally offer a limited menu and very rapid but low-intensity service. Fast-casual establishments, the industry's fastest-growing segment, provide menu options that are generally slightly higher in price than QSRs, although fast-casual options do not generally include table service. Casual restaurants are considered to be those that provide table service to guests and serve moderately priced food in an informal atmosphere. Finally, fine-dining operations offer guests the highest-quality food and full table service, differing from other restaurant segments by providing higher-quality product, more attentive service, and more devotion to overall ambience.

4. **Explain the differences between commercial and noncommercial foodservice operations.**

   A commercial foodservice operation is open to the general public. In most cases, its goal is to generate a profit for the owner of the business. Noncommercial foodservice operations are not typically open to the general public. The goal of most noncommercial operations is to serve quality meals to a special group of diners such as students, patients, workers, or military personnel. In some cases a noncommercial entity may operate a facility that is open to the public. In such a case, however, the primary purpose for operating the facility would still be to support the mission of the organization operating it rather than to maximize profits.

APPLICATION EXERCISE

Consider a restaurant or foodservice operation you may want to own or manage someday.

Write the answers to the following questions using no more than two or three sentences for each question:

1. To which income level will your establishment appeal? Why?

2. To which background types will your establishment appeal? Why?

3. To which age group will your establishment appeal? Why?

4. To which lifestyle groups will your establishment appeal? Why?

5. Under which restaurant segment would your establishment fall? Why?

REVIEW YOUR LEARNING

Select the best answer for each question.

1. **What is the first step in the decision-making process used by consumers making a purchase?**
   A. Information gathering
   B. Purchase assessment
   C. Research of alternatives
   D. Recognition of need or want

2. **What is an example of a promotion likely to attract customers of a similar background?**
   A. Reduced prices for senior citizens
   B. Buy one, get one free children's platters
   C. Discounted fish sandwiches during Lent
   D. Free appetizers with the purchase of an entrée

3. **What factor would likely prevent most customers from eating every night at their area's most exclusive establishments?**
   A. Income
   B. Lifestyle
   C. Household status
   D. Peer group affiliation

4. **Which establishment is most likely to attract someone with a health-conscious lifestyle?**
   A. A fine-dining establishment with a knowledgeable sommelier
   B. A casual restaurant with multiple big-screen televisions
   C. A fast-casual operation with organic entrées
   D. A QSR with a children's playground

5. A college student who eats at a pizza establishment because most of his friends recommend it is influenced most heavily by which factor?

   A. Age

   B. Gender

   C. Peer group affiliation

   D. Household status level

6. In which restaurant and foodservice industry segment will menu prices likely be the lowest?

   A. QSR

   B. Fast-casual

   C. Casual

   D. Fine-dining

7. Valet parking is most likely to be found at which type of restaurant or foodservice operation?

   A. QSR

   B. Fast-casual

   C. Casual

   D. Fine-dining

8. What is the fastest-growing restaurant and foodservice industry segment?

   A. QSR

   B. Fast-casual

   C. Casual

   D. Fine-dining

9. Which of these statements is an example of suggestive selling?

   A. Happy hour appetizer pricing

   B. Beer pairings with entrées

   C. Kids-eat-free promotions

   D. Fixed price salad bar

10. Which is a noncommercial foodservice operation?

    A. Hotel

    B. Hospital

    C. Shopping mall

    D. Amusement park

FIELD PROJECT

Consider your favorite local establishment. Identify the restaurant and foodservice industry segment that would include that operation. Then complete the following exercise.

1. Identify five restaurant or foodservice operations in your area that are in the same segment and that compete directly with your favorite establishment.

2. Create a chart like the following one. In this chart, list each of the competitors you named in Question 1. Determine whether each competitor competes with your favorite establishment on the basis of product or service, or both.

Competitor	Product	Service Level	Both
1.			
2.			
3.			
4.			
5.			

5

Preparing a Marketing Plan

CHAPTER LEARNING OBJECTIVES

After completing this chapter, you should be able to:

- Explain the purposes of a business plan and a marketing plan.

- Identify the key components in a business plan.

- Describe how managers develop a marketing plan.

- Describe how managers develop a marketing budget.

- State how managers implement marketing plans.

KEY TERMS

alternative revenue source (ARS), p. 110

barriers to success, p. 104

business plan, p. 98

co-branding, p. 111

concept statement (business plan), p. 100

corporation, p. 103

dba, p. 102

executive summary (business plan), p. 100

financial plan, p. 98

marketing activities schedule, p. 119

marketing mix, p. 109

market positioning, p. 106

partnership, p. 102

partnership agreement, p. 102

pro forma, p. 113

shareholder, p. 103

sole proprietorship, p. 102

start-up funds, p. 98

SWOT analysis, p. 104

value statement, p. 107

CASE STUDY

"I can envision the restaurant in my head, I just have a hard time putting it into words. I'm not a writer, I'm a food guy. That's where I was hoping you could help me," explained Carl.

Carl was talking with Shingi. Shingi had graduated from the hospitality management program at State College two years earlier. She had taken her first job with a large national restaurant chain. It was there that she met Carl, a kitchen supervisor at the restaurant. Shingi also helped manage.

"I've been in the business for 20 years," continued Carl. "I know this city, and I know my new restaurant will be a big success. I've saved some money, but not enough. When I talked to my bank, they said they would be glad to consider me for a loan after they see my business plan and a marketing plan."

"So what's the problem?" asked Shingi.

"The problem is that I don't have a written business plan or a written marketing plan to show them. I mean, I know what I want to do and I know how I'm going to do it, but I don't even know where to start in writing it down. That's where I need your help, Shingi!" explained Carl.

1. Why do you think Carl's bank wants to see his written plans before it would be willing to consider making a loan to him?

2. If Carl wanted to seek start-up finding from members of his own family or his friends instead of a bank, do you think he would still need to put his plans into writing? Why or why not?

OVERVIEW: BUSINESS AND MARKETING

A **business plan** is a formal statement of business goals, an explanation of how the goals can be achieved, and the detailed steps for reaching the goals. A business plan may also contain background information about the organization or individuals associated with the proposed establishment. A well-written business plan includes clear information about many important business matters.

In most cases, a business plan will include a marketing plan as well as a financial plan. Recall from chapter 1 that a marketing plan is a guide for an operation's marketing efforts because it tells what will be done to attract the number of customers needed to achieve the operation's revenue targets. The marketing plan also includes a detailed listing of specific activities designed to help an establishment meet its revenue goals.

A **financial plan** is an estimation of the cash needed to open a business or buy an existing business. A financial plan includes information about the amount of money an owner currently has on hand, as well as the total amount needed to start the business, called **start-up funds**. If a financial plan includes the use of borrowed money, the plan also explains how and when the money will be paid back.

A well-developed business plan can help minimize the risk of failure for

Exhibit 5.1

establishments that have not yet opened (*Exhibit 5.1*). It can do the same for those that are already in operation. Business plans detail the goals a business seeks to achieve. Managers responsible for developing marketing plans to support those goals should understand how business plans are developed and the important information they contain. When they do, they are better able to use the information found in business plans to help develop their marketing plans.

THE BUSINESS PLAN

Because of the challenges associated with opening new operations, owners and managers who wish to open a new establishment must give a great deal of thought to the business even before beginning to write a formal business plan. While the development of every new establishment will be somewhat unique, there are key developmental issues to address when the creation of a new restaurant or foodservice operation is under consideration:

- Location
- Concept or brand
- Menu
- Building layout and design
- Marketing
- Financing

Not surprisingly, many of these are the same issues typically addressed in various parts of a comprehensive business plan.

Creating a comprehensive business plan takes time. Generally, the more time devoted to the process, the better the final plan. A well-developed business plan should serve three distinct purposes:

- The plan should be a communication device that provides a clear understanding of the operation's concept and proposed location.
- It should serve its owners and managers as an operating tool that establishes a timeline for the establishment's development and financial targets for its ongoing operation.
- The plan should assist in fund-raising by describing the operation's need for financing and explain how borrowed start-up funds will be repaid by the business.

There is no legally mandated requirement for the information that must be included in business plans; however, they typically include the following components:

- Executive summary
- Concept statement
- Operating plan
- Competitive assessment
- SWOT analysis
- Vendor assessment
- Marketing plan
- Financial plan
- Appendices as needed

OPEN FOR BUSINESS

RESTAURANT TECHNOLOGY

Some owners and managers are not confident about their writing skills. Fortunately for them, a variety of companies have developed business plan, marketing plan, financial plan, and even media plan software to assist them.

These software programs are designed to help in the actual writing of a business plan. Many of the programs address all aspects of the business plan process: completing the written plan, forecasting close-to-reality financial results with feasibility checking, as well as preparing presentations suitable for use in seeking start-up funds.

To see an example of the kind of business plan templates offered by companies such as these, enter "business plan software" into your favorite search engine and view the results.

THINK ABOUT IT . . .

Banks are nearly unanimous in requiring companies seeking start-up funding to submit a business plan. Would you want to see a business plan before you lent money? What information would you expect in the plan?

Executive Summary

An **executive summary** provides readers of a business plan with the highlights of the plan. Even though the topic appears first in the printed document, most business plan developers leave the writing of the executive summary until the end because the summary typically includes information taken from other sections of the plan. Put another way, the plan cannot summarize something that has not been written.

Producing a clear and compelling case for a restaurant or foodservice establishment in the executive summary portion of a business plan is critical. Readers must be convinced at the outset that the rest of the plan is worth reading.

The executive summary portion of the business plan is usually brief. One to two pages is common. Major points in the business plan are presented in this section, along with short supporting statements of one or two sentences. In a typical restaurant or foodservice business plan, the first paragraph of the executive summary should generally include the following information:

- Business name
- Business location
- Brief description of the establishment
- Purpose of the plan

The next paragraph should highlight important points, such as projected sales and profits, and keys to the operation's success. Many times, business plan writers will also include in this section a graph or bar chart that shows sales, expenses, and profits before interest and taxes for the next three years. The data in the graph or chart are then explained in the body of the text.

Concept Statement

The **concept statement** is the part of a business plan that details exactly what type of establishment will be created. Recall from chapter 4 that the restaurant and foodservice industry is comprised of several identifiable and widely understood segments: quick-service, fast-casual, casual, and fine-dining establishments. Each of these segments contains a wide range of restaurant or foodservice concepts.

The concept statement allows plan developers to be very specific about which segment they are targeting. It also allows them to describe their unique position within that segment. These are specific topics that should be addressed in this segment of the business plan:

- Menu items to be sold
- Proposed price point
- Unique or distinguishing features

MENU ITEMS TO BE SOLD

A variety of individuals will read the business plan, so it is important to explain clearly the products and services the proposed establishment will offer. For example, an owner who seeks to open a casual restaurant featuring "American fare" should explain what this description means from a menu item and service perspective. Readers will want to know what American fare means to this owner. Providing specific menu examples paints a clear picture of what the proposed establishment will offer.

PROPOSED PRICE POINT

Operations in each industry segment can charge prices that range from very inexpensive to very expensive, relative to the segment. Developers of business plans should specify where in that range their establishment would fall. For example, if an owner plans to open a quick-service restaurant (QSR) featuring hamburgers, he or she should explain whether the proposed restaurant's pricing structure will place it in the lower, middle, or higher range of its competitors' pricing structures. Managers can obtain competitor's prices simply by visiting these operations and comparing their prices with those of the operation described in the business plan.

UNIQUE OR DISTINGUISHING FEATURES

Defining a restaurant or foodservice operation in terms of what makes it unique in the eyes of customers differentiates it from its competitors. It also gives those considering financing the new establishment a clear idea of why it is needed and why it will be popular with the target market.

This portion of the business plan should explain why target customers would be more attracted to the proposed operation than to competitive operations. This section should clearly articulate the specific features and benefits provided to customers. For example, a plan developer might highlight that his or her establishment will feature healthy and nutritious menu items in a fast-casual setting, or that it will offer fine dining in an atmosphere that takes advantage of a spectacular ocean view. Or maybe the operation will highlight features that make it a fun place to eat.

WHAT'S THE FOOTPRINT?

Researchers monitoring the purchasing behavior of restaurant and foodservice customers increasingly find that guests are doing more than just seeking out environmentally friendly operations. Indeed, a majority of these guests are actually willing to pay more to dine in facilities they believe are helping protect the environment.

All restaurant and foodservice operations try to communicate to their guests that the food and beverages they prepare are of good quality and that service levels will be high. It is now clear that the implementation of green practices such as use of organic food or Leadership in Energy and Environmental Design (LEED) certification can also be marketed as a major point of difference for those establishments willing to implement environmentally friendly policies and practices. In the highly competitive restaurant and foodservice industry, real opportunities such as these make it easy to stand out from competitors.

Operating Plan

The operating portion of a business plan details the business structure, explaining who will own and operate the establishment. It also addresses why these individuals are qualified to do it.

Some restaurant and foodservice establishments are operated as a sole proprietorship. A **sole proprietorship** is an operating business structure in which one individual owns, and frequently operates, the business. A sole proprietorship is the least complex business structure available to restaurateurs. In this structure, the proprietor of the business will own all of it and will be held personally responsible for all of its debts.

A sole proprietorship can be legally used as the operating structure of any size establishment. Under this structure, the owner is responsible for 100 percent of the debts that may be incurred by the operation. From a potential lender's perspective, it is critical that the individual seeking funding is clearly identified in this portion of the plan. This portion of the plan should also establish that the owner would take personal responsibility for and have the financial ability to repay any loans given to the business.

In many instances, a sole proprietor's business is operated under a different name. When that is the case, both the name of the business and the individual owning it will be legally registered with the appropriate governmental agency—usually in the state in which the business is operated. This practice allows those who will be doing business with the operation to know the identity of its owner. For example, if Allisha Miller started a fast-casual restaurant, used the sole proprietorship business structure, and called her restaurant Miller's Bar-B-Q, the legal name of the business would be "Allisha Miller; dba Miller's Bar-B-Q" where **dba** means "doing business as."

Many restaurant and foodservice establishments are operated by partners. A **partnership** is a business structure consisting of two or more owners who agree to share in the profits and losses of a business. A partnership is very similar to a sole proprietorship. While a partnership may be formed orally, it is best formed by a written contract. The terms of the contract, also called a **partnership agreement**, detail the rights and responsibilities of each co-owner of the business.

Items that should be addressed in a partnership agreement may include how much time and money each owner will contribute to the business and who will operate it. An agreement may also address how profits will be split among the owners and who is responsible for any losses that may be incurred by the business.

The issue of responsibility for losses is especially important because, as is true in a sole proprietorship, the partners in a general partnership are held personally responsible for any debts incurred by their business. For this reason, potential lenders to a new operation will want to know the identity of each partner as well as each partner's proposed contribution to the business. And, as with a sole proprietorship, lenders will want to know which partners are committing to the repayment of any loans made to the business.

In many cases, restaurant and foodservice operations are operated as corporations—a formal business structure recognized as a legal entity having its own privileges and liabilities separate from that of its owners. When a corporation is formed, its owners are called shareholders or stockholders, because their investments in the corporation were used to form or run the business. A shareholder is simply an individual or group that owns one or more portions (shares) of a corporation. A corporation can legally borrow money, own property, hire employees, sue, and be sued. Corporations are different from sole proprietorships and partnerships because the corporation itself, not its shareholders, is responsible for all of its debts. This structure is a great advantage to shareholders because it removes them from individual liability for the debts of a business operated by the corporation. Lenders reading a business plan submitted by a corporation, however, will want to know a great deal about the financial stability of the corporation for the very same reason.

After the business structure has been clearly identified, the operating portion of a business plan should detail the education and experience of the establishment's owners. Again, lenders will look for experience in the industry that assures them that the operation can survive and provide a return on their investment. The education and experience of the operation's managers should also be presented if it is known at the time the business plan is being prepared.

Finally, many business plan experts also recommend including the resumes of key owners and managers in the business plan. While this approach is a good idea, resumes should be provided to support and validate the information included in the operating plan portion of the business plan, not as a replacement for it.

Competitive Assessment

This section of the business plan details those establishments with which the proposed operation will compete. It may be tempting to state that the proposed operation will have no competition because its food, service, or location will be superior to all other operations. However, regardless of how good it is, nearly every establishment will face some form of competition. Readers of the business plan will want to know that its writers recognize this fact.

A competitive assessment may mention other operations such as in the QSR or fast-casual segments; for example, "Our new pizza operation will compete with five other businesses currently offering carryout pizza." Alternately, it

Exhibit 5.2

SWOT ANALYSIS

| Strengths | Weaknesses |
| Opportunities | Threats |

may mention one or more specific operations as in "Bill's Bar-B-Q will be the biggest competitor of Miller's Bar-B-Q." The assessment portion may also include information regarding how much of the potential market competitors control and how the proposed business will compete to take some of this market share.

SWOT Analysis

Increasingly, establishment owners and investors like to see a SWOT analysis included in a business plan. A SWOT analysis identifies an operation's strengths and weaknesses and examines its opportunities and threats (see *Exhibit 5.2*). This analysis helps managers set goals and focus on plans that maximize the business's strengths and capitalize on its greatest opportunities.

SWOT analysis considers the proposed establishment's strengths, weaknesses, opportunities, and threats from the viewpoints of the owners, managers, employees, and customers. A realistic SWOT analysis also considers strengths and weaknesses in relation to competitors. For example, if all of the competitors in an industry segment maintain spotless establishments, then a clean operation is a necessity, not a strength.

STRENGTHS

In this part of the SWOT analysis, an owner or manager indicates all of the strengths of the operation. These are areas in which the business excels. Examples of strengths include a well-trained staff, a good location, well-kept and clean facilities, strong marketing abilities, high food quality, and service that consistently exceeds customer expectations.

WEAKNESSES

This part of the SWOT analysis identifies any weaknesses in a business. This analysis is done so that the weaknesses can later be eliminated or turned into strengths. Some examples of weaknesses are a boring menu, dirty premises, limited abilities or resources for marketing, undifferentiated products, poor-quality products, poor service, high staff turnover, and poor reputation.

In addition to weaknesses, there may be certain barriers to success—things outside the establishment that might cause a weakness. For example, if the products to be produced are difficult or take a long time to prepare because of a lack of skilled labor, the establishment will not easily be able to prepare a high-quality product.

Some barriers can be overcome by proper planning and execution. For example, to overcome the lack of skilled labor mentioned in the previous example, an owner or manager might implement a training program, modify the recruiting efforts, or even change the menus or recipes.

OPPORTUNITIES

In this section of the SWOT analysis portion of a business plan, the plan developer should address realistic opportunities to either increase revenue or decrease costs. Examples of such opportunities include opening additional locations, tapping previously untapped target markets, or launching a new delivery or takeout service (*Exhibit 5.3*). One way to determine opportunities is to look at strengths with an eye for building on them and to look at weaknesses to see if eliminating them can create opportunities.

Exhibit 5.3

THREATS

Threats can come from a variety of sources. Identifying possible threats to a business is important to ensure that the threats are addressed or controlled before they can do much damage. Examples of possible threats that could be included in the SWOT analysis portion of a business plan include an increased number of competitors, a price war with a competitor, increased taxes, poor economic conditions, evolving demographics of potential customers, or road construction that disrupts current traffic patterns.

To conduct a successful SWOT analysis, owners and managers must be realistic about the strengths and weaknesses of their operations as well as the opportunities and threats they face. *Exhibit 5.4* presents an example of possible characteristics of a business that may be identified during a SWOT analysis.

Exhibit 5.4

POSSIBLE CHARACTERISTICS IDENTIFIED IN A SWOT ANALYSIS

Strengths	Weaknesses
Location of the operation	Location of the operation
Good capabilities of management and staff	Poor capabilities of management and staff
Being a new operation that offers a diverse level of service and products	Lack of marketing expertise
Quality of meals and service	Poor quality of meals and service
Few or no competitors	Numerous competitors
	Dated operation with a stagnant menu

Opportunities	Threats
Ability to expand services	Competitor offering lower prices
Ability to increase number of menu items offered	Competitor coming in with new or innovative menu and service
Newly formed target markets	Negative publicity
Competitors leaving or coming in	Competitor mimicking a certain aspect of your service or menu
New promotional campaigns	Competitor changing operation concept
Technology	
Competitor changing operation concept	

chain emphasizes its "fresh-baked bread" as a key component of its value statement and thus its advertising campaigns. In this case, it is likely that managers and staff will, because of the emphasis placed on the bread's quality, pay special attention to its production. As a result, the quality of the bread products will remain high, reinforcing the validity of the company's value statement.

The external worth of a value statement is demonstrated when potential customers can easily understand and recall the key benefits or features most emphasized by a business. Consider, for example, the QSR chain that, for several years, used the slogan "Have it your way" to emphasize the fact that guests in their operations were allowed to select the toppings of their choice when ordering sandwiches.

In most cases, a well-conceived value statement can provide real worth to managers and to their customers. The value statement may focus on an operation's features or its benefits. For example, feature descriptions or feature references included in a steakhouse establishment's value statements may include these ideas:

- Made with real Angus beef
- Choice grade
- Twelve ounces in size
- Thick cut or hand cut
- Cooked to order on an open flame
- Accompanied by French-cut green beans sautéed in extra virgin olive oil
- Served on good dinnerware with silver-plated utensils

Alternatively, the same operation might choose to address the benefits its guests will receive when they visit. These benefits may include the following:

- Wonderful taste sensations
- Effortless dining without having to prepare food and do the dishes afterward
- Pleasurable dining experience
- Pleasant décor
- Courteous waitstaff
- Being seen by others while dining at a very nice establishment

Only an operation's owners and managers know the very best features and benefits to mention in their value statements. In all cases, however, the value statement for a target market must directly address the question: "Are the benefits worth the cost?" In other words, what benefits does the product provide that the target market considers worth purchasing? Remember, guests buy benefits, not features.

When customers buy food and beverages, they do so because they expect to receive *more* in benefits than they invested in cash, time, or convenience. It is important to note that in nearly all cases, it is the manager, not the customer, who develops the value statement.

It is also important to recognize that customers do not automatically think that an operation's menu prices equal the value they will receive when they visit the establishment. Most knowledgeable customers are cautious when they hear words such as the following used to describe a product or service:

- The best in town
- Number one
- Finest food and service
- The area's favorite
- None better

Simply from a commonsense perspective, customers assessing any value statement are very likely to remember *caveat emptor*, the Latin phrase for "let the buyer beware." As a result, an operation's value statement must include only those things that can, in fact, be delivered to guests at a high level of quality and consistency. It is important to remember that only when guests feel they have received value in excess of what they have paid that a beneficial exchange has occurred.

Value must always exceed price paid if customers are to become repeat customers. When managers are confident their guests will receive good value on a consistent basis they can begin to develop and implement effective marketing plans.

Finally, know that managers developing their marketing plans will use a number of different activities and strategies designed to attract customers. Collectively, these activities constitute the operation's marketing mix: the strategies and tools managers use to effectively market their operations. Many of these tools and strategies are addressed in later chapters of this book. It is important to recognize, however, that the more detail included in a business plan about an operation's marketing mix, the better the plan.

Financial Plan

While location is often mentioned as the single most important ingredient in an establishment's success, proper financing is considered by many to be the second most important. A new operation's expenses accrue long before it opens and begins to make a profit. Financing provides the income the establishment needs during this period of unprofitability. In nearly every case, an establishment that lacks proper start-up funding will not be able to pay its bills until it becomes profitable enough to do so. Start-up costs incurred vary based on location and concept, but all operations typically incur the pre-dopening costs shown in *Exhibit 5.5*:

Exhibit 5.5
COMMON PRE-OPENING COSTS
Land and building acquisition or lease
Legal fees
Required licenses
Required insurance
Utility deposits and prepayments
Kitchen equipment and tools
Dining-room furnishings
China, flatware, and glassware
Employee uniforms
Initial food and beverage inventories
Pre-opening marketing costs
Pre-opening payroll costs

Even after a new establishment is open, it may take many months or even years before it reaches targeted levels of profitability. As a result, an establishment must have access to enough cash or credit to pay its bills in a timely manner starting from the very first day it opens.

Savings, short-term and long-term loans, and available grants are among the most commonly used sources of financing. The decision regarding which of these sources will be used and how much money must be secured must be known prior to the writing of the business plan. Also, realistic estimates of how quickly the establishment will reach its targeted level of profitability must be developed because these estimates are integral parts of the formal business plan.

One of the first steps that should be taken when considering the development of the financial section of a business plan is to learn about alternative revenue sources available. An **alternative revenue source (ARS)** generates money in addition to that raised from other funding sources such as loans and personal savings.

There are three types of ARS opportunities:

- Co-branding partnerships

- Grant opportunities

- Potential new sources of revenue

CO-BRANDING PARTNERSHIPS

Co-branding is what happens when two companies join together to share the expense of marketing the products and services each company offers to its own customers. Working together, each company can do a better job of marketing than it could do working alone.

The business term *co-branding* is a relatively new one. The most common co-branding arrangement involves two or more businesses that can help each other. For example, a restaurant near a baseball stadium may choose to market itself to sports fans who might visit the operation before or after ballgames. Similarly, the baseball stadium may market its games to the establishment's diners. By joining forces, both of these organizations may be able to reach a larger number of potential customers because each offers something both of these businesses' customers may want to buy. In some cases, two different establishments may even share a building or parking lot.

It is often helpful for managers to evaluate co-branding opportunities by answering four questions:

- Which co-branding opportunities offer the best chances for success?
- What will the co-branding arrangements consist of?
- How can the co-branding arrangements best be implemented?
- How will the effectiveness of the arrangements be evaluated and when?

GRANT AND LOAN OPPORTUNITIES

Restaurant and foodservice operations owners and managers who want to market effectively to grow and expand their businesses are sometimes surprised to learn there are others who want to help them do just that. Government grant and loan programs often target exactly the types of activities managers undertake to market their operations. In other cases, operations may qualify for grant assistance in nonmarketing areas.

The number and size of available grants and low-interest loans can change quite often, so it is important that managers stay up-to-speed on their availability. Examples of currently available grant, tax credit, and loan programs include the following:

American Recovery and Reinvestment Act (ARRA) Grants

The U.S. Department of Labor's Education & Training Administration offers several grant opportunities under the ARRA of 2009. Projects under these grants provide training and placement services in the energy efficiency and renewable energy industries for workers impacted by national energy and environmental policy, as well as other unemployed workers. In many cases, these unemployed workers can make excellent restaurant or foodservice employees.

THINK ABOUT IT . . .

Consider your ability to create a business plan. Which parts of the plan would be easy to write? Which parts would be more difficult? Where would you go to get help on the challenging parts?

Work Opportunity Tax Credits (WOTC)

The Work Opportunity Tax Credit (WOTC) is a federal tax credit granted to businesses that hire individuals from 12 target groups that have consistently faced significant barriers to employment. The main objective of this program is to enable the targeted employees to gradually move from economic dependency into self-sufficiency as they earn a steady income, learn new skills, and become contributing taxpayers. Participating employers are compensated by being able to reduce their federal income tax liability. Tax credits secured by employing workers in these targeted groups can also free up other money that can then be made available for marketing efforts.

Special Small Business Administration (SBA) Loans

The U.S. Small Business Administration (SBA) dedicates its energy and resources to providing support to small businesses and small-business owners across the nation. The SBA does not make grants, but it does offer a variety of loan programs. Because of its focus on small businesses, in many cases these loans are made to owners.

Like tax credits, loans secured from special SBA loan programs can free up an owner's other funds so that money can be made available for operation marketing efforts.

Owners and managers can stay informed about grant, loan, and tax credit programs for which they may qualify by consulting their tax accountants and attorneys, as well as by their active membership in groups such as the National Restaurant Association, the professional trade association for members of the restaurant and foodservice industry.

POTENTIAL SOURCES OF NEW REVENUE

A final ARS that all managers should consider prior to initiating their formal marketing efforts does not rely on other companies or outside entities for implementation. These potential sources of revenue can arise when managers creatively assess what their establishments are selling now and what they might sell in the future.

For example, consider a downtown operation that is very popular with the business community. This establishment has an excellent reputation and is highly successful. One way for this business to achieve even greater revenue could be to implement an off-site lunch delivery program (*Exhibit 5.6*). In this program, selected menu items could be offered for delivery to downtown office workers who are too busy to take a long lunch break. Customers could call in their orders, and their menu selections could be delivered directly to them. In such a program, the additional sales generated by the establishment could be significant.

Exhibit 5.6

Additional sources of potential new revenue for many operations may include the following:

- The rental of excess dining-room capacity for private events
- The development of a carryout program to encourage take-away food sales
- Home delivery of meals
- Off-site catering

Effective managers carefully assess all possible ARSs, and evaluate the ones that could be best for their own operations. These managers take the following steps:

- Assess the financial impact of each potential ARS.
- Choose the best ARS for their own operation.
- Take the steps needed to secure or implement the ARS.
- Monitor the effectiveness of the new revenue source.
- Take corrective action if needed to continue the favorable impact of the ARS.

Finally, note that because potential lenders may place differing requirements on businesses, the information needed in the financial portion of a business plan may vary somewhat. However, the plan will almost always include a three-year financial **pro forma**, a detailed estimate of the income, expenses, and profits achieved by a business over a specific time period. If start-up funds will be borrowed, the financial plan should also detail how and when the business will pay back that money.

Manager's Memo

Some business owners need help when writing their business plans. The U.S. Small Business Administration (SBA) is a governmental agency that provides help to those who are preparing business plans. Its template for a business plan can be accessed at this Web site: *web. sba.gov/busplantemplate/ BizPlanStart .cfm.*

Many community colleges, universities, and nonprofit groups such as SCORE also provide business plan–related assistance. SCORE is a nonprofit association dedicated to educating entrepreneurs and helping small businesses start, grow, and succeed nationwide. SCORE is a resource partner with the SBA and has been mentoring small-business owners for more than 40 years.

Exhibit 5.7

SAMPLE BUSINESS PLAN CONTENT CHECKLIST

- ☐ Cover sheet with establishment name and plan preparer's contact information
- ☐ Date of plan preparation
- ☐ One- to two-page executive summary
- ☐ Table of contents
- ☐ Description of the establishment's concept
- ☐ Legal description of the organization developing the operation
- ☐ Market analysis
- ☐ Financial projections
    - ☐ Three-year balance sheet
    - ☐ Three-year income and expense (profit and loss) statement with assumptions
    - ☐ Three-year statement of cash flows
- ☐ Other documents
    - ☐ Organizational chart
    - ☐ Resumes of owners
    - ☐ Resumes of managers
- ☐ Sample menu
- ☐ Copies of items
    - ☐ Leases
    - ☐ Licenses
    - ☐ Insurance policies
- ☐ Blueprints or floor plans

While each business plan is as unique as the operation it describes, *Exhibit 5.7* details one suggested format for a restaurant or foodservice business plan. Note that this template suggests potential areas to be addressed or documents to be included in appendices to the plan. These appendices, when applicable, may include such items as owners' and managers' resumes, sample copies of menus, executed leases, purchase agreements, and building plans.

THE MARKETING PLAN

For those seeking to open a new restaurant or foodservice operation, a well-developed marketing plan is an essential part of an overall business plan. However, all managers should have a marketing plan. Having a solid marketing plan for an existing establishment is just as important as having such a plan for a new one.

As outlined in chapter 1, managers follow several steps to develop their marketing plans. Each of these steps seeks to address one of the following questions:

- What marketing activity should be undertaken?
- How much money will be needed to do it?

- Who will do it?

- When will it be done?

- How will the plan's results be measured?

Managing an effective marketing plan involves several steps. First, the plan must be developed. Then, plan developers must create a budget to fund the plan. Finally, the plan must be put into action.

Developing the Marketing Plan

The development of a marketing plan is a complex process. It cannot be completed in an hour or two. The best restaurant and foodservice managers will set aside some time each week or month to collect the information they will need for the next year's marketing plan.

It can be difficult for managers to find the uninterrupted time required to develop a marketing plan during regular operating hours. Many managers set aside specific times to work on their marketing plans. These can be times when their operations are closed, or when other managers can prevent interruptions to the planning process (*Exhibit 5.8*).

A manager may write the marketing plan alone or with help from others in the business who can provide valuable information or insight. Involving others in the process can be beneficial because it can result in greater commitment to the plan.

Exhibit 5.8

A well-developed marketing plan should do the following:

- Review the operation's target market
- Assess the operation's competitors
- Identify the operation's revenue and financial goals
- Use a SWOT analysis to assess the operation and its current marketing environment
- Identify marketing objectives
- Identify marketing strategies and supporting tactics
- Establish a marketing budget
- Create a marketing activities schedule that conforms to the budget

As with the business plan, it is easy to understand the marketing plan by examining each of the sections within it.

REVIEW THE OPERATION'S TARGET MARKET

In the first section of the marketing plan, managers identify the guests the establishment seeks to attract. As noted in chapters 3 and 4, managers can use customer demographics and psychographics to describe existing customers and others the operation seeks to serve.

Remember that few operations can be successful if they try to be all things to all people. The needs and wants of customers in different market segments vary greatly. Instead, successful managers must carefully identify those segments that they can serve best (*Exhibit 5.9*). Experienced restaurant and

Exhibit 5.9

Your target market is those people you want as customers.

foodservice managers know that a thorough understanding of who they want to attract will help them make many marketing-related decisions.

When preparing this section of the marketing plan, managers must consider possible changes in their target customers. Are they increasing in age? Are they eating new things? Are they going out to eat more or less frequently? Any of these trends, as well as others like them, can create changes in a target market that must be addressed by managers.

Recall from chapter 3 that secondary information may exist to help in this area and that in many cases the information can be obtained free of charge. For example, data may be available from city, state, or federal governments or to members by trade groups such as the National Restaurant Association or the State Restaurant Association.

ASSESS THE OPERATION'S COMPETITORS

A business plan requires an assessment of the competitive environment within which a business will operate. In the marketing plan, managers address the specific impact of their direct competitors. In most cases, managers will not have access to the financial records of other competing operations. Knowing the size of a specific competitor's marketing budget, if sales are increasing or decreasing, or even whether or not the competitor is profitable simply may not be possible. Instead, in many cases information about an operation's direct competitors is collected by observation only. Information about a competitive operation's physical attributes such as location, number of seats, and items served on the menu may be easily assessed.

It is important to understand, however, that a competitive analysis is much more than an assessment of physical characteristics. Managers accurately assessing competitors look at the quality of food and service consistently delivered to guests for signs indicating the existence of solid employee training programs, and for evidence of guest loyalty. Strong competitors do the things that make their customers want to come back.

IDENTIFY THE OPERATION'S REVENUE AND FINANCIAL GOALS

The establishment of revenue and financial goals provides direction for the entire marketing plan. These goals should be identifiable and measurable. Consider, for example, the following revenue and financial goals:

- Sell more food
- Sell more drinks
- Increase total sales
- Increase profits

While these are goals nearly every manager seeks to achieve, they are not easily quantifiable or measurable. Now consider the following revenue and financial goals:

- Increase food check average each month by 5 percent when compared to the same month in the previous year.
- Increase annual beverage sales by $50,000 over last year's sales.
- Increase total revenue by $10,000 each month when compared to last year's monthly sales levels.
- Make an annual profit that is 5 percent higher than last year's profit.

Note that the achievement of the goals is both identifiable and measurable. Most important, establishing quantifiable goals of this type allows managers to assess the effectiveness of marketing efforts throughout the year and at year's end.

USE SWOT ANALYSIS TO ASSESS THE OPERATION AND ITS CURRENT MARKETING ENVIRONMENT

After managers have evaluated their customers, their competitors, and the realistic financial goals they have set for themselves, they can then assess the market conditions they face. Recall from chapter 3 that a market environment consists of external forces and events that can directly affect an establishment. Whereas the specific forces affecting an individual operation will vary, the economic, legal, and vendor environments will each contribute to a given set of market conditions in a given year. With information about market environment, restaurant and foodservice managers can prepare a detailed SWOT analysis that outlines the marketing-related strengths, weaknesses, opportunities, and threats associated with the current market conditions.

IDENTIFY MARKETING OBJECTIVES

Some managers have difficulty clearly identifying their marketing objectives. In some cases that is because they state their objectives in terms of vague phrases or slogans such as, "We will be the number one establishment in our market" or "We will be the leader in customer service." These phrases or sentiments, good as they may be, are not objectives. Just as financial objectives must be quantifiable, a marketing objective should meet these criteria:

1. Expressed in monetary terms; for example:

    Breakfast sales will increase 5 percent.

    One hundred dinners per night will be served.

    Drive-through customer check average will exceed $10.

2. Indicate an appropriate time frame; for example:

    Within six months

    By the end of the year

    By June 1

IDENTIFY MARKETING STRATEGIES AND SUPPORTING TACTICS

Marketing activities can be classified as either strategic or tactical. Strategic activities address an operation's basic business objectives. These strategic activities include identifying target markets, determining which products and services will be offered for sale, and determining the direction of the business.

Tactical marketing activities are used to implement marketing strategies. For example, if one marketing strategy is to increase dinner sales between 5:00 P.M. and 6:00 P.M., a tactic to do so might be advertising directly to a portion of the target market that prefers to eat their meals early in the evening. Remember that for each marketing strategy designed to achieve an operation's marketing objectives, one or more accompanying tactics should be clearly specified.

ESTABLISH A MARKETING BUDGET

If financial resources were unlimited, carefully identifying how much should be spent on marketing would not be important. Unfortunately, marketing funds are not unlimited. In all cases, the marketing budget must be large enough to fund all of the identified strategic and tactical efforts. The process used to establish a marketing budget will be addressed separately in the next major section of this chapter.

CREATE A MARKETING ACTIVITIES SCHEDULE THAT CONFORMS TO THE BUDGET

Once the marketing tactics have been identified and the amount of money available has been established, managers create a **marketing activities schedule** that identifies what will be done, when it will be done, and who will do it. This schedule is used to guide marketing efforts. Because this portion of the marketing plan must conform to the marketing budget, it will be addressed in detail after examining the way managers develop their marketing budgets.

Developing the Marketing Budget

Budget constraints must be considered when creating a marketing plan. Managers develop marketing budgets using one of four methods:

- Estimate of what the business can afford after other costs are paid

- Percentage of actual or forecasted revenue

- Amount spent on promotions by competitors of the business

- Marketing plan objectives and the actions needed to achieve them

The first two methods—what the business can afford and the percentage of revenue—are the simplest methods used to determine a marketing budget. In the first instance, a manager might develop the marketing budget by looking at revenue and costs from the previous year and projected revenue and costs

REAL MANAGER

PREPARING A MARKETING PLAN

Once a marketing plan is in place, a "run of show" or "day of event" checklist should be used to ensure all details of the event have been secured. We held a huge parking lot party in Houston on hot summer day. One of the specials was ice-cold beer served out of beer tubs. The beer was secured as well as beer tubs and signage placed all over the parking lot. One big item was overlooked: the beer was not iced down before the event started. Having a checklist with the item "ice down beer" would have ensured that the beer would have been iced down hours before the event started!

for the year in question to gain a sense of what additional monies might be available for this year's marketing budget.

In the case of a marketing budget tied to a percentage of revenue, a manager would forecast monthly sales, determine monthly percentage for marketing, and sum the 12-month marketing amounts to arrive at the annual marketing budget. To illustrate, consider the manager whose revenue forecast for the next 12 months is presented in the marketing budget worksheet in *Exhibit 5.10*. In this example, the marketing budget for January would be $5,000:

> **$100,000 monthly revenue forecast × 0.05 marketing budget percentage = $5,000 marketing budget**

The annual marketing budget would be $77,500:

> **$1,550,000 annual revenue forecast × 0.05 marketing budget percentage = $77,500 marketing budget**

Note that because both of these methods are tied to revenue, if sales decrease, so does the marketing budget. Such budget reductions are generally badly timed, as the need to promote an establishment is even greater during periods of declining sales.

Basing a marketing budget on the amount competitors spend on their promotions is relatively simple, although obtaining accurate information needed to do so may be difficult. In some cases managers can get an idea of

MANAGER'S MATH

Assume that your establishment is creating an annual marketing budget. As part of the process, you are forecasting revenue levels and designating 3% for marketing. Consider the data and then answer the questions that follow.

Month	Revenue Forecast	Marketing Budget at 3% of Revenue
January	$80,000	$2,400
February	75,000	
March	90,000	
Total	$	$

1. How much money from February and March sales will be reserved for marketing?

2. What will be the total amount of money reserved for marketing from the revenue generated in January, February, and March, assuming the revenue forecasts are correct?

(Answers: 1. February $2,250, March $2,700; 2. $7,350)

Exhibit 5.10

MARKETING BUDGET WORKSHEET

Month	Revenue Forecast	Marketing Budget at 5% of Revenue
January	$ 100,000	$ 5,000
February	110,000	5,500
March	120,000	6,000
April	140,000	7,000
May	140,000	7,000
June	150,000	7,500
July	150,000	7,500
August	150,000	7,500
September	120,000	6,000
October	120,000	6,000
November	120,000	6,000
December	130,000	6,500
Total	**$1,550,000**	**$77,500**

this figure by researching industry averages. However, a savvy manager is aware that the information used by competitors to determine marketing budgets may not apply to his or her operation (see *Exhibit 5.11*).

The final method, basing the marketing budget on the marketing plan's objectives, helps keep marketing efforts goal focused. This method is the ideal one to use; however, it can also be the most complex method because it entails accurately forecasting cost information for potential marketing suppliers such as media outlets, advertising agencies, and vendors selling promotion products and services.

Exhibit 5.11

Different establishments will have different marketing budget needs.

Implementing the Marketing Plan

When the marketing plan and budget are in place, managers turn to executing against their plans. At the start of the implementation phase, managers break the plan into discrete tasks, assigning resources to each one. They also plot the tasks on a calendar to determine when each task will start and end.

MARKETING TASK ASSIGNMENTS

A typical marketing plan will include a variety of marketing tasks and activities. Consider, for example, the marketing plan that calls for advertising a Thanksgiving Day buffet in the local newspaper. If this task is to be completed in a timely manner, someone must be responsible for it. Contacting the newspaper to determine specific steps needed for ad placement, assisting in the creation of the ad, and approving the final invoice for the advertisement are all tasks that must be accomplished if this marketing activity is to be successful.

In many cases, the manager will undertake the marketing tasks. In all cases, it is the manager's job to identify who is responsible for each activity included in the marketing plan.

Marketing Activities Schedule. A marketing activities schedule contains three key listings:

- What is to be done?
- When will it be done?
- Who will do it?

Exhibit 5.12

SAMPLE MARKETING ACTIVITIES SCHEDULE

Marketing Objective	Supporting Marketing Activity	Date to Be Initiated	Date to Be Completed	Assigned to

This part of the marketing plan need not be complicated. *Exhibit 5.12* is an example of a form that can be used to build an operation's marketing activities schedule.

A marketing activities schedule can be thought of as a "to-do" list for marketing. The advantage of the schedule is that it not only states what is to be done, and when, but it also tells its readers who is responsible for doing it. Such a schedule provides accountability to ensure that all tasks are completed by the assigned resource. It is important to note that managers may delegate to others the responsibility for completing one or more marketing activities, but managers must still follow up to ensure the activities have been completed.

Once the marketing budget and activities schedule are in place, managers should validate their draft plan with others prior to implementing it. Owners, other experienced managers, and supervisors may all have input that will help improve the plan. In addition, providing these key individuals a chance to shape the plan may be helpful when it comes to getting their support for implementing it. Finally, once the plan has been reviewed and is finalized, it should be distributed to all those who have a stake in its successful implementation.

SUMMARY

1. **Explain the purposes of a business plan and a marketing plan.**

   A business plan is developed to present the goals of a business and to explain, in detail, how the goals can be achieved. Business plans provide an overview for potential lenders and a roadmap for implementation. A business plan may also contain background information about the organization or individuals attempting to reach the objectives set for a business.

A marketing plan is part of a business plan and is a detailed listing of specific activities designed to reach the revenue goals of an establishment. It is a guide for an operation's marketing efforts because it tells what will be done to attract the number of customers needed to achieve an establishment's revenue goals.

2. **Identify the key components in a business plan.**

   While there is no legally mandated requirement for the information that must be included in a business plan, plans will typically include the following key components:

   • Executive summary

   • Concept statement

   • Operating plan

   • Competitive assessment

   • SWOT analysis

   • Vendor assessment

   • Marketing plan

   • Financial plan

   • Appendices as needed

3. **Describe how managers develop a marketing plan.**

   To create marketing plans, managers first review their target markets. Then they assess their competitors. They also outline the measurable revenue and financial goals for their operations and conduct a SWOT analysis to identify operational strengths, weaknesses, opportunities, and threats and to assess the marketing environment faced by the operation.

   Once the analysis phase is complete, managers create marketing objectives, outlining the strategies and tactics that will be used to achieve the objectives. Finally, managers prepare a marketing budget and an activities schedule that outlines how the objectives will be met.

4. **Describe how managers develop a marketing budget.**

   There are several approaches to developing a marketing budget. Managers can allocate funds based on predictions of costs or of revenue. Managers can also match competitors' marketing budgets. Finally, managers can create budgets based on the anticipated costs involved in achieving each of the marketing objectives.

5. **State how managers implement marketing plans.**

   The first step to implementing marketing plans is to create a marketing activities schedule that identifies what tasks will be done, when they will be done, and who will do them. Then managers validate their approach by sharing the document with owners, their peers, and members of the operation's management team. Finally, to complete the implementation process, managers share their marketing plans with all those who have a stake in the plan's success.

APPLICATION EXERCISE

The manager of a large establishment has a marketing plan that calls for a variety of activities to be undertaken in the coming year. Consider the following activities and then answer the questions that follow.

Participate in citywide "Chili Cook-off" contest sponsored by the area chamber of commerce.

Make weekly updates to the operation's social media site.

Identify three new menu items to be included on the list of "Summer Fling" menu specials.

Call all customers who booked holiday parties in the prior year to determine interest in rebooking for this year.

1. For the Chili Cook-off activity, how important will be the participation of the operation's chef or kitchen manager to the quality of product served? How important will be the visible participation of the operation's chef or kitchen manager on the day of the event?

2. For the social media activity, what skills would be required to complete this task? Who should decide what would be said in the weekly message?

3. For the inclusion of the new menu specials, what groups in the establishment should be consulted prior to finalizing the list of new menu items? Who should make the final decision about which new menu items will be included on the list?

4. For the holiday party activity, who should be assigned to make these calls? If you were a previous holiday party customer, would it matter to you who made the calls? Why or why not?

REVIEW YOUR LEARNING

Select the best answer for each question.

1. **In which part of a business plan would a reader find pro forma statements?**
   A. Vendor assessment
   B. Marketing plan
   C. SWOT analysis
   D. Financial plan

2. **In which part of a business plan would a reader find information about the threats a business might face?**
   A. Executive summary
   B. Concept statement
   C. SWOT analysis
   D. Operating plan

3. **What does the term *dba* indicate?**
   A. That a partnership is being formed to start a new business
   B. That the shareholders of a corporation own and are operating a business
   C. That a name has not yet been chosen for a business operated by a corporation
   D. That a sole proprietor is operating a business with a name different from the owner

4. **What is the purpose of a partnership agreement?**
   A. To explain how the partners in a business will market it
   B. To detail the rights and responsibilities of each partner in the business
   C. To list a business for sale on terms agreeable to all the partners in a business
   D. To ensure vendors are in agreement with partners about the prices to be paid for products

5. How is a corporation's business structure different from a sole proprietorship or a partnership?

   A. A corporation is a legal entity separate from its owners.

   B. A corporation is prevented from taking out business loans.

   C. A corporation can have only one owner.

   D. A corporation may be sued.

6. What part of a marketing plan explains marketing-related actions to be taken and who will take them?

   A. SWOT analysis

   B. Marketing budget

   C. Vendor assessment

   D. Activities schedule

7. An establishment has an excellent location. In which portion of a SWOT analysis would that fact be noted?

   A. Threats

   B. Strengths

   C. Weaknesses

   D. Opportunities

8. Which is a potential alternative revenue source (ARS) for an establishment?

   A. A change in menu item portion sizes

   B. A tax credit for employing targeted workers

   C. A suggestive selling training program for servers

   D. The replacement of the establishment's china and glassware

9. What is the SBA?

   A. A form of paid advertising

   B. A part of the marketing plan

   C. A government agency that helps small businesses

   D. The method used to develop an operation's marketing budget

10. Laura forecasts her operation's revenue next year will be $500,000. She wants to establish her marketing budget at 4% of revenues. What will be her marketing budget for next year?

    A. $1,250

    B. $2,000

    C. $12,500

    D. $20,000

6 Setting Menu Prices

INSIDE THIS CHAPTER

- Understanding Pricing
- The Importance of Proper Pricing
- External Factors Affecting Pricing
- Internal Factors Affecting Pricing
- Choosing a Pricing Strategy
- Calculating Selling Prices

CHAPTER LEARNING OBJECTIVES

After completing this chapter, you should be able to:

- Contrast pricing as viewed from the perspectives of sellers and of buyers.
- Explain the importance of proper pricing.
- Identify external factors that influence pricing decisions.
- Identify internal factors that influence pricing decisions.
- Describe how managers choose an appropriate pricing strategy.
- Explain four methods managers can use to calculate selling prices.

KEY TERMS

à la carte menu, p. 128

business cost, p. 129

competitive analysis, p. 131

contribution margin (CM), p. 143

direct labor cost, p. 138

external pricing factors, p. 131

food cost, p. 136

food cost percentage, p. 137

fringe benefits, p. 138

gross profit, p. 143

internal pricing factors, p. 135

labor cost, p. 138

other operating costs, p. 139

pricing strategy, p. 140

prime costs, p. 144

prix fixe menu, p. 128

profit formula, p. 135

profit-oriented pricing, p. 140

sales-oriented pricing, p. 140

standardized recipe, p. 137

status quo pricing, p. 141

target profit, p. 135

CASE STUDY

"Well, I'm just saying, I don't think this is going to go over well with our regulars," said Christina, one of the day shift servers at Don's Diner.

"Look, Christina," Don, the owner, explained, "I don't like it either. But what can we do? The cost we pay for coffee is up almost 20 percent from last year. We need to raise the menu price on coffee just to stay even with last year."

"I understand what you're saying," Christina explained, "but I can tell you that when you raise the price of coffee from $ 2.00 to $2.50, our customers will notice and they will not like it."

"But they'll still get free refills," defended Don.

"It isn't that. It's that we were already 25 cents higher on coffee than the Bullet. My regulars remind me of that all the time," said Christina, referring to the Bullet Diner, Don's main competitor.

"We've talked about that before," replied Don patiently. "They're lower than us on coffee, but a lot higher for a burger and fries. They just use low coffee prices to get people in the door," said Don.

"Well, if that worked for them before, it's gonna work even better when you raise our coffee prices," said Christina.

1. Why do you think Don feels his higher costs should be passed on to his customers?

2. Why do you think Christina feels the prices charged by Don's competitors should influence the prices Don charges his customers for similar items?

UNDERSTANDING PRICING

Menu prices are an important part of a restaurant or foodservice operation's marketing strategy. When establishing pricing, managers must balance the needs of the seller and the buyer. Managers with a strong understanding of menu pricing use food and beverage prices to build customer loyalty while ensuring the revenue needed to meet an establishment's financial targets. The ability to set menu prices is one of a manager's most important skills.

The Seller's View of Price

All sellers must set prices. In many cases, sellers do so with the goal of attracting as many customers as possible. Recall from chapter 4 that an establishment's target market must have both the desire and the ability to buy an item. However, different customers have different levels of willingness and ability to pay. From a marketing perspective, a manager's prices must be low enough to attract guests with lesser levels of willingness or ability to pay, and high enough to make profitable sales to those with greater willingness and ability to pay. Managers may use à la carte menus, where each item is priced separately, to provide a range of lower- and higher-priced items (*Exhibit 6.1*). This pricing is in contrast to a prix fixe menu (pronounced "prefix"), which consists of predetermined items presented as a multicourse meal at a set price.

Some managers argue that the ability and willingness of customers to buy is not the most important factor in menu pricing. These managers point out that unless a seller receives more money for a product than was required to

---

Exhibit 6.1

SOUP & SALADS

Baked Italian Vegetable Soup / $5.30
A bowl of our homemade Italian vegetable soup, topped with melted mozzarella cheese and garlic croutons

Soup and Salad / $7.95
A bowl of our homemade Italian vegetable soup, a dinner salad with choice of dressing, and hot garlic bread.

Southwest BBQ Chicken Salad / $10.95
Assorted lettuce, black beans, corn, tomatoes, cucumbers, and grilled chicken breast tossed with our homemade BBQ Ranch dressing and topped with fried tortilla strips

Hail Caesar! / $9.95
Crisp Romaine, garlic croutons, parmesan, grilled chicken and our homemade Caesar dressing * *Contains raw eggs*

Salad Caprese / $9.95
Mixed field greens with fresh sliced tomatoes and fresh mozzarella cheese with balsamic vinaigrette

Mixed Field of Green Salad with Grilled Chicken Breast / $9.95
Assorted baby lettuce and mixed greens tossed with house Italian balsamic vinaigrette, black olives, red onion, and grilled chicken breast.

produce it, that seller will ultimately go out of business. These managers maintain that costs, or expenses, dictate prices. A **business cost** is the price paid to obtain or produce an item required to operate a business. Food, labor, supplies, and rent are all examples of costs incurred in the restaurant and foodservice industry. Although it is certainly possible to offer "loss leader" menu items that are priced very low to attract new customers, in the long run, an establishment must charge prices high enough to cover all of its costs or it will not be able to stay in business. The best managers know they must consider their customers *and* their costs when they establish their menu prices.

The Buyer's View of Price

While sellers must consider costs when establishing prices, customers are typically indifferent to them. For buyers, only one factor is important: perceived value. Recall from chapter 2 that consumer rationality is the tendency of consumers to make buying decisions based on the belief that the purchase will be of direct benefit to them. From the customers' vantage point, price reflects only the amount of value they feel they receive in a business transaction.

In nearly all cases in the restaurant and foodservice industry, it is the seller that establishes menu prices. But it is important to understand that customers do not *automatically* assume a seller's price will provide great value. Rather, both before and after a purchase is made, customers carefully consider their own views of value. If the products and services purchased convince buyers that they have received real value for their money, they will likely become repeat customers. If, however, customers do not feel they received good value for the price paid, they are unlikely to buy from that establishment again and may tell their friends about their negative dining experience.

In summary, the long-term price of an item cannot be higher than what customers are willing and able to pay for it. When priced too high, an item does not sell. Every manager whose business is not flourishing implicitly understands this issue. In essence, these managers' customers are saying, "For what you are selling and what value I would be getting, your price is too high to make me willing and able to pay." However, if prices are too low, a business may not be able to operate profitably. Menu pricing requires a delicate balance to ensure that customers are willing and able to buy without managers sacrificing the overall financial health of the operation.

THINK ABOUT IT . . .

Are there establishments you would like to visit, but you feel they are too expensive for you? What could the manager of one of those operations do to get you to become a customer?

THE IMPORTANCE OF PROPER PRICING

The process of setting prices in the restaurant and foodservice industry is important and complex. To better understand why, consider that the three major areas of business are manufacturing, retailing, and service. Manufacturers convert raw materials into products. Prices for manufactured products must cover the expense of the raw materials as well as any costs incurred in the production of the item. Retailers purchase pre-made products from manufacturing suppliers and sell those products at a markup to the consumer. A retailer's prices must cover the cost of the products and the operating expenses incurred in selling them.

Restaurant and foodservice pricing is more complicated than either manufacturing or retail pricing because often establishments both produce and resell items. Managers must know how to price the products they manufacture such as muffins and bakery cakes, as well as pre-made items offered for retail sale like ice cream and alcoholic beverages. In addition, restaurant and foodservice businesses also sell service, like the convenience of a QSR drive-through or the elegance of a fine-dining meal. Also, unlike products, service is an intangible item. As established in chapter 2, the subjective nature of services makes establishing appropriate prices for them very challenging.

Proper pricing is both a science and an art. The science of pricing requires managers to use math skills to calculate costs and arrive at suggested menu prices. The art of pricing means managers recognize the subjective customer perception-related aspects of pricing. The art of pricing takes into account these intangible aspects when arriving at final selling price decisions. Examples of customer perception-related issues and their impact on pricing decisions include those shown in *Exhibit 6.2*.

Exhibit 6.2

SUBJECTIVE PRICING ISSUES AND APPLICATION

Pricing Issue	Practical Application
Should the amount purchased at one time affect price?	Should a large order of fries sell for twice the price of a small order if it is twice as big?
Should the amount purchased over time affect price?	Should frequent guests be rewarded for their loyalty with reduced prices on some or all items they buy in the future?
Should competitors' prices affect price?	Does it matter if the operation is considered expensive or inexpensive relative to its competitors?
Should the method of ordering affect price?	Should those who order for delivery via the Internet pay different prices than those charged to walk-in customers?
Should the form of payment used to purchase items affect price?	Should those who pay in cash be charged the same amount as those who use other payment forms?

Managers responsible for pricing should remember these three points when making their final pricing decisions:

1. **Prices act as signs to buyers:** When prices are low, they deliver a "buy" signal to customers, who can now better afford the items they want and are willing to pay for. When prices are too high, they discourage customers from buying.

2. **Prices must reflect real costs:** Proper pricing recognizes that food, labor, and other operating expenses must be considered when calculating menu prices.

3. **Prices must be considered fair:** Because buyer perceptions of price affect purchase decisions, it is essential that customers feel they receive real value for the money they spend. Buyers seek value and do not feel responsible for ensuring the profitability of an operation. In fact, most customers are absolutely disinterested in the profits achieved by a business, unless those profits are perceived as being too high.

EXTERNAL FACTORS AFFECTING PRICING

Managers must consider several external pricing factors, or conditions outside their own control, when pricing their menu items. These are some examples of external factors:

- Competition
- Economic conditions
- Food trends
- Seasonality of products
- Pricing-related laws

Competition

Before managers establish prices, they often research what competitors charge for their products and services. An important step in understanding the competition is the completion of a competitive analysis. This type of analysis looks at other establishments that offer similar products. The analysis lists what specific products these operations offer, the characteristics of the items (e.g., weight, size, number), and their prices. When reviewing competitors' prices, managers see the potential price ranges for offerings, and determine the high and low ends of the pricing scale. An example of this type of analysis is shown in *Exhibit 6.3* on the next page.

Exhibit 6.3

COMPETITIVE ANALYSIS OF ENTRÉES

Restaurant	Filet, 8 oz	Hamburger, 1/2 lb	Ribs, full slab	Veal, 7 oz	Salmon, 9 oz	Prime rib, king cut	Roast Chicken, half of whole	Tuna, 8 oz
Branson Chophouse	$18.50	$9.00	$13.50	$19.00	$20.50	$24.00	$10.50	$23.00
Will's Steakhouse	21.50	7.50	N/A	20.00	16.95	31.00	13.50	26.00
Carriage House	15.95	9.00	16.50	18.00	18.00	N/A	11.50	22.00
The Lantern Seafood and Steakhouse	21.00	9.00	18.50	22.00	17.50	N/A	16.50	28.00
The Coventry	26.50 (9 oz) 19.00 (6 oz)	8.00	19.50	21.00	19.50	29.00	11.50	25.00
Your Steakhouse	$23.50	$7.50	$21.50	$20.00	$18.50	$27.00	$11.95	$19.00

Consider the manager of Your Steakhouse, whose competition includes the other establishments listed in *Exhibit 6.3*. After reviewing this information, the manager may realize that his or her prices are in line for the filet, hamburgers, veal, salmon, prime rib, and chicken. Here are other considerations:

- The full slabs of ribs at Your Steakhouse may be priced too high at $21.50. The manager may want to consider lowering the price to fall between $17.00 and $18.00.

- At Your Steakhouse, the tuna at $19.00 is priced considerably lower than that of competitors. The manager may want to raise the price to fall between $24.00 and $25.00.

Exhibit 6.3 illustrates an assessment of entrées only. To gain the best understanding of the prices charged by competitors, the manager would want to conduct a competitive analysis of the prices of other menu items such as appetizers, desserts, wine, beer, other special beverages, meal-sized salads, and other items similar to those served in his or her establishment.

Economic Conditions

Some experts say that the restaurant and foodservice industry is economy-proof because everyone has to eat. However, it is *where* people eat that is important to a restaurant or foodservice manager. Managers should ask themselves the following questions related to the economy and how it may affect their operations:

- How is the quality of life in the operation's market area?
- Is the area growing or declining in population?
- What is the unemployment rate?
- Are people spending their discretionary income—the money available to spend after expenses are paid?
- If so, how are they spending it?

If the economy is not doing well, people may be less inclined to eat out, especially if an establishment's prices are perceived as high.

In difficult economic times customers want to feel they received a good value for their purchase, but what that means is different for each customer. Each time a customer makes a buying decision, the customer must weigh the value of the product and service received against the cost of obtaining them (see *Exhibit 6.4*).

In spite of periodic downturns in the economy, America's restaurants and foodservice establishments continue to grow, currently employing nearly 13 million Americans and adding nearly $2 trillion to the economy. This growth gives the economy and the country a much-needed financial boost. Savvy managers are aware that economic conditions tend to change over time. For that reason, managers must continually monitor the economic conditions of their local market area.

Food Trends

A manager's prices also are affected by the popularity of what is on the menu. The popularity of food products tends to be one of four types: constant, a trend, a temporary fad, or seasonal.

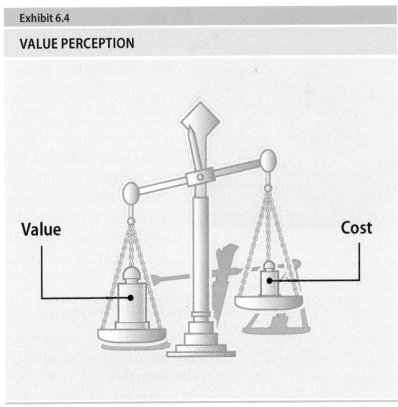

Exhibit 6.4

VALUE PERCEPTION

Value   Cost

Offering the right menu items at the right time at the right price can assist in realizing profits for an operation. Being on top of popular food trends might enable you to offer a trendy product at a premium price. For example, tiramisu recently was an extremely popular dessert, and due to the high demand for this product, managers were able to charge a premium price.

Food trends also can work against a manager if the trend requires investment in special equipment or training for a food trend that disappears. For example, if a certain type of frozen dairy dessert is experiencing a temporary surge in popularity, investing in a machine that is complex to operate and makes only that type of dessert would likely be unwise. Managers should be wary of making any radical food fad–related changes in their operation unless they are sure they can survive a possible decline in the food's popularity.

Exhibit 6.5

Seasonality of Products

The seasonality of a food product will help determine its price. There are various types of seasonality, such as agricultural seasonality, taste seasonality, and tourist seasonality. An example of agriculture seasonality is the serving of strawberries in the winter, while taste seasonality would be the desire for soups and stews when the weather gets cold (*Exhibit 6.5*). An example of tourism-related seasonality would be operations having plenty of clam chowder during the summer vacation season at Cape Cod, an area noted for summer tourists.

Depending on an operation's approach to pricing, managers can charge different prices when the food is in season or is in high demand. For example, a manager could charge higher prices when a product is in season because that is when it is usually the best quality or the only time it is available. Or, a manager might charge lower prices because his or her costs are lower when the product is in season. Conversely, when an establishment is able to obtain out-of-season items, managers can charge premium prices for providing these items, provided the quality is equal to or better than the typical in-season items.

Pricing-Related Laws

Consumer protection laws enacted at the state and federal level are designed to ensure customers are informed, in advance, of the prices they will pay for the items they buy. Prices must be presented fairly, but the question of how to ensure prices are presented fairly is an important one.

Certainly it is fair for managers to use their knowledge of customer buying habits to predict how their customers will react to different pricing strategies. For example, managers whose menu prices end in $0.95 or $0.99 can do so fairly. These managers know, for example, that customers do not perceive much difference between a price of $7.50 and $7.99 for an item, but would perceive the difference between $7.95 and $8.44 as quite large despite the fact that, in both cases, one price is 49 cents higher than the other. Hidden charges, however, such as an undisclosed service charge for small groups would always be met with resistance. In nearly all cases, hidden charges are neither legal nor ethical and should not be assessed.

INTERNAL FACTORS AFFECTING PRICING

Establishing a pricing strategy is directly associated with a manager's goals for an establishment, its menu offerings, and its staff skills. Setting and achieving financial goals are vital in determining a manager's success or failure. All restaurant and foodservice owners have the same high-level objectives: increase sales and decrease expenses. It is a matter of how and to what extent managers achieve these objectives that determines whether the operation generates an acceptable level of profit. As a result, internal pricing factors affect pricing decisions. These are some internal factors:

- Financial goals
- Food costs
- Labor costs
- Other operating expenses

Financial Goals

Every owner and manager knows that revenue minus expense equals profit. This equation can be expressed in a profit formula:

Revenue − Expense = Profit

Most of this book focuses on ways managers can increase the revenue portion of the profit formula through the application of professional marketing strategies and tactics. Of course, controlling expenses is also a critical part of the profit formula and of a manager's job.

An understanding of the profit formula allows a manager to establish his or her target profit: the amount of profit an owner hopes to achieve. Target profit can be established as either a number or a percentage. To illustrate, consider the owner who is estimating revenue, expense, and target profit for

THINK ABOUT IT . . .

Establishments must make a profit if they intend to stay in business. Do you think the amount of profit made by an operation should be different for those in different industry segments? Why?

MANAGER'S MATH

Robin is preparing her target profit forecast for next year. Help her complete the following form and then use the information to answer the questions.

Operating Estimate	Target Profit by Amount	Target Profit by Percentage
Revenue	$750,000	100%
Expense		90
Profit		

1. What is the amount of expense Robin is forecasting for next year?

2. What is the target profit amount Robin is forecasting for next year?

3. What is the target profit percentage Robin is forecasting for next year?

(Answers: 1. $675,000; 2. $75,000; 3. 10%)

Exhibit 6.6

TARGET PROFIT BY AMOUNT AND PERCENT

Operating Estimate	Target Profit by Amount	Target Profit by Percentage
Revenue	$1,000,000	100%
Expense	$ 850,000	85%
Profit	$ 150,000	15%

next year. Using the profit formula, the owner could establish his or her target profit using the information in either the Target Profit by Amount or Target Profit by Percentage column shown in *Exhibit 6.6*.

Target profit is important when assessing the overall value of an operation, but it is also important in establishing menu prices. The operation's total revenue is the sum of all the individual prices paid by its customers. If prices are too low, insufficient revenue may prevent the operation from meeting its target profit goals. In other cases, low prices could allow an establishment to meet its revenue goals, but in doing so generate so much expense that target profit goals cannot be met. If the prices are too high, customers may not come to the establishment in large enough numbers to achieve the business's revenue goals. In this case, a revenue shortfall could prevent the operation from achieving its target profit even if it did a good job of controlling its expenses.

Exhibit 6.7

FOOD COST COMPONENTS

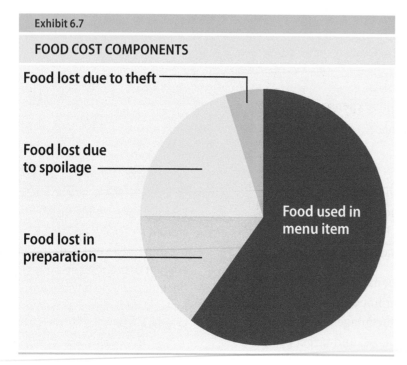

Food lost due to theft

Food lost due to spoilage

Food lost in preparation

Food used in menu item

Food Costs

Food cost is the expense of the food products used to make the menu items an operation sells. It is one of the major expenses of every restaurant or foodservice operation. The amount paid for all forms of food, from bulk, uncut menu ingredients to portion-controlled food that is ready to prepare and serve all contribute to overall food cost. Food cost also includes the amount paid for the food delivered to an operation, and it includes all applicable transportation costs and any taxes to be paid.

In addition to the obvious costs, there are several other contributors to food cost (see *Exhibit 6.7*):

- **Food used in menu items:** This contributor is literally the cost of the food put on the plate. This cost can include extra food due to overportioning.

- **Food lost in preparation:** In every kitchen there are mistakes that result in food being thrown away. While managers try to minimize this, mistakes are often unavoidable.

- **Food lost due to theft:** This contributor is the cost of food stolen by employees, customers, or suppliers. Suppliers steal food when, for example, they charge and receive payment for food that was not delivered.

- **Food lost due to spoilage:** This contributor is the cost of food that had to be discarded due to improper storage or excessive age.

All of these factors combined result in the overall food cost. In some operations, minor paper costs related to wrapping and serving food are also included in food cost (*Exhibit 6.8*). All food costs must be considered when managers arrive at their menu selling prices.

A single food cost is generally determined for an entrée or entire bundled order, rather than separate food costs for each of the parts. For example, perhaps a steak dinner consists of the steak, potatoes, vegetable, side salad, and beverage. The food cost of the steak dinner is the sum of the food costs for all five items. Supplementary products like appetizers and desserts typically have individual food costs.

Recall that an important goal in a restaurant or foodservice operation is to control or reduce expenses without sacrificing quality. Since food cost is an expense, it should be reduced as much as is feasible while maintaining quality standards. Each type of food cost can be a target for expense reduction.

The first food cost expenses managers should address are those resulting from theft and spoilage. Both of these costs are simply throwing money away. Second, managers can direct their attention to minimizing preparation waste and errors. One technique to reduce this kind of food cost is to use a standardized recipe: a recipe that gives a known quality and quantity at a known cost.

The goal for many establishments is to achieve a certain food cost percentage: the percentage of the revenue that goes to the cost of purchasing food. Mathematically, food cost percentage is the food cost divided by the revenue

Manager's Memo

Two things must be in place to calculate food cost. First, standardized recipes must be used so the manager will know what ingredients and the amount of each that were used. Second, the current cost of all ingredients must be known.

Most establishments sell an entrée for a specified price. For example, a chicken dinner may include the chicken entrée, salad with dressing, potato or vegetable, and bread or roll and butter. The food cost for each of the meal components must be added together to calculate the total food cost for menu item pricing purposes.

Exhibit 6.8

generated from the sale of the food. For example, a manager sold a menu item for $8, and the cost of the food was $2. The manager would use the following formula to find the food cost percentage:

Food cost ÷ Selling price = Food cost percentage

This example would be calculated as follows:

$2.00 food cost ÷ $8.00 selling price = 25% food cost percentage

In this example, the manager would have a food cost percentage of 25 percent. Using the food cost percentage to set pricing will be covered later in this chapter.

A manager's targeted food cost may be established per menu item, per item group (e.g., beverages, salads, entrées, or desserts), or as an overall operational total. It is also determined by the operation's overall pricing strategy. In all cases, however, the manager establishing an operation's menu selling prices must consider the cost of food required to make each item prior to determining its selling price.

Labor Costs

The other main expense of every food operation is labor, and it should also be studied for ways to minimize cost while maintaining quality. **Labor cost** is the amount paid to employees for preparing and serving each meal. It includes the costs of managers and all other workers.

Calculating labor cost is more challenging than it might first appear. For example, if an employee is paid $10 per hour and works 8 hours, it would be easy to figure out that the employee has cost the operation $80.

8 hours × $10 per hour = $80

In one respect, that would be correct. In this example **direct labor cost**, the cost for preparing and serving all guest meals in that eight-hour period, would be $80 for that employee. The direct labor cost is calculated by multiplying employees' hourly wage by the number of hours worked. Because direct labor costs are easy to calculate, many managers strive to keep direct labor cost at or below a certain percentage—30 percent, for example.

Note that the direct labor costs do not paint the whole labor cost picture because direct labor cost does not include contributions for payroll taxes, social security, state and local taxes, and any other required employer payments. Direct labor costs also exclude the costs of **fringe benefits**, which can include labor-related items such as employee health care, dental, vision insurance, vacation and sick leave pay, holiday pay, retirement contributions, and other benefits that may be paid all or in part by the employer to benefit the employees.

The type of operation and the type of menu offered by an establishment play a large role in determining the number of workers needed, their skill levels, and subsequent labor costs. For example, if an operation has a very extensive menu with many difficult-to-prepare items, it will require a more skilled staff. Establishments offering a limited number of easy to prepare items may need fewer, less-skilled employees that can be paid less per hour.

Regardless of the operation type, the manager establishing an operation's menu selling prices must have an awareness of the operation's labor costs. And a consideration of the labor costs must inform decisions related to setting prices.

Other Operating Costs

The final expense category to consider prior to establishing a pricing strategy is that of other operating costs, those expenses that are not related to food or labor. In some operations, other operating costs can be equal to 15 percent or more of all revenue.

Other operating costs can be separated into controllable expenses and noncontrollable expenses. Controllable expenses include items such as management salaries and employee meals—basically, costs that managers can directly control. Noncontrollable expenses include rent and utilities—basically any costs over which managers have little or no control. *Exhibit 6.9* lists some of the other operating costs incurred in many restaurant and foodservice operations. While not every operation will incur each cost listed, all establishments do incur some other operating costs and managers must consider these prior to establishing their selling prices.

Exhibit 6.9

COMMON *OTHER OPERATING COSTS* FOR ESTABLISHMENTS

• Advertising	• Internet access
• Bank charges	• Kitchen equipment
• Bar supplies	• Laundry and dry cleaning
• Building alterations	• License fees
• China, flatware, and glassware	• Menus and wine lists
• Cleaning supplies	• Musicians or other entertainment
• Employee awards and prizes	• Office equipment
• Pest control	• Outdoor signs
• Floors and carpets	• Paper supplies
• Flowers and decorations	• Refrigeration
• Franchise fees	• Rent
• Furniture	• Uniforms
• Gardening and grounds maintenance	• Utility services
• Insurance	• Waste removal

CHOOSING A PRICING STRATEGY

As noted, there are several considerations to address when pricing a product. Before beginning to price individual menu items, managers must first choose a pricing strategy: a rule that guides the price-setting effort. Pricing strategies are also known as pricing objectives. There are several types of pricing strategies:

- Profit-oriented pricing
- Sales-oriented pricing
- Status quo pricing

Profit-Oriented Pricing

Under the profit-oriented pricing strategy, target profits drive prices. Recall that target profits can be a particular dollar amount or a percentage of revenue. In some cases, these target profits are set. In other cases, the target is not specified. Rather, the goal is to achieve the highest profit possible.

Setting pricing based on target profits requires solid forecasting of both costs and customer demand. Attempting to achieve a particular dollar amount as a target profit is an easier short-term goal because accurately predicting each factor is less difficult in the immediate future. It is often better to set the target profit as a percentage as a longer-term strategy, when there are more potential changes or unknowns.

Sales-Oriented Pricing

In the sales-oriented pricing strategy, the goal is to maximize sales volume, or total revenue, rather than profit. Sales-oriented pricing is used to increase sales and market share. In the short term, coupons offering discounts and sales of particular menu items may increase sales volume. In the long term, pricing is very competitive with similar establishments.

The drawback to the sales-oriented pricing strategy is that, although it may lead to increased sales, building more volume may not lead to increased profits. This pricing strategy can work only if all of the following are true:

- Services are very limited.
- There are no extra amenities provided.
- The product is easily produced.
- The costs of providing the product can be kept low.

Status Quo Pricing

The motivation behind the status quo pricing strategy is to maintain an establishment's competitive position relative to the other operations in its market. In this type of pricing, competitors try to match prices for similar offerings.

While remaining competitive is important, every operation has different operating costs associated with providing its products and services. With similar pricing structures, an operation with low costs could be profitable while a different operation with higher operating costs might not be. If status quo pricing is the selected strategy, close attention to costs, prices, and actual profits is necessary to keep costs low and remain competitive.

CALCULATING SELLING PRICES

Managers responsible for marketing recognize the importance of price in brand positioning. Proper pricing means prices that help the operation meet its financial goals while providing the exceptional value to customers that will keep them coming back. Pricing is too important to be left to guesswork. The best managers use objective methods when calculating their menu prices. Although there are several approaches to objective menu prices, these are four of the most commonly used methods:

- Food cost percentage pricing method
- Contribution margin pricing method
- Prime cost pricing method
- Ratio pricing method

Food Cost Percentage Pricing Method

The food cost percentage pricing method is very popular in the restaurant and foodservice industry. The method goes by several names including the *simple markup method* and the *factor method*. While the various names used to identify the method may make it seem confusing, this method is actually the simplest of all menu pricing methods because it is based only on the cost of food required to make a menu item.

If a manager is pricing an item with the food cost percentage pricing method, he or she can use the cost of the food and the food cost percentage to arrive at a suggested menu price. Assume a manager needs to achieve a 33 percent food cost percentage and that a particular item has a food cost of $4.95. The manager would calculate the suggested menu price (*selling price*) using the following formula:

Food cost ÷ Food cost percentage = Selling price

MANAGER'S MATH

The food cost percentage method is often referred to as the *markup method* or *factor method* because managers can use a factor as a shortcut to calculate selling prices. Dividing any targeted food cost percentage into 1.00 yields a factor that can be multiplied by an item's food cost to yield its selling price. This factor table shows the factors that result for several popular food cost percentage targets.

Target Food Cost Percentage	Factor
20	5.00
25	4.00
28	3.57
30	3.33
32	3.12
34	2.94
36	2.77
40	2.50
42	2.38

Assume that the food cost of the item is $2.00 and the targeted food cost percentage is 25%. Using the factor from the table, the selling price would be calculated using this equation:

Food cost × Factor = Selling price

This example is calculated as follows:

$2.00 food cost × 4.00 factor = $8.00 selling price

This example is calculated as follows:

$4.95 food cost ÷ 33% food cost percentage = $15.00 selling price

Recall that earlier in this chapter the formula for a food cost percentage was stated as follows:

Food cost ÷ Selling price = Food cost percentage

In this example, applying this formula would yield the following food cost percentage:

$4.95 food cost ÷ $15.00 selling price = 33% food cost percentage

By applying basic algebra, the use of the formula means that if any two of the numbers in the formula are known by a manager, the third number can easily be calculated. Thus, if food cost and selling price are known, this is the formula to compute food cost percentage:

Food cost ÷ Selling price = Food cost percentage

If food cost and targeted food cost percentage are known, this formula is used to compute selling price:

Food cost ÷ Food cost percentage = Selling price

If targeted food cost percentage and desired selling price are known, this is the formula to compute food cost:

Selling price × Food cost percentage = Food cost

In the previous example, if the manager wanted to sell an item for $15.00 and knew that the targeted food cost was 33 percent, then the allowable food cost would be calculated as follows:

$15.00 selling price × 33% food cost percentage = $4.95 food cost percentage

After mastering the basic formulas, the food cost percentage pricing method is simple to use. However, the selling price that results from using this method is often simply a starting point. To illustrate, assume an item costs $4.11 to make. The manager has a 35 percent target food cost. Using the food cost percentage formula yields this selling price:

$4.11 food cost ÷ 35% food cost percentage = $11.74 selling price

In this case, the managers would likely round the selling price to $11.75, $11.95, or even to $11.99 to take advantage of menu marketing-related pricing strategies. These strategies will be covered in more detail in chapter 10.

Be aware that applying the same division or multiplication factors to all menu items may not be in the operation's best interest. Some managers feel the food cost percentage pricing method tends to overprice high food cost items and underprice low food cost items such as soups, pasta, chicken, beverages, and desserts. An additional weakness some managers point out is the fact that the food cost percentage pricing approach ignores the cost of labor. Using the food cost percentage approach, even if a menu item has a higher labor cost, it will sell for the same price as an item that is prepared quickly if the food costs of the two items are identical.

Market factors, what potential customers are willing to pay for specific menu items, and what the competition is charging should all influence pricing decisions. Prices should be adjusted up or down based on psychological pricing considerations and other subjective factors. These adjustments may result in the selling prices for many menu items being set at a food cost percentage higher than management might desire, but there will be others with a lower than average food cost percentage. The goal is for the total menu to average out to a targeted food cost percentage.

Contribution Margin Pricing Method

Contribution margin (CM) is what is left over after the food cost of a menu item is subtracted from the menu selling price. That amount is what each item contributes to paying for labor, other operating expenses, and profit. CM is often referred to as **gross profit** because that is the amount each item can contribute to paying for labor and all other operating expenses and to providing a profit. The CM figure, once known, is then added to the cost of each item to determine that item's price.

The CM pricing method is easy to use if managers know or can estimate several variables:

- The number of customers they will serve in a budget or time period
- Their nonfood operating costs
- Their desired profit

To illustrate, assume that a manager has created a budget that indicates the operation will serve 80,000 customers in the coming year and that all nonfood costs (labor and all other operating expenses) will be $412,000. The operation's target profit goal is $56,000. To use CM pricing, managers would follow these two steps:

Step 1. Calculate the average CM per customer:

**(Nonfood costs + Profit) ÷ Number of customers
= Average CM per customer**

MANAGER'S MATH

Dave is calculating proposed menu prices for three new menu items. Using the following information, calculate the selling price Dave should charge for each new menu item and then use the information to answer the questions that follow.

Item	Food Cost	Target Food Cost Percentage	Selling Price
Hanger steak	$5.50	40%	
Tuscan chicken	2.51	20	
Lake perch	3.50	25	

1. What is the selling price for hanger steak resulting from the formula's calculation?
2. What is the selling price for Tuscan chicken resulting from the formula's calculation?
3. What is the selling price for lake perch resulting from the formula's calculation?
4. If you were Dave, would you adjust any of these prices up or down prior to printing them on the menu? Why?

(Answers: 1. $13.75; 2. $12.55; 3. $14.00)

This example is calculated as follows:

($412,000 Nonfood costs + $56,000 Profit) ÷ 80,000 Customers = $5.85 Average CM per customer

Step 2. Determine the selling price for the menu item by adding the food cost to the CM: For example, the base selling price for a menu item with a $6.15 food cost would be as follows:

$6.15 Food cost + $5.85 CM = $12.00 Selling price

CM menu pricing is easy to use because the necessary information is generally in the establishment's operating budget or forecast. CM is practical when the nonfood costs required to serve each customer are basically the same and the only difference in menu items is the food cost itself. Managers who use the CM pricing method consider the contribution margin per menu item to be as important as, if not more important than, food cost in the individual menu item pricing decision. This pricing method reduces the range of selling prices because the only difference in the selling price is the cost of the individual food item.

Prime Cost Pricing Method

In the restaurant and foodservice industry, food costs and labor costs together are considered prime costs. The prime cost pricing method requires managers to consider the labor cost required to make a menu item as well as the item's food cost. This formula is used in prime cost pricing:

(Labor cost + Food cost) ÷ (Target labor cost percentage + Target food cost percentage) = Selling price

Use of the prime cost pricing method requires management to determine the cost of direct labor spent on preparing an item. This amount is added to food cost to determine the prime cost. For example, assume the food cost for an item is $3.00 and the labor cost is $1.00. The item's prime cost would be $4.00.

A manager derives the selling price based on prime cost by first establishing a combined labor and food cost percentage. This figure is called a prime cost percentage. If the manager desires a 10 percent labor cost and 35 percent food cost, the prime cost percentage would be 45 percent:

10% + 35% = 45%

In this example, the selling price formula would be as follows:

($1.00 Labor cost + $3.00 Food cost) ÷ (10% Target labor cost percentage + 35% Target food cost percentage) = Selling price

$4.00 Prime cost ÷ 45% Prime cost percentage = $8.89 Selling price

The item with a $4.00 prime cost would be divided by 45 percent to arrive at an $8.89 menu selling price.

Managers tend to use the prime cost pricing method if menu items vary widely in their preparation time and costs. This pricing method allows for the true cost of the labor to be associated with each individual menu item.

Ratio Pricing Method

The ratio pricing method considers the relationship, or ratio, between food and nonfood costs. The ratio is then used in a three-step process to develop base selling prices. To illustrate, assume that the operating budget for an establishment indicates food costs of $320,000, nonfood costs of $640,000, and a profit goal of $51,000.

Step 1. Calculate the ratio of food cost to nonfood costs and profit:

(Nonfood costs + Profit) ÷ Food cost = Ratio

In this example:

($640,000 Nonfood costs + $51,000 Profit) ÷ $320,000 Food cost = 2.16 Ratio

Now the manager knows that for each $1.00 of revenue to pay for food costs, he or she must generate an extra $2.16 in revenue to satisfy nonfood and profit requirements.

Step 2. Calculate the nonfood and profit requirement amount for the menu item: In this next step, the manager multiplies the menu item's food cost by the ratio determined in Step 1.

Food cost × Ratio = Nonfood and profit requirement

In this example, assume that the food cost is $4.10. The formula applied would look like this:

$4.10 Food cost × 2.16 Ratio = $8.86 Nonfood and profit requirement

Step 3. Determine the menu item's selling price by adding the nonfood and profit requirement to the menu item's food cost:

Food cost + Nonfood and profit requirement = Selling price

In this example:

$4.10 Food cost + $8.86 Nonfood and profit requirement = $12.96 Selling price

When managers have accurate budget information, the ratio pricing method can be a reliable way to ensure adherence to the operation's financial goals when pricing menu items.

OPEN FOR BUSINESS · RESTAURANT TECHNOLOGY

To use objective pricing methods, managers must have standardized recipes pre-costed with current financial information. Pre-costing involves determining the cost to produce one serving of a recipe. It considers the required ingredients, current costs for the ingredients, and the number of servings a recipe will produce. Often, the most challenging calculations involve determining the food cost for each recipe ingredient. Today, advanced recipe management software programs are readily available to help managers make the calculations they need to accurately pre-cost recipes and arrive at proper menu prices.

SUMMARY

1. **Contrast pricing as viewed from the perspectives of sellers and of buyers.**

   All sellers must set their prices, and they do so with the goal of attracting as many customers as possible. Some managers point out that the willingness of customers to buy is not the most important factor in menu pricing. These managers correctly state that unless a seller receives more money when selling a product than was required to produce it, that seller will ultimately go out of business. As a result, sellers must consider both customers and costs when setting prices. On the other hand, from a buyer's perspective, only his or her own perception of value received for price paid is important.

2. **Explain the importance of proper pricing.**

   Managers know that proper prices act as clear signals to buyers. When prices are low they deliver a buy signal. If prices are too high, however, they discourage customers from making purchases. Pricing correctly also requires managers to consider costs. Food cost, labor costs, and all other operating expenses must be considered when calculating selling prices. Of most importance, however, is the fact that customers must consider prices to be fair. When prices are fairly established, guests receive good value and will become loyal customers.

3. **Identify external factors that influence pricing decisions.**

   A variety of external factors directly affect the prices managers set for their products. The prices set by competitors are important because customers compare prices. Economic conditions affect pricing because difficult economic times can restrict a manager's ability to raise or even maintain prices. Food trends impact pricing because managers can charge more for foods that are highly popular but must often charge less for foods that have reduced levels of popularity. Seasonality of food ingredients also impacts pricing decisions as foods that are out of season may be higher in price and as a result, menu prices must be increased to account for the higher costs. Finally, there are laws designed to ensure consumers are informed of prices in a fair manner. These laws can directly influence how managers establish and communicate prices to their customers.

4. **Identify internal factors that influence pricing decisions.**

   Internal factors can also impact menu pricing. Included in the list of internal factors are the overall financial goals of an operation, food costs, and labor costs. Labor-intensive operations must charge prices high enough to recover the wages and salaries paid to the operation's workers. Finally, other operating costs, such as rent and utilities, incurred by an establishment can have a large impact on pricing.

5. **Describe how managers choose an appropriate pricing strategy.**

   Managers choose from three basic strategies when determining how much to charge for their menu items. Managers using the profit-oriented pricing strategy set their prices to achieve a targeted level of profit, either as a dollar amount or a percentage of overall revenue. Managers using the sales-oriented pricing strategy seek to maximize revenue, not profit. Sales-oriented pricing is a shorter-term strategy most often used to increase volume and market share. Managers electing a status quo pricing strategy seek to maintain their pricing position relative to other operations in their market area.

6. **Explain four methods managers can use to calculate selling prices.**

   Managers can choose from a variety of menu pricing methods. Four of the most popular ones are the food cost percentage, contribution margin, prime cost, and ratio pricing methods. When using the food cost percentage pricing method, managers seek to price their items in a way that yields a predetermined food cost percentage. Those managers using the contribution margin pricing method seek to ensure each menu item price includes an amount needed to cover the average nonfood costs and targeted profit per guest served. The prime cost pricing method includes detailed labor and food costs in the calculation of a menu item's price. Finally, the ratio pricing method requires managers to consider all operating expenses and desired profit when pricing a menu item.

APPLICATION EXERCISE

Review the competitive analysis of services in *Exhibit 6.10*. Based on this analysis, what changes would you make to your services in order to be more competitive? Explain your answer.

Exhibit 6.10

COMPETITIVE ANALYSIS OF SERVICES

Restaurant	Valet parking	Parking lot	Coat check	Doggie bags	Cloth linens	Family style dining	Private room	Wine steward
Branson Chophouse	Free	No	$2.00	Yes	Yes	No	$50.00	No
Will's Steakhouse	$5.00	No	No	Yes	Yes	Yes	No	No
Carriage House	$8.00	Small	Free	Yes	Yes	No	Free	Yes
The Lantern Seafood and Steakhouse	$6.00	Large	No	Yes	Yes	Yes	$75.00	No
The Coventry	Free	Large	Free	Yes	Yes	No	Free	Yes
Your Steakhouse	**No**	**Small**	**Free**	**Yes**	**No**	**Yes**	**$150.00**	**No**

REVIEW YOUR LEARNING

Select the best answer for each question.

1. **What two factors are most likely to affect a seller's perception of a price?**

   A. Quality of raw materials and cost

   B. Customers' perceptions and service style

   C. Industry segment and taxes paid on all profits

   D. Costs and concern for customers' perceptions

2. **What most affects a buyer's perception of a price?**

   A. Seller's costs

   B. Perceived value

   C. Profit needs of seller

   D. Taxes paid on the purchase

3. **Which is an example of a food trend that could affect menu pricing decisions?**

   A. The requirement to identify the calorie counts in all desserts sold by an establishment

   B. The decline in popularity of an establishment's best-selling menu item

   C. The decreased popularity of trans fats for deep frying foods

   D. The unavailability of fresh raspberries during the winter

4. **What are the three components of the profit formula?**

   A. Revenue + Expense = Profit

   B. Revenue ÷ Expense = Profit

   C. Revenue × Expense = Profit

   D. Revenue − Expense = Profit

5. **A menu item costs $3 to make and it sells for $12. What is the item's food cost percentage?**

   A. 20%

   B. 25%

   C. 36%

   D. 40%

6. **Which pricing strategy emphasizes revenue maximization over all other factors?**

   A. Status quo pricing

   B. Profit-oriented pricing

   C. Sales-oriented pricing

   D. Contribution margin pricing

7. **In which pricing strategy do managers set their prices with the goal of being similar in price to their competitors?**

   A. Profit-oriented pricing

   B. Sales-oriented pricing

   C. Status quo pricing

   D. Ratio pricing

8. **A manager using the food cost percentage pricing method has an entrée whose ingredient costs are $2. The manager's food cost target is 25%. What pricing factor will the manager use to determine the menu price of this entrée?**

   A. 2

   B. 3

   C. 4

   D. 5

9. **What are the two factors used to calculate menu prices using the prime cost pricing method?**

   A. Target profit and other operating costs

   B. Contribution margin and food cost

   C. Labor cost and advertising cost

   D. Food cost and labor cost

10. **A manager using the ratio pricing method has an entrée whose ingredient costs are $4.00. The manager's nonfood and profit ratio is 2.5. What will be the selling price of the item?**

    A. $6.50

    B. $10.00

    C. $12.50

    D. $14.00

FIELD PROJECT

Select three restaurant or foodservice operations of the same type (QSR, fast casual, casual, or fine dining). Obtain copies of their menus or visit the establishments and copy the names, prices, and sizes of their entrées. Prepare a competitive analysis of four similar entrées served by these establishments. Use the following table as a template. Then complete the competitive analysis exercise that follows.

Establishment	Entrée 1	Entrée 2	Entrée 3	Entrée 4	Average Entrée Price per Establishment
1	$	$	$	$	$
2	$	$	$	$	$
3	$	$	$	$	$
Average Price per Entrée	$	$	$	$	$

1. Determine the average entrée price per establishment by summing the individual entrée prices for a given establishment and dividing by the total number of entrées. Which establishments have the highest and lowest overall averages? Which establishments, if any, may want to raise or lower their overall average prices based on the overall pricing of the competition?

2. Now conduct a similar process for each entrée. What is the average price per entrée for each entrée? For each entrée, which establishments have the highest and lowest prices? For each entrée, which establishments, if any, may want to consider raising or lowering their prices based on the competition's pricing?

3. Finally, assume that you are opening an operation that will compete with the three establishments listed here, serving the same entrées. Using the results of your competitive analysis, determine a price for each entrée for your operation.

7

Communication Channels

CHAPTER LEARNING OBJECTIVES

After completing this chapter, you should be able to:

- Identify the principles of effective print-based advertising.

- List the principles of effective broadcast-based advertising.

- State the principles of effective mail-based advertising.

- Summarize the effective use of Web sites and email in marketing.

- Explain the importance of social media in marketing.

- Describe the importance of cell phone applications (apps) in marketing.

KEY TERMS

broadcast communication channels, p. 156

cell phone application (app), p. 167

communication channels, p. 152

contacts, p. 165

direct mail, p. 153

frequency, p. 160

graphics, p. 155

Internet-based communication channels, p. 163

junk mail, p. 160

reach, p. 160

snail mail, p. 161

social media networks, p. 165

spam, p. 165

spot (broadcast), p. 157

wireless communication channels, p. 163

CASE STUDY

"It doesn't make sense to me that we would create a special 'Summer Fresh Menu' and then not tell our customers about it," protested Harry, the chef at the Point's End restaurant.

"Our customers will find out about it when they come in," said Lucy, defensively. Lucy was the establishment manager and in charge of its marketing efforts.

"But that's just my point," Harry continued. "Part of the reason for creating this seasonal menu was to draw in new customers. New customers won't come in to try the menu if they don't know about it."

"OK," said Lucy, "we do have some funds in the marketing plan that we could use for advertising the menu. I will just have to decide on the most effective approach."

"I think you should decide soon," replied Harry. "We're launching the new menu next week!"

1. Is Harry correct that the Point's End restaurant has an important new message that should be communicated to its current and potential guests?

2. How might Lucy's decision regarding how to communicate the "Summer Fresh" menu to guests impact the establishment's financial goals?

Communication is by far the most common use of the Internet. From the earliest days of email and chat rooms, users relied on the Internet as a fast and convenient way to talk to each other. Today, managers can use the Internet and other forms of electronic communication to speak directly to their customers.

In the past, customers used word of mouth to tell others about their dining experiences. Today, the Internet offers consumers a variety of communication tools to recount dining adventures. When managers use the Internet to send messages that attract customers and then deliver on their promises, the customers use "word of mouse" to relay to others their positive dining experiences.

COMMUNICATION CHANNEL OVERVIEW

Restaurant and foodservice managers must develop good products, price them properly, and establish excellent service standards. But they must also communicate to potential customers about their establishments. To do so, managers develop a marketing plan that guides their communication efforts. That marketing plan involves determining the establishment's **communication channels**, or the means by which a business talks to its customers. In the past the communication channel was seen as being one-way, from the operation to its customers. Today, communication channels also include ways for customers to talk to businesses.

Determining the most effective customer communication channel begins with planning the message. First, consider the purpose of the message and the desired response. In most cases, the desired response is simply that customers will visit the operation. But there are other reasons to communicate. Consider, for example, the manager who wishes to implement a program that thanks frequent diners for their business. In this case, the primary purpose of the message is to demonstrate appreciation to good customers.

Remember that to be successful, a message must be clear and concise. If not, customers will not receive the intended message and will not react to it. A commonly used model for creating effective messages uses the acronym *AIDA*:

- **Attention:** Get the audience's attention.
- **Interest:** Interest the audience in the message.
- **Desire:** Create a desire for the product or service.
- **Action:** Prompt the audience to take the desired action.

Adherence to the AIDA principles will ensure the message is concise, yet effective.

In addition to the message itself, managers must consider a few other message-related factors:

- **Promotional messages of competitors:** A successful promotional message is one that is unique and specific. Managers should monitor their competitors' promotional messages and advertising and avoid duplicating those messages.
- **Regulations regarding truth in advertising:** Managers must know what they can and cannot say or portray. The Federal Trade Commission (FTC) specifies that "advertising must be truthful and nondeceptive."[1] Advertisers must have evidence to back up their claims and advertisements must be fair. For example, if a manager is making claims

[1] From business.ftc.gov/documents/bus35-advertising-faqs-guide-small-business (accessed December 3, 2011).

related to nutrition, they need to understand what can be categorized as "healthy." In addition, they must be familiar with any state and local advertising-related regulations.

- **Brand image of the establishment:** A message should align with the establishment's concept. For example, a quick-service restaurant and a fine-dining establishment need to convey very different images. The use of media, color, and music in messages all affect customers' perceptions of an operation and its image.

- **Optimal use of the communication channel:** Each communication channel has things it does well and things it cannot do or does poorly. For example, radio does not allow the opportunity to use visual images. Outdoor advertising cannot be used to communicate with small target audiences. The right communication channel should always be selected to communicate the right message.

The previous rules hold true for all marketing messages, regardless of the communication channel. However, as noted in the final item, each type of communication channel has its own special guidelines. Communication channels can be broken down into traditional and interactive channels. Traditional channels include newspapers, magazines, flyers, telephone, radio, television, and direct mail, which is mail sent to the home or workplace of potential customers. Traditional communication channels generally can be broken into three broad subcategories: print, broadcast, and media.

Interactive channels leverage rapid technological advances, including the Internet and wireless communications, and consist of several subcategories including websites, social media sites, and cell phone applications.

Regardless of the methods used to communicate with customers, the operation's messages must be clear and cost-effective.

TRADITIONAL COMMUNICATION CHANNELS

Print, broadcast, and mail are effective forms of business communication. Experienced restaurant and foodservice managers carefully consider the use of these traditional tools as they seek to inform their target markets about the products and services available to customers.

Print

Print is one of the oldest forms of communicating with customers. The main goal of any print advertisement is simple: Make the reader *want* to read it. Understand that few readers will want to read an ad about a business. Instead, readers are more interested in what a business can do for them. While this principle applies to any communication channel, it is especially true of printed materials.

Exhibit 7.1

POPULAR PRINT FORMS

Billboards	Brochures	Calendars	Coupons
Directories	Flyers	Magazines	Menus and menu flyers
Newsletters	Newspapers	Pamphlets	Signs

Print advertising takes many forms. *Exhibit 7.1* shows many of the most popular print forms. Communication experts agree that when dealing with any of these print forms, there are several principles to follow to ensure effective communication.

PRINCIPLE #1: USE A SIMPLE LAYOUT

Readers avoid reading things that are perceived as being too hard to read. If a printed piece looks cluttered, readers will simply turn the page, put down the piece of paper, or look elsewhere. Simple layout also means the use of easy-on-the-eyes type styles and minimizing the number of pictures or images used in the same ad.

PRINCIPLE #2: MAKE THE MESSAGE CLEAR

In most cases, a single idea is easier to communicate than several ideas. The more focused a message can be, the greater the impact of the printed piece.

PRINCIPLE #3: STRESS BENEFITS

Customers buy features to gain benefits. Printed pieces should highlight these features. For example, an operation could use a print ad to describe its quality food or excellent service. The use of graphics in print-based ads can also be powerful. A print ad that includes a picture of a mother serving takeout food to her family communicates the labor savings and convenience of takeout food. It also sends a message of time freed to spend with family. In this and in all other cases, the most memorable print ads explain clearly to customers how the features offered by an operation translate into features that will benefit customers personally.

PRINCIPLE #4: USE PICTURES WHEN POSSIBLE

Print communication may carry large or small amounts of information. Managers should recognize, however, that most people are visually oriented. Readers will remember less than 10 percent of what they read, but can recall up to 50 percent of what they have seen.[2] For this reason, the pictures in a print promotional piece are very important.

In advertising, pictures are referred to as graphics—visual representations that may include photographs, drawings, numbers, symbols, maps, and diagrams. In the restaurant and foodservice business, photographs of single menu items or full plates of food are common graphics used in print promotional pieces (see *Exhibit 7.2*).

Many people also like to look at photographs of other people. Print ads with graphics showing other people typically draw more attention than photographs of things. The best restaurant and foodservice print ads use real people enjoying real food in real settings.

Exhibit 7.2

PRINCIPLE #5: INCLUDE PICTURE CAPTIONS

Photo captions are the second-most-read part of any advertisement, after the headline. Where it makes good sense, put captions under each photo. A caption is a second opportunity to sell, so it should be written as carefully as the headline of the printed piece.

PRINCIPLE #6: USE COLOR IF POSSIBLE

Many forms of printed material may be produced in black and white or in color. In general, colored print material is more expensive to produce but is better received by readers. The decision to print in black and white or color is often an economic one. However, printers report that their customers feel that materials printed in color have more impact than those same materials printed in black and white.[3]

---

[2]From Terence A. Shimp, *Advertising, Promotion, and Other Aspects of Integrated Marketing Communications*, Seventh Edition (Cincinnati, OH: South-Western College Publishing), 34.

[3]From www.ebaprinting.com/impact_of_colors_in_advertisements/ (accessed December 3, 2012).

PRINCIPLE #7: PROOF THE AD CAREFULLY BEFORE IT IS PRINTED

Every manager who has ever been confronted by a customer pointing out a spelling or grammar error on the operation's menu knows how embarrassing it can be to make a mistake on an important printed document. Far worse are coupons or ads that contain textual errors that offer unintended discounts. In general, the more individuals given a chance to proofread a printed document, the lower the chance for error. Experienced managers show review copies of print materials to a wide group of proofreaders, including those who are highly skilled in the use of language.

PRINCIPLE #8: TRACK THE RESPONSE IF POSSIBLE

One criticism of print ads is that it is difficult to know how many people have actually read a given ad. For example, a newspaper may have a daily readership of 100,000 individuals. However, it is unrealistic to assume that every reader will read every ad in a given day. Similarly, a printed magazine may have a circulation of 10,000, but this figure does not translate into 10,000 sets of eyes reading the magazine. The number could be many more than 10,000 if the magazine was passed on by its original recipient, or it could be much less if readers tend to not read every page of the publication. For this reason, many managers include calls to action such as coupons to use in a dining establishment, an 800 number to call, or a Web site to visit to track the effectiveness of a given print ad. These mechanisms give managers a better idea of the number of customers who have seen and read the promotional piece.

THINK ABOUT IT . . .

Pick up a recent magazine and page through its ads. Which ads made you stop and want to read them? Which of the principles listed here do you see demonstrated in the ads?

Broadcast

Broadcast communication channels include radio and television, media that were originally broadcast over the airwaves. Broadcast media are effective because they reach very large numbers of customers. Restaurant and foodservice operations have traditionally used radio extensively to reach their customers. Larger establishments and many restaurant chains regularly use television to spread their advertising messages. Sometimes broadcast media are referred to as mass marketing because national and worldwide audiences may view the same messages delivered using a particular broadcast communication channel.

The purpose of a broadcast ad or promotional message is the same as that of a printed one. Both types seek to clearly communicate a message to current and potential customers. However, unlike print advertising, broadcast advertising is subject to monitoring and limitations imposed by the Federal Trade Commission (FTC).

There are three rules that all ads must follow under the Federal Trade Commission Act:

- Advertising must be truthful and nondeceptive.

- Advertisers must have evidence to back up their claims.

- Advertisements cannot be unfair.

In general, an ad will be determined to be deceptive if it is likely to mislead consumers acting reasonably under the circumstances and if the deception itself is "material"—that is, if it is important to a consumer's decision to buy or use the product. For example, if the number of calories in an entrée item is listed, the seller must have specific data supporting the statement.

In general, an ad will be determined to be unfair if it causes or is likely to cause substantial consumer injury that a consumer could not reasonably avoid and it is not outweighed by the benefit to consumers. Radio and television stations are required to ensure that commercials meet FTC standards before agreeing to broadcast them.

In addition to the FTC, other agencies regulate various aspects of food advertising. Each state has consumer protection laws that govern ads broadcast in that state. The Food and Drug Administration (FDA) oversees food labeling, and the Bureau of Alcohol, Tobacco, Firearms and Explosives (ATF) has jurisdiction over alcohol labeling and advertising. Alcohol ads by their content or placement may not be directed to underage consumers. Some broadcasters and publishers place additional restrictions on where or when alcohol ads can run. Finally, there are also special regulations related to the use of words such as *lite, low-calorie,* and *healthy*. Some of these important and legally defined terms will be addressed in detail in chapter 10.

When managers decide to use radio or television as their communication channel, they purchase a spot. A **spot** is typically a 15- or 30-second broadcast time period on either radio or television, although occasionally it may run up to 60 seconds. In most cases, the longer the spot, the more it will cost to broadcast it. In addition to length, however, there are a variety of factors that affect the cost of a radio or television spot:

- **The popularity of the station broadcasting the spot:** Spots on very popular stations cost more than spots played on less popular ones.

- **The number of viewers or listeners who will likely see or hear the spot:** Spots during radio and television programs with high listener or viewership cost more than the same length of spot played during a less popular program.

- **The time of day:** Radio spots are most expensive during early morning hours and late afternoon hours, when the number of listeners is highest. Television spots cost most during "prime" viewing times, generally during evening programming.

Manager's Memo

For guidance on how the FTC evaluates claims made in food ads, managers should contact the FTC to ask for a free copy of the *Enforcement Policy Statement on Food Advertising*.

For information about food product labeling, managers can visit the FDA's Web site (*www.fda.gov*) or call the FDA Inquiry Line: 1-888-INFO-FDA.

For information about advertising related to meat and poultry, managers can visit the Department of Agriculture (U.S.D.A.) Web site (*www.usda.gov*) or call the USDA's Center for Nutrition Policy and Promotion: 202-418-2312.

- **The number of spots purchased at one time:** Like many businesses, broadcasters frequently offer significant discounts to large-quantity customers. Thus, the price per spot is likely to be much lower for a manager purchasing 20 spots than for the same manager purchasing only 2.

- **The number of spots purchased over time:** Again, like many other businesses, broadcasters often offer lower prices to customers who buy regularly from them than to customers who buy only on rare occasions.

RADIO BROADCASTS

Just as there are principles for using print communication channels, there are principles that guide the use of broadcast channels. Managers developing radio ads should follow these five principles:

Principle #1: Get the Listener's Attention Immediately. In a radio ad, a business has only a few seconds to create listener interest. Many radio listeners are multitasking while listening to the radio, such as driving or working. For that reason, an effective radio message must grab the attention of the listener quickly and must maintain it throughout the spot.

Principle #2: Picture the Listener. Consider that the listener is standing right in front of the announcer who is delivering the message. A good radio spot should convey all the personality and enthusiasm present in a personal conversation. If the radio voice sounds insincere, mechanical, unenthusiastic, or lacking conviction, it will have a negative impact on the message being communicated.

Principle #3: Read Proposed Copy Aloud Prior to Broadcasting. Just as it is important to proof copies of printed material, it is critical to listen to the radio spot before it is broadcast. People do not usually talk the same way they write. To illustrate, the first sentence that follows is grammatically correct, but formal. The second sentence is casual, the type of statement a friend might make to another friend in a quick conversation.

1. It is truly the best steak that I have ever eaten!

2. It's the best steak I ever ate!

Note that the formality and familiarity implied by the speaker of each statement is quite different. Each could, perhaps, be appropriate in a properly constructed radio spot, but the choice of which to use is one a manager should make only after hearing each of them read aloud, in context.

Principle #4: Summarize the Message. A radio ad should summarize its single most important point at the end of the message. Of course, that assumes the listener has been sufficiently interested to stay tuned throughout the entire message. Summarizing the message is done to enhance message retention and explains why so many broadcast advertisements end with a statement that starts, "So remember . . ."

Principle #5: Make Ads Stand Out. Radio ads work best when they create mental images for the listeners. Listeners may picture themselves eating dinner in a beautiful dining room or on a relaxing outdoor patio with a beverage. They may even picture themselves splurging on an item for which they have been saving money. But these mental pictures develop only when a manager is able to make his or her ad stand out from the barrage of other ads listeners hear in a given day. The use of music or other sounds, humor, irreverence, and clever writing are all methods those who produce radio ads employ to make their ads stand out, be memorable, and be effective.

TELEVISION BROADCASTS

Because of television's ability to convey visual images, the broadcast principles for this medium vary somewhat from those of radio. There are four television-specific principles managers should follow:

Principle #1: Choose Programming Partners Carefully. Managers communicating via television should carefully match the networks and programs on which they are advertising with their own brand image and with their target customer demographics. Most basic cable networks offer a wide variety of programming to fit the needs of viewers. Managers can capitalize on the growing number of television stations to direct their messages to specific groups. For example, an establishment has created a new "Healthy Fresh" summer salad menu featuring seasonal and locally grown fruits and vegetables. The establishment manager wants to communicate this fact especially to female customers. In this case, choosing a network whose viewership is targeted more toward women could effectively capture that audience.

Principle #2: Look Professional. Broadcast network advertising can be expensive, but managers should not skimp on production costs in this media any more than they would skimp on print costs. Television viewers are sophisticated and will reject commercials that are badly scripted or poorly produced.

Tammy is the manager of Armand's Hyde Park restaurant. She is considering buying spots on a popular local radio station. The station manager is offering Tammy two different packages. The first package includes 20 spots of 30 seconds each. The second package includes 50 spots of 30 seconds each. The first package sells for $1,000, whereas the second package sells for $2,250. In each case, the ads will run during the same time periods and on the same days.

1. How much will Tammy spend per spot if she purchases the first package?

2. How much will Tammy spend per spot if she purchases the second package?

(Answers: 1. $50 per spot; 2. $45 per spot)

Principle #3: Understand Reach and Frequency. In broadcasting, **reach** is the estimated number of unduplicated audience members that tune in to a particular channel or program at least once during a reported time period. **Frequency** is the average number of times a single viewer is exposed to an ad during a given time period. Many experts believe a television commercial must be seen multiple times if it is to achieve its maximum impact. Therefore, careful consideration of these two similar, but not identical, terms is essential because both are used often in reference to broadcast advertising.

Principle #4: Show, Don't Just Tell. Like radio, television lacks the ability to effectively measure response to its ads. It can measure viewership, but not the subsequent action taken by those viewers. It is essential that the medium does what it does best—present a visual image. Television is a visual as well as audio form of media. The importance of using television to "show" as well as "tell" is continually affirmed by those who use television to creatively tell their story using pictures and sound.

The geographic scope of television advertising ranges from advertising within localized communities using local-only channels on cable stations, to coverage using nationally distributed channels such as ABC, NBC, CBS, and FOX. Regardless of the broadcast partner, managers have a powerful communications ally when they choose to broadcast their promotional messages.

MAIL

Direct mail is one of the easiest communication channels to use. Unfortunately, it is also one of the most often misused channels. **Junk mail**, the type of mail that is routinely seen as a nuisance and that is often discarded without opening, is not an effective communication device. But traditional direct-mail services can be creatively combined with high-quality print pieces to create and send items such as personal letters, flyers, newsletters, and coupons.

With the advent of email, some managers may feel using traditional mail services no longer makes sense as an effective way to reach customers. Other managers, however, recognize that an effective mail piece can be a very powerful way to communicate a message.

The principles of creating print-based communication pieces covered previously apply to items mailed to customers. There are several additional principles to consider when using the mail communication channel:

Principle #1: Handwrite Addresses. Hand writing addresses on mailings sent to smaller groups of targeted customers make a mailer stand out from the stacks of junk mail potential guests regularly receive. Fairly or unfairly, preprinted

address labels shout "mass mailing!" and "junk mail!" In contrast, addressing by hand adds a personal touch.

Principle #2: Use Colored Envelopes. Because most mail comes in white envelopes, colored envelopes immediately seize a recipient's attention. The use of colored envelopes is a very simple and low-cost way to make mailings stand out.

Principle #3: Use Real Stamps. Put stamps on the envelope (instead of using a meter) for the same reason addresses should be handwritten—to personalize the mailing. This principle is even more effective when the stamps have food or travel themes related to the hospitality business.

Principle #4: Keep a Consistent Look. Keep a consistent look for repeat mailings. Target customers will come to recognize an establishment's mailings, menus, newsletters, postcards, or other communications on sight.

Some managers will no doubt continue to believe that email has made so-called snail mail (the traditional form of mailings) obsolete, but that is certainly not true. When managers take the time to target the right audience and to make traditional mailings interesting and attractive (*Exhibit 7.3*), they consistently discover just how effective mail can be!

WHAT'S THE FOOTPRINT?

Whether it is called direct mail or junk mail, everyone who has a mailbox knows that it is a large and growing problem. Increasingly, eco-concerned customers are opting out of receiving advertising-related mail because of its negative environmental impact.

Junk mail delivered to an "address" rather than an individual used to be seen merely as an annoyance. Today, its senders are just as likely to be seen as doing real damage to the environment, and that is certainly *not* a message establishment managers want to send to their customers!

Exhibit 7.3

Personalized touches help mailings stand out.

Pros and Cons of Traditional Communication Channels

Managers who use traditional communication channels realize that each has its strengths and weaknesses. No one communication channel is perfect for every operation, every situation, or every budget. Managers must select the channel based on a number of considerations. *Exhibit 7.4* summarizes the pros and cons of some of the most popular forms of traditional communication channels typically used by establishment managers.

Exhibit 7.4

TRADITIONAL COMMUNICATION CHANNEL PROS AND CONS

Type of Medium	Pros	Cons
Television	• Can target specific markets • Can reach a large population • Provides video and audio • Provides specific timing of ads	• Usually has higher costs • Provides limited time for conveying message • Technology exists that enables viewers to avoid commercials • Is transitory; viewer cannot look at ad again
Radio	• Has lower cost • Can target specific markets • May reach a relatively large population • Provides specific timing of ads	• Lacks visuals • Allows limited time for conveying message • Is transitory; listener cannot listen to ad again
Newspaper	• Can target a local area • Usually has lower costs compared to other channels • Provides shorter lead time for ads	• Is highly competitive with other ads • Has shorter life span; usually discarded daily • Provides lower production quality
Magazine	• Can target very specific markets • Has longer life span • Provides high-quality production	• Provides longer lead time for ads • Is usually most costly print media
Direct Mail	• Can target very specific markets • Provides greater control over content	• Requires accurate, timely data • Is easy to ignore • Has high cost per exposure • Creates negative image
Outdoor	• Provides high reach rates • Has lower cost per exposure for broad target audiences • Allows targeting an audience by location	• Is ineffective for targeting small markets • Is sometimes limited by local regulations • Has longer lead time for ads

INTERNET-BASED AND WIRELESS COMMUNICATION CHANNELS

While the traditional methods of communicating with target customers are still extremely useful, there can be no denying the increased importance of Internet-based and wireless communication channels. **Internet-based communication channels** include those computer programs that allow for one-way or two-way communication between Internet users. **Wireless communication channels** include those computer-based and non-computer-based systems that deliver information via public airwaves. Today's managers can take advantage of several such systems: web sites, email, social media, and cell phone applications (apps).

For example, if an establishment creates its own Web site and then uses that site to post information about a new fall menu, the operation is using an Internet-based communication channel (Web site) to deliver one-way communication to its target customers. If the same establishment uses a cell phone app that allows customers to give the managers feedback about the proposed menu, the establishment is using a wireless communication channel.

Some Internet-based and wireless communication channels permit two-way communication between a business and its customers. The advantages to businesses of providing two-way communication opportunities are clear. Using the Internet to provide only one-way communication would be the equivalent of a telephone conversation in which the message sender could say anything he or she wished but the person receiving the call could not respond. In the same way, one-way communication approaches do not take advantage of the full range of possibilities that the Internet and many wireless communication options now offer.

It is most likely that managers will continue using traditional communication channels to send messages to their customers. It is equally likely, however, that the use of nontraditional communication channels will continue to grow. For that reason managers should become very familiar with the effective use and management of Web sites, email, social media, and cell phone apps.

Web Sites

Restaurant and foodservice managers have traditionally favored localized communication channels ranging from radio spots to printed telephone directory advertisements. The managers' reason for using these channels was sound: It helps them reach local consumers who are their primary target markets because these individuals are the ones who actually visit the establishment. The use of a Web site broadens the reach of an operation tremendously; however, the fact that Internet users can access a local establishment's Web site across the globe does not mean that the establishment's target market has expanded across the globe.

The reach of the Internet is important for managers to understand. To illustrate, consider the manager of an Irish-themed establishment who hires a company to increase the quality of Internet search results when potential customers search for "Irish Pub." If the establishment is in a city with a large number of out-of-town visitors, it may make sense to widen the reach of the establishment's Web site beyond the local area. However, if the operation is not catering to tourists, such an Internet presence may be a waste of scarce marketing dollars.

The principles of effective Web design could fill many books. Many of the print-based communication principles used to create effective hard-copy documents, such as using easily readable type and carefully proofreading written work, apply to the onscreen print of an operation's Web site. Similarly, the principles of high-quality television advertising, such as ensuring professionalism in the final product and the effective use of imagery, are applicable to videos posted on a Web site. Because Web sites offer more than just print and videos, there are some additional aspects of managing the communication-related portion of a Web site that managers should understand. These include the placement of critical information on the operation's site:

- Location and driving directions
- Hours of operation
- Menu
- Promotions
- Links or instructions for making reservations (if applicable)
- Links or instructions for placing carry-out orders (if applicable)
- Links to social media sites
- Contact information by email and phone number

Email

Email is certainly one of the most commonly used marketing tools. Like many other technologies unique to the Internet, email communication is sent and received primarily via the use of text and graphics. Communicating effectively involves taking the same care and time involved in creating print-based messages.

When communicating via the Internet, managers must understand that there are risks involved in taking an overly casual approach to communications. Tech-savvy managers understand that every email they write has the potential to be posted across the globe. It is, after all, the World Wide Web! The marketing implications of email communications being posted for millions to see are many. Managers should be careful not to give out personal information about themselves or others. They must be aware of the real risks involved in communicating with people they cannot see and may never meet in person. It is extremely important to stay professional and to avoid inappropriate humor and sarcasm, as well as commenting on sensitive religious, political, or social issues. Managers can never assume that emails will remain private, so they must be very careful about what they write in them.

Establishment managers should follow proper protocol in the development and distribution of their operation's emails:

- Use the "subject" line to emphasize the main point of the email; for example a "special" or an "upcoming event."

- Begin with a greeting.

- After the greeting, get straight to the point.

- Remember that the email could be read by, literally, everyone in the world and thus is a public document.

- Be polite and respectful of the reader.

- Keep it short.

- End with a call to action (for example, "contact us for more information" or "book your reservation now").

- Close by signing the email with the sender's full name and contact information.

- Proofread very carefully before hitting "Send."

Managers should recognize that there are also ethical and legal issues related to using the Internet for communication. Unsolicited email or other forms of communication is called **spam**. Spamming sends large numbers of unsolicited emails. There are many spammers and the amount of unsolicited email grows daily. Spam costs productivity and may result in potential damage related to fraud and infected files. As a result, consumers are increasingly wary about opening emails unless they are from a trusted source, and spamming has been the subject of legislation in many jurisdictions. Managers using email as a communication device must recognize these concerns and heed them. Managers planning to use email extensively are well advised to seek the counsel of legal advisers familiar with applicable Internet communication-related laws.

Social Media

Increasingly, Internet users participate in social networks. **Social media networks** consist of individuals who stay electronically connected for reasons that include friendship, common interest, romantic relationship, or shared knowledge. Some individuals in a social network, called **contacts**, spend significant amounts of time maintaining the connection. Others may spend much less time.

> **THINK ABOUT IT . . .**
>
> If you received an email from an establishment you had previously visited, would you open it? Would your response be the same if you had not visited the establishment?

From a manager's perspective, the most important aspect of social media is that it readily allows customer-to-customer communication. The result is that managers cannot control this nontraditional communication channel. However, managers should not underestimate how much they can influence it.

Rapidly increasing numbers of customers of all ages consult social network sites prior to making dinner reservations, ordering takeout food, or choosing a pizza delivery company. As a result, those managers who use social media sites most effectively position themselves for success. Those who do not risk being left behind. Managers need to understand how social media networks operate and how they can be effectively used as an emerging nontraditional communication channel.

It is important to understand that communication is the primary reason for the existence of social networking sites. Users of social media sites register to use the sites, create content, connect with like-minded contacts, and exchange information. Creative managers have employed a variety of strategies designed to create an active social media presence to attract large numbers of contacts. Those that been successful recognize that when it comes to having meaningful social media conversations, there must be someone available to communicate. Some managers mistakenly assume a social media page is simply a Web site. However, the two are not synonymous. In most cases, Web site visitors seek information. Social media users seek two-way communication. A social media page that does not allow for two-way communication is unlikely to return positive results.

A second major mistake some managers make is using their social media presence only to advertise specials. In essence, these pages become Web-based flyers intended only to increase sales. While this approach may attract some attention in the short run, this limited use of the two-way communication channel underuses the more dynamic features of social media networks by stifling the ability for customers to provide insight and feedback.

Visitors reviewing an establishment's social media presence want to know about new and exciting things happening at the establishment and how these changes might impact them. Following are examples of the types of information an operation might post on a social media site:

- Descriptions of new menu items

- Lists of daily or weekly specials

- Articles about locally or nationally famous guests who have dined in the establishment recently

- Releases related to the hiring of a new chef, server, or bartender

- Links to positive reviews posted on other social media sites

- Details on events or promotions

- Coupons

- Holiday greetings

Many establishments also now give customers the ability to make reservations from social media sites. This type of information sharing allows customers to feel a part of the operation, which in turn leads to greater customer loyalty.

Viral communication is another characteristic of social media. In traditional communication channels, a business communicates directly with a customer and, perhaps, the customer provides feedback. With viral communication, a business communicates directly with a single user or set of users. Those users share the message with their friends. The message sharing is user driven, as friends share with other friends. The potential for a message to reach more customers is incredibly powerful and relatively inexpensive.

The world of social media, like the restaurant and foodservice world, continues to evolve. The most popular social media sites of today may or may not be the most popular sites of tomorrow. However, it seems likely that social media sites will continue to provide a virtual platform where everyone can communicate more freely. Social media sites can help coax feedback from those who may not be comfortable giving it in person. They may also help members strengthen their social relationships with others. Managers who understand social media networking and seek two-way communications with their guests can take advantage of these networks.

Whether they are in charge of a single operation or a chain, today's managers recognize that social media conversations are a huge and still-growing part of how guests form and share opinions with each other. Being part of that guest-initiated conversation allows these managers to be proactive in shaping how their establishments can advance in an evolving communication environment.

Cell Phone Applications (Apps)

A cell phone application (app) is a computer application that runs on advanced cellular phones. A cell phone app is an add-on or collection of data that allows cellular telephones to do things that are usually unrelated to making telephone calls.

The vast popularity of cell phones has created yet another nontraditional communication channel. This wireless communication channel sometimes bypasses the Internet and sometimes incorporates it. In both cases, customer

[4]From shgww.com/archives/885?pfstyle=wp (accessed December 7, 2011).

THINK ABOUT IT . . .

Which social media sites do you use? How would you recommend managers use those sites to effectively communicate with their customers?

OPEN FOR BUSINESS

BY THE CUSTOMER/ FOR THE CUSTOMER

The complete list of social media sites is ever changing and includes a variety of target-market-specific sites. Here are some of the most popular social media sites of which technology-savvy managers should be aware:

- Facebook

- FourSquare

- Google +

- Groupon

- LinkedIn

- MySpace

- Orkut

- TripAdvisor

- Twitter

- Urbanspoon

- Wikipedia

- Yelp

- Zagat

Current consumer research indicates that nearly 90 percent of computer users look at online ratings and reviews of establishments and nearly 50 percent will refuse to book a reservation without first reading a review[4]

demand and changes in customer lifestyle have resulted in the need for managers to better understand this increasingly popular communication channel.

When dealing with nontraditional communication channels, it is important to keep up to date with recent technological trends and advances. For example, in the 2010s, teenagers in large numbers abandoned the use of email in favor of texting and social media. At the same time, large numbers of older consumers increased their use of email, which, to these users, is still a new form of communication. As a result, products and services geared toward teens may be better marketed through social media and cell phone apps, while email may be the preferred method for reaching older consumers.

Popular apps allow users to surf the Internet, post information to their social media accounts, or play games. Like all communication channels, the goal for a cell phone app is to allow enhanced interaction between a business and its customers. Restaurant- and foodservice-related apps allow users to get directions to establishments, preview menus and promotional materials, make reservations, and post reviews to social media sites. Social couponing apps allow users to download discount coupons directly to their phones, rather than having users print out the coupons. Some apps even allow customers to track delivery orders and pay for their food using the phone. Customers like the mobility, utility, and convenience using innovative cell phone apps. As handheld computing devices become more widely adopted, managers should track this communication channel to improve two-way communication with customers (*Exhibit 7.5*).

Exhibit 7.5

Managers using cell phone apps can implement a variety of activities:

- **Data Collection:** Managers can ask customers to join their loyalty programs by texting them via their mobile phones. Managers can also group their customers under various lists and subgroups and can allow customers to easily unsubscribe from messages by sending a text message to the operation. Mass texts can be used to communicate a variety of information to guests.

- **Event Promotion:** Mobile marketing technology lets operations hold mobile marketing campaigns, where restaurant and foodservice guests have a chance to win a free dinner, coupon, or gift card for a special upcoming event. When customers come in the door for the special event or promotion, instead of a paper coupon they can show the message on their phone that brought them to the operation for a special drink, reduced dinner price, or waiver of entrance fee.

- **Cell Phone App Marketing Campaigns:** Managers can tailor mobile marketing campaigns based on customer's personal information and preferences or even the day's weather forecasts. These marketing campaigns allow establishments to have locally based, dynamic campaigns that create personalized, direct marketing. Some text-messaging software applications that are tailored to the restaurant and foodservice industry are easy to use, Web based, affordable, and do not require installing any special software. Managers should continually monitor advances in this rapidly changing area.

THINK ABOUT IT . . .

What phone apps do you use most frequently? What additional features would you like to see added to this app?

SUMMARY

1. **Identify the principles of effective print-based advertising.**

   Print is one of the oldest and easiest means of business communication. The best print-based communication pieces use a simple layout. They send a single clear message and stress benefits to readers rather than the seller's product or service features.

   To increase effectiveness, the best print pieces include pictures and other graphics. Print pieces use captions when they include photos. Despite the higher cost, the use of color is highly desirable. Finally, high-quality print-based communication pieces are very carefully proofread prior to their printing.

2. **List the principles of effective broadcast-based advertising.**

   Broadcast media typically refers to radio and television. An effective radio spot immediately grabs the attention of the listener. It seeks to talk to the listener as if the announcer were in the same room. Radio spots should be carefully proofread prior to broadcast, should be summarized near the end of the spot, and most important, must stand out from other ads.

   The best television ads are professionally produced and are placed on networks and programs that reflect the target markets of the operation being advertised. Managers using this medium understand reach and frequency as well as the importance of using creative imagery to produce memorable communication pieces.

3. **State the principles of effective mail-based advertising.**

   While sometimes neglected, traditional mail service can still play a critical role in a manager's marketing plan. To be effective, mailing addresses should be handwritten and the pieces should be mailed in colored envelopes using stamps, not stamp meters. Consistency of look is also important for mailings, so that customers can immediately recognize the mailed piece as coming from the same establishment.

4. **Summarize the effective use of Web sites and email in marketing.**

   The effective use of Web sites in marketing calls for managers to recognize that a Web site can combine the best features of print and video. The information to be listed on an operation's site should include such items as the operation's location, hours of operation, menu, and current promotions. Other key areas that lead to effective marketing include instructions for making reservations or placing orders. Managers should also ensure their sites are easily located by those using search engines to aid in their establishment selections.

   Emails can also be used as an effective marketing tool. Areas of importance when using emails for marketing include recognizing that emails are public documents that may be viewed by many people. Offensive language or images should never be included in a manager's email. To be most effective, emails should be short and targeted and allow for easy opting out by those who no longer wish to receive them.

5. **Explain the importance of social media in marketing.**

   The use of social media network sites is virtually exploding. Managers can use these popular networks to communicate new menu items or specials, provide details on upcoming events or promotions, and link to positive reviews posted on other social media sites. It is important that managers understand communication via social networks is a two-way process. Using social networking sites only to sell products to those on the network is a poor long-term strategy. A better strategy is to use social networking sites to develop strong two-way communication links and, as a result, create customer loyalty.

6. **Describe the importance of cell phone applications (apps) in marketing.**

   The continued creation of new and innovative cell phone apps will likely ensure that this channel's rapid expansion continues. Cell phone apps allow users to see menus, make reservations, track deliveries, and pay for products. As digital communication steadily moves away from traditional computers and toward wireless devices, the smaller size and portability of cell phones no doubt makes them a communication channel that will continue its rapid expansion.

APPLICATION EXERCISES

Exercise 1

Write a statement suitable for posting on your establishment's social media site (200 words maximum) that announces the hiring of a new chef. Remember to focus on how this news benefits your customers, not just about how it benefits the establishment. Be creative as well as professional in the creation of your posting.

Exercise 2

Compose a short message suitable for sending to your customers' cell phones (100 to 150 characters maximum) that announces a two-for-one appetizer special available at your establishment next Friday only. Be creative as well as professional in the creation of your tweet.

1. Do you think your customers will want to read your two entries?

2. How do your two messages address the AIDA areas you learned about in this chapter?

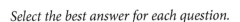

REVIEW YOUR LEARNING

Select the best answer for each question.

1. **What does the letter *I* represent in the AIDA communication concept?**
   A. Interest
   B. Integrity
   C. Innovation
   D. Inclusiveness

2. **Which is the oldest form of customer communication?**
   A. Mail
   B. Print
   C. Radio
   D. Television

3. **What type of photo would likely draw the most attention to an ad?**
   A. Closeup of the establishment's printed menu
   B. Exterior shot of the establishment's building
   C. Cooks preparing food in the kitchen
   D. People eating in the establishment

4. **Which factor is most likely to impact the price of a radio spot?**
   A. The operation's service type
   B. The type of food advertised in the spot
   C. The number of listeners who will hear the spot
   D. The market segment of the establishment purchasing the spot

5. An establishment specializes in family-friendly cuisine. Which of the following types of television networks would likely be the best fit?

   A. A news network

   B. A travel network

   C. A sports network

   D. A cartoon network

6. Which is one way that managers can increase the likelihood that a mail piece will be read?

   A. Using plain white envelopes

   B. Using preprinted address labels

   C. Using stamps rather than a meter

   D. Using a different graphic design for each mailing

7. Which communication channel has features that allow customers to get real time–updated driving directions to establishments of their choice?

   A. Web sites

   B. Printed maps

   C. Social networks

   D. Cell phone applications

8. Which Web sites would make the best link partners for a manager of a fast-casual restaurant?

   A. Web sites for professional food societies

   B. Web sites for attractions located near the establishment

   C. Web sites that provide real-time stock market reporting

   D. Web sites promoting economic development in the operation's city

9. How should managers begin their emails used for marketing their operations?

   A. With a call to action

   B. With a greeting to the reader

   C. With information about who should read the email

   D. With the name and contact information of the sender

10. Approximately what proportion of computer users have viewed online guest reviews prior to selecting an establishment?

    A. 1 to 25%

    B. 26 to 49%

    C. 50 to 74%

    D. 75 to 100%

FIELD PROJECT

Consider two pieces of print, broadcast, or mailed pieces of advertising from one or more establishments in your area. Carefully evaluate the messages of these two communication pieces. Then answer the following questions for each piece.

1. How does each piece's message address the key AIDA areas:

   - Attention
   - Interest
   - Desire
   - Action

2. Describe the target market each piece seeks to reach.

3. How might you transform each piece of one-way communication into an interactive, two-way communication?

8

Advertising and Sales

CHAPTER LEARNING OBJECTIVES

After completing this chapter, you should be able to:

- Describe how managers establish advertising objectives.

- Explain how to develop an advertising schedule.

- State the methods managers use to evaluate advertising effectiveness.

- Describe objective measures of personal selling effectiveness.

- Explain the method managers use to evaluate event and suggestive selling effectiveness.

- List and describe the components of an effective on-site merchandising program.

KEY TERMS

CASE STUDY

"You don't have to tell me. I know that gift cards are popular," states Josh. "I read just yesterday that gift cards are one of the top two things people mention when they're asked what's on their holiday gift list. I have a couple myself."

"That's why I decided to make them available to our customers," replied Amy, the manager of the Peanut Barrel Bistro.

Amy was discussing with Josh, the dining-room manager at the Peanut Barrel, a new promotional idea she wanted to implement at their restaurant. Amy had arranged to have 300 Peanut Barrel gift cards with a value of $25 each made up and delivered to the establishment. Now she is discussing with Josh how the cards could best be marketed to customers.

"I don't know," said Josh. "We've always had gift certificates available, though I have to admit we haven't sold that many of them. How are gift cards going to be any different for us?"

"Gift cards are like mini-billboards in our customers' wallets," replied Amy. "Customers carry them around. Besides being a convenient way to pay, they're a constant reminder to our customers to stop in and see us. That's huge."

"Well, it will be huge only if we can sell some of them," said Josh. "How are we going to do that? My servers are pretty busy already just taking orders and getting food to our customers."

1. How important do you think it is that Amy gain Josh's full support for her new idea?

2. How important will it be to the success of Amy's idea that she and Josh implement an effective in-house gift card selling program?

ADVERTISING AND SALES OVERVIEW

Advertising is one important way managers communicate marketing messages to target audiences. Technically, advertising is any form of marketing message that managers pay for and deliver in an identifiable but nonpersonal way. Advertisements include, for example, newspaper ads, commercials played on the radio or television, and the placement of ads in a Web site. Advertising is different from personal selling. Personal selling is the presentation of a marketing message delivered by one or more employees of a business for the purpose of making a sale.

Exhibit 8.1

Personal selling can be undertaken by managers and by service staff. When managers engage in personal selling it is often referred to as event sales, or simply as "sales." When personal selling is undertaken by service staff it is often referred to as suggestive selling because it takes the form of making recommendations or suggestions to guests about items the guests might be interested in buying, as shown in *Exhibit 8.1.*

A manager incurs costs for both advertising and personal selling. This chapter explains how managers plan, implement, and evaluate their establishment's advertising and personal selling programs. It also explains how managers can implement on-site merchandising programs that combine advertising and personal selling.

ADVERTISING

Recall that managers use customer demographics and psychographics to identify target markets and that these managers create marketing campaigns to reach these markets. Advertising is often the most visible part of a company's marketing efforts. A well-planned advertising campaign is a coordinated series of advertisements and promotions used in the same time frame to meet certain objectives. An effective advertising campaign can achieve many operational goals:

- Communicating a message to a large audience, often using a variety of media
- Generating awareness of and interest in a product or service
- Persuading the audience to take action, such as purchasing a product
- Strengthening existing customer preferences and loyalty
- Creating or reinforcing an image of a product or organization
- Differentiating an operation's products and services from its competitors

Advertising is often used to create awareness of sales promotions and public relations events.

Sales promotions come in many forms, such as coupons, contests, and giveaways. For example, if an operation's target market is families, it might offer a "free meals for children" promotional coupon to parents and helium balloons to children.

Like advertising, promotions are designed to increase customer awareness or sales; however, sales promotions usually provide customers with a more urgent incentive to purchase a certain item. Sales promotions typically offer the customer a distinct benefit in exchange for his or her business, often within a limited time frame.

Public relations events (addressed in detail in chapter 9) are those activities designed primarily to increase customer awareness of an operation, rather than to immediately increase its sales. For example, an establishment might use advertisements to distribute coupons that create awareness of a charity event it is hosting.

Given the benefits of advertising, one might expect that all operations should include advertising in their marketing mix. However, advertising also has disadvantages, and it is not always the best choice for every situation. Before integrating advertising into an establishment's marketing plan, a manager must first understand how to use its advantages and how to counteract its disadvantages (see *Exhibit 8.2*).

Advertising may be seen as impersonal and therefore is not as persuasive as an individual in a one-on-one conversation. To counteract this, managers introduce elements to personalize their advertisements. For example, are there opportunities to present the management or staff within the advertising? Can the image portrayed by the establishment be more personal? By making advertising more personal, the public will make a personal connection to the operation and will be more likely to remember the advertisement.

Exhibit 8.2

SUMMARY OF ADVERTISING DISADVANTAGES AND WAYS TO DEAL WITH THEM

Disadvantage	Counteraction
Advertising is impersonal.	Personalize the advertisement.
Advertising must compete for customer attention.	Make your ad stand out.
Advertising is costly.	Look for cost-saving opportunities, such as cooperative advertising.

Advertising also must compete for attention. The public is selective about what it will respond to or pay attention to since it is bombarded with advertising through multiple media on a daily basis. As a consequence, the most effective ads stand out from the others. Having an ad stand out may mean using a less traditional type of media, such as an Internet banner ad or using an innovative slogan or motto.

Finally, advertising can be costly. Depending on the media used, the production quality of the ad, and the amount of exposure purchased for the advertising, the costs can vary dramatically. For example, the cost of producing a television commercial and airing it in a large, urban market will be very high compared to the cost of creating a small print ad and running it in a college newspaper.

When considering the costs of advertising, managers must keep in mind that advertising should be considered part of a long-term investment in the success of an operation. Normally, people need to be exposed to an ad several times before they notice and remember it. Therefore, it sometimes may take weeks, months, or even years of advertising and marketing efforts to bring in a significant number of additional customers.

Establishing Advertising Objectives

After identifying a target market (see chapters 3 and 4), the manager's job becomes one of knowing where the targeted audience currently stands in relation to the establishment and where it must be moved. In most cases that means assessing customers relative to a number of factors, several of which seek to provide results that are objectively measurable:

- Awareness
- Trial
- Usage
- Brand building
- Traffic building

AWARENESS

In some cases a target audience may be completely unaware of an operation. This may be the case, for example, when the business has recently opened or when an existing establishment changes its name. For these operations, the first step in developing awareness is simply to get the establishment's name known among its target market or in its target market area. In most cases, this involves a paid advertising message; however, some operations also have success using a distinctive building shape or signage to help build name awareness.

It is important to recognize that people forget things easily. Names, places, and dates are among the things most easily forgotten, which means that building name recognition is a constant process. Even the most well-known restaurants and other foodservice operations spend part of their marketing budgets simply maintaining name awareness. An advertising campaign that focuses on name awareness not only seeks to have customers remember the name of an operation, but also to have customers remember that name before they recall the names of competitors. Awareness is not an easily measurable concept. That is, if the goal of an advertisement is to increase awareness of an operation in the minds of 10,000 persons who make up an operation's target market, measuring increased awareness within that population may not be easily achieved. Awareness can, however, be indirectly measured by increased levels of business.

TRIAL

If an operation has succeeded in creating a high level of name recognition among its target market, it has achieved a significant goal. However, the operation must do much more. To see why, assume that the following new establishments had recently opened in a target market: The Bluebird; Stewart and Blake's; Hobnob; Stanley's; Le Fontaine. The names alone do not tell customers much about the establishments. What kinds of food do these operations offer? Where are they located? How expensive are they? Without knowing this information, **trial** (the term used to describe the purchase and use of a product or service for the first time by a particular customer) is unlikely.

To increase trial, marketers know they must provide information beyond that of name recognition only. Sometimes managers can increase trial simply by providing more information about their product or service. In other cases, managers decide to give customers the chance to sample their product for free or at a very low price.

By offering low-cost trial to prospective customers, managers offer two things of value to their customers. First, managers show that they are confident in the value being offered. Customers know that a business cannot offer "low-cost" or "no-cost" products for long and still stay in business. As a result, the message received by customers is "Give us a try. We are so sure that after you visit our establishment you will be back to pay our regular price that we will give you the first 'trial' at a very low price." Second, by offering trial at no or low cost, managers eliminate a common question posed by first-time customers: "What if I don't like it?"

Having an "invitation only" grand opening, distributing printed coupons for no- or low-cost appetizers, or offering "X dollars off" the total price of your first visit are all examples of advertising techniques operation managers can use to help build trial. Unlike awareness, increases in trial may be measured, for example, by the number of discount coupons redeemed, the number of new items sold, or the number of new customers served.

> **THINK ABOUT IT . . .**
>
> Consider your own buying behavior. How do you usually respond when a seller gives you the option to try its product for free or at a very low cost?

USAGE

Many potential customers may recognize the name of an establishment and some may even have visited and liked it. For an establishment to be very successful, however, customers must come to *prefer* the establishment to others they may also like. **Usage** is the term marketing professionals use to indicate the number of times a particular customer frequents a business in a specific time period.

The concept of usage in the restaurant and foodservice industry is very different than the concept of usage in other industries. Consider the manufacturer that sells washing machines. Most customers who buy a washing machine will need one only every 10 to 15 years. For that seller, good customer usage would mean one sale to a given customer every decade. Meanwhile, a manufacturer of running shoes may be able to make a sale to its customer every few months or years. A local gas station may sell to its best customers on a weekly basis. In each of these cases, the product or service sold dictates the definition of high customer usage.

Exhibit 8.3

In most cases, restaurant and foodservice operations cannot reasonably expect customers to eat every meal with them. In some quick-service restaurants (QSRs), customer frequency may be very high. In this segment, a target customer may visit the establishment two or more times every week. By contrast, many of a fine-dining establishment's customers may choose it only for special occasions (*Exhibit 8.3*). This may be two or more times per year, but it may not be realistic to assume it would be two or more times per week.

It would be a mistake, however, to think that the average customer usage rates for lower-priced establishments are always greater than those of higher-priced ones. In the QSR industry segment, prices are comparatively low but the competition levels are very high. As a result, QSR customers have many choices and may not elect to visit an operation on a weekly or monthly basis, even if they like it.

The challenge for a manager of a particular operation is to understand what usage level is realistic for his or her operation. With this understanding, a manager can design an advertising message to drive usage for the individual establishment and can then measure increases in customer counts.

BRAND BUILDING

Recall from chapter 2 that *brand* is the single term used to describe an establishment's distinguishing features. Brand identifiers are the name, logo, signage, employee uniforms, décor, pricing, service level, and other characteristics that, when taken together, make one operation different from another.

When managers use advertising to build brand awareness, they seek to elevate the value, quality, or convenience of their operations in the minds of their target customers. Branding can be considered the sum total of what customers really think about an operation. Good branding differentiates an operation's products and services in a positive way that sticks in the minds of potential customers. In the restaurant and foodservice business, there are two key elements of effective branding:

- A logo that is attractive and easy to read
- A memorable tag line

Logos. A logo is a graphic mark or emblem used by a business to aid and promote instant public recognition. An effective logo meets the following criteria:

- Presents a strong image with no clutter to its look
- Is distinctive, making it easy to recognize at a glance
- Has a graphic imagery that is appropriate for the business
- Works well with the name of the business
- Is easy to read
- Looks good in black and white as well as in color

Tag Lines. A second key branding element is an effective tag line. A tag line is a three- to seven-word phrase (or slogan) that accompanies a logo. Often it is created to convey an establishment's most important benefits or what it wants its target customers to remember about its brand. Tag lines can be considered as the words an operation wants to linger in the minds of its customers. KFC's use of the tag line "Finger lickin' good" is an example of an effective tag line, easily remembered by customers.

When managers use advertising to build brand awareness, they are not just presenting logos and tag lines; they are communicating important information about who they really are to their most valuable current and future customers. Like awareness, the effectiveness of brand-building activities may be challenging to measure. It may be indirectly measured, however, by an increase in the number of customers served.

TRAFFIC BUILDING

In many cases, when managers are asked why they advertise, the answer is "To get more customers!" Traffic is the term marketers use to identify the total number of customers served by a business. Total traffic consists of first-time customers as well as repeat customers with both high and low usage. Improvements in traffic as a result of an advertisement are easily measured by monitoring the total number of guests served in an operation.

> **THINK ABOUT IT . . .**
>
> To illustrate the power of a tag line, consider the words "When you care enough to send the very best." Do you recognize this tag line? Were the company's branding efforts successful?

In the restaurant and foodservice industry, advertising with the objective of increasing traffic can take many forms. As demonstrated in chapter 7, identifying the right message and the appropriate communication channels is essential. Creative managers use a variety of strategies to "get the word out" about their operations.

To illustrate some such creative approaches, consider how some operations use vehicle graphics to advertise their brand and location. Whether the graphics are on the manager's personal vehicle, delivery cars, or catering vans, the colorful images create a moving advertisement that captures attention in the target market area. Other establishments use postcards with bright photographs that showcase their facility or food. These postcards may be given away in the establishment or displayed in places where they can be distributed to potential customers. Still other establishments create clever signage displaying their advertising message to use in booths or carts at local festivals and events. In each of these cases, managers use effective advertising in creative ways to increase traffic counts and build revenues.

Exhibit 8.4

COMMON ADVERTISING OBJECTIVES

Developing Advertising Strategies

As illustrated in *Exhibit 8.4*, when managers develop marketing strategies they choose ads that target awareness, trial, usage, brand building, or traffic building as they assess which advertising objective they seek to achieve. The specific measurable advertising objectives set by managers will vary based on their businesses and financial goals, but some objectives are common to most operations:

• Increase awareness of the operation

• Increase new customer trial

• Increase current customer usage

• Elevate all customers' understanding of the operation's brand

• Increase total customer count (traffic)

Regardless of the specific advertising choices managers make, an effective advertising plan requires the use of an advertising calendar or schedule. An **advertising schedule** is a calendar that tracks advertising and other promotional activities (see chapter 5) on a weekly, monthly, or seasonal basis.

Exhibit 8.5

SAMPLE ADVERTISING SCHEDULE

The Port May Restaurant   **Month/Year**_____

	Sun.	Mon.	Tues.	Wed.	Thurs.	Fri.	Sat.	Budget
Week 1	Draft newspaper ad			Submit newspaper ad				Newspaper ad $350
Week 2		Birthday of the month letters for next month						Birthday letters and postage $200
Week 3				Contact printer for monthly in-house flyer	Replace tabletop menu inserts			In-house flyer $150 Tabletop menu inserts $175
Week 4		Approve radio ad				Run weekend radio ad		Radio ad $600

Advertising schedules help managers see how they are addressing their target markets and if there are any long gaps in advertising activities. *Exhibit 8.5* shows an example of a simple advertising schedule that could be used by an establishment.

An advertising schedule helps managers plan for success. The schedule can help managers visualize what needs to be done and when to do it. It also allows them to coordinate in-house or external promotional activities and advertisements with each other. Finally, plotting out expenses on the advertising schedule can help managers save money. For example, after reviewing the schedule, a manager may decide to skip every fifth week of a radio ad campaign to save money to be used for some other activity. Perhaps the most important advantage of an advertising schedule, however, is that it simply helps keep managers from "forgetting" important advertising tasks!

After ads have been placed in the market, an advertising schedule helps managers measure the effectiveness of one advertisement against another. Combining information about when an advertisement was placed in the market and the ad's impact on revenue can help managers make better ad placement and timing decisions.

Evaluating Advertising Effectiveness

Once advertisements are in place, managers need to assess the effectiveness of their ads. Managers can choose from a variety of approaches to do so. Each approach requires the use of an objective measuring device. An objective measure is a measure that can be used to evaluate real changes in data. Two or more people can use the same measuring tool and come to the same conclusions about improvements in performance. For example, if an ad campaign can be measured to have increased operation revenue by 10 percent, the measure is objective, and any person undertaking the measurement would get the same result.

A change in a subjective measure, however, takes place only in the mind of the evaluator. Two different evaluators could come to two different conclusions about performance change if it is measured subjectively. To say that business "has picked up" is a subjective measure in which one manager's view of picking up may or may not be consistent with another manager's view. Prior to initiating an advertising campaign, managers should seek to identify, whenever possible, objective measures of the ads' effectiveness.

Measuring the effectiveness of any marketing effort is important, and advertising is an especially important area for assessment. Competitive business environments mean that managers must make good use of all resources, including those devoted to advertising.

Today's managers have many advertising choices at their disposal, including the Internet, radio, television, and print. As a result, there are several reasons why measuring advertising programs makes good sense. First, measurement gives managers an indication of the effectiveness of their advertising efforts. Objective measurements give managers the information necessary to determine whether the ads have helped the managers achieve their goals.

Second, accurate measurement gives managers the information they need to modify, improve, or increase their advertising efforts. When results are measured, managers can wisely choose to increase the use of specific communication channels and decrease the use of others to arrive at the right marketing mix. Finally, as will be discussed in chapter 11, when managers have accurate data they can calculate the financial return on their advertising expenditures.

Most managers do not have the budgets, expertise, or time to conduct detailed measurement and analysis of their advertising efforts; therefore, their measurement tools and techniques should be practical ones they can easily apply. To do so, managers should use the following steps.

STEP 1: IDENTIFY SPECIFIC AND MEASURABLE ADVERTISING OBJECTIVES WHERE POSSIBLE

When managers define specific, measurable objectives for their advertisements, they can determine if they have, or have not, achieved them. The more specific the objective, the easier it is to measure it. To illustrate, consider the following two advertising objectives:

- Effectively introduce the new 12-ounce petite filet mignon
- Sell 125 orders of the newly introduced 12-ounce petite filet mignon in 30 days

The first objective is not easily measurable. It does not relate to either sales or revenue. The second objective is highly measurable. The number of orders served can be easily counted and the orders may be tracked back to specific advertising methods used to sell the steaks. Note also that there is a specific time frame for achieving the objective. The best managers establish their marketing objectives prior to the implementation of their advertising. When they do, they know how the impact of the advertisement can be measured.

STEP 2: CHOOSE EFFECTIVE MEASUREMENT TOOLS

When managers know what they will measure, they can select appropriate measurement tools. Appropriate measurement tools can include any of the following examples:

- Number of items sold
- Changes in number of items sold
- Changes in reservations made
- Increases in revenue
- Total revenue
- New customers

Fortunately, point-of-sale (POS) systems can easily generate much of these data. Other forms of information may be gathered directly from customers.

STEP 3: MEASURE AND ACT

In most cases, the measurement will involve accumulating data during a specific start and stop time period. The data should be summarized properly and kept up to date if they are to be usable. Most important, they need to be analyzed and put to practical use. Even accurate data, if left sitting on a shelf in the manager's office, are of little value.

Gathered and properly analyzed, good information can be used to demonstrate the impact of advertising on sales and profitability and can be used to modify future advertising programs. Managers do so by improving or eliminating advertising efforts that were not effective and retaining advertisements that worked well.

OPEN FOR BUSINESS

RESTAURANT TECHNOLOGY

Most establishments have Web sites. These sites can be powerful means of advertising. Like any other form of advertising, however, managers must evaluate the effectiveness of their sites. Some managers make the mistake of focusing solely on the number of hits to the site's home page. In this day of advanced search engine optimization (SEO), most of the traffic will enter a site one or even two pages deep. These pages may include the driving directions, the menu, the operating hours, or any other of the operation's information-specific site pages. Managers should assess the traffic drawn to their Web sites, but they must resist the temptation to obsess about home page hits. Instead, it is important to consider the overall traffic to the site.

PERSONAL SELLING

Although most establishments do not have a person designated to do personal selling on a full-time basis, personal selling is one of a manager's most powerful revenue-enhancing tools. Personal selling is an activity that can be undertaken by both managers and their staffs.

Personal Selling by Managers

Although those outside the industry may think that all customers come in based on their own dining decisions, there are a variety of situations in which one customer makes the buying decision for a large number of others. This type of business can be very profitable to a restaurant or foodservice operation. These situations can include a variety of special events:

- Holiday parties
- Anniversary parties
- Weddings
- Wedding rehearsal meals
- Birthday events
- Bereavement meals
- Off-site catering opportunities

There are five specific steps to be taken as managers seek to improve operational revenues through the sale of special events:

1. **Prospecting**, which involves trying to find new customers

2. Communicating, or informing current and potential customers about what is for sale

3. Selling, consisting of making contacts with the customer, answering questions, and trying to close (finalize) the sale

4. Servicing, which involves providing any needed support to the customer before and after the sale is made

5. Gathering information, or learning about the market to improve the selling process in the future

Like most other forms of promotion, there are advantages and disadvantages to using personal selling as part of a marketing mix. Perhaps the greatest advantage to personal selling is that it is a face-to-face activity, so customers receive a high degree of personal attention. In addition, the sales message can be customized to meet the needs of individual customers.

The two-way communication between managers and potential guests involved in personal selling allows managers to respond directly and promptly to customer questions and concerns. In a restaurant or foodservice setting, a face-to-face sales meeting may also give the sales force the chance to allow customers to sample menu items or tour facilities. Frequent meetings between managers acting as salespersons and their customers also provide an opportunity to build good long-term relationships.

While there are many advantages to personal selling, some businesses still do not devote a significant amount of time to this task. The main disadvantages cited against personal selling are the time and costs involved. Full-time salespeople are expensive. In addition to their time, there are often significant costs involved in personal selling, including car and other travel expenses, meal and entertainment costs, and phone charges. In addition, a salesperson can usually call on only one customer at a time, which makes it an expensive way to reach a large audience.

Managers undertaking their own personal selling activities or supervising the activities of others face the same challenges in establishing objectives as they do when considering advertising objectives. Thus awareness, trial, usage, brand building, and traffic building can all be identified as important personal selling goals.

Those who are experienced in restaurant and foodservice sales, however, know that focusing on buyer type is another good way to establish personal selling objectives. For example, a restaurant recently decided that hosting holiday parties for companies and organizations will be an important revenue source. Potential customers include three distinct buyer types or groups:

- **Group 1:** This group includes those who have not held holiday parties in the past.
- **Group 2:** This group includes those who will be holding a holiday party this year.
- **Group 3:** This group includes those who held a holiday party at the establishment in the past.

Personal selling related to those potential customers in group 1 might focus on the reasons holiday parties are a good business investment, the rationale for holding such a party this year, and the availability of the establishment to host it. While this could be a lucrative group, it is important to recognize that they may be the hardest group to sell to because members of this group have not held holiday parties in the past. In this illustration, a manager could, for example, decide to make two sales calls per month on decision makers in this group. It would be important to know who the decision makers are because these individuals are the ones who actually approve or do not approve purchases within their areas of responsibility.

Buyers in group 2 are already aware of the benefits of holding a holiday party. Now decision makers in this group must be convinced that this particular establishment is the best location to hold their parties. In some cases, customers within this group may have held parties in the past at other locations. These customers may be happy with the previous locations and may be hesitant to move their events. In this case, the selling effort will focus on the advantages to the customer of moving the event, the suitability of the operation, its reputation for quality, and the special features and benefits the establishment can offer the customer. Because decision makers in this group have already decided to hold a party somewhere, the manager may decide to make 10 sales calls per month to members of this group.

Surprisingly, customers in group 3 are among those who often receive the least amount of a manager's attention. This is especially surprising because every group 3 customer is a potential group 2 customer for the operation's competitors! For that reason, a manager may decide to make two informational sales calls per past customer on a schedule that allows him or her to contact 100 percent of the past holiday party customers in the first six months after their last party was held and a second call within nine months of the event.

Note that the sales calls to group 1, 2, and 3 members could be objectively measured and have a specific time frame attached to them. Some managers develop a personal selling schedule similar to their advertising schedule (see *Exhibit 8.5*) to help them plan, monitor, and complete their own personal selling tasks.

Developing Personal Selling Strategies

Managers who emphasize personal selling as part of their marketing efforts know that there are identifiable characteristics of salespersons who consistently generate significant amounts of revenue for their establishments. They are as follows:

SET HIGH TARGETS AND GOALS

The best salespeople set goals that are both ambitious and measurable. For example, a salesperson may set a goal of booking five wedding rehearsal dinners that will take place in the month of June.

PLAN CAREFULLY

Successful salespeople plan quarterly, monthly, weekly, and daily schedules. Because most operations do not employ full-time sales staff, this often means the manager or other designated staff person must devote an identifiable part of his or her own week to personal selling efforts.

DETERMINE THE OBJECTIVE FOR EACH SALES CALL

The best salespeople know exactly what they want to accomplish in each sales call, be it a face-to-face meeting or a telephone call, before they meet with the customer (*Exhibit 8.6*). The purpose may be to increase awareness of the

Exhibit 8.6

establishment or finalize a sale, but the objective is always clearly identifiable and tied to the overall targets and goals (see the first characteristic listed).

ASK RELEVANT QUESTIONS

Good salespeople know that it is better to get information from a prospect than it is to give it. Asking relevant questions helps salespeople target their sales presentations to the needs of their customers without the risk of providing information that may not be relevant to the customer's needs.

LISTEN ATTENTIVELY

Asking the right questions is important, but listening to customers is even more important. When customers present their needs, effective salespeople can explain how their establishments can provide solutions to the customer's needs.

WAIT PATIENTLY

The best salespeople wait to present their establishment's products and services until they know exactly what the customer is trying to buy or seeking to accomplish. Ineffective salespeople may jump too quickly into a sales pitch, but the best performers are patient and wait until they understand the customer's needs before presenting their operation's features and benefits.

ADAPT QUICKLY

Effective sales staff members modify their sales presentations if they learn that their original understanding of the customer's needs was incorrect or that the customer's needs have changed.

FOCUS ON CUSTOMERS MORE THAN THEMSELVES

Ineffective salespeople too often want to tell customers about themselves and their establishment. Many times this can include information that is of little interest to the customer. The better approach is to keep the conversation, as well as the focus of the sales call, firmly centered on the customer's needs.

PREPARE FOR OBJECTIONS

An objection is a reason given by a potential customer that could justify a decision not to buy. In the restaurant and foodservice business, objections often given by customers include those that state perceived shortfalls of the establishment:

- It is too expensive.
- It is too large or too small.
- It is too far away.
- It does not offer enough menu variety.
- It does not have adequate parking.
- It opens too late.
- It is not open late enough.

Manager's Memo

Some managers overlook prospective customers they already know well. Personal and business contacts, such as accountants, attorneys, grounds-keepers, food suppliers, equipment repair companies, religious leaders, realtors, friends, dentists, physicians, and hairstylists are all potential special events' customers. Each of these individuals may also be able to provide referrals for others they know who may need the services an operation provides. All managers need to do is ask for the referrals.

In some cases, these individuals may also allow the manager to place business cards or flyers in their offices or on their bulletin boards. People like to buy from people they know. And because of the social nature of the job, most restaurant and foodservice managers know a lot of people!

In each case, effective salespeople are prepared, in advance, to address their customers' objections with important and honest information about how those objections can be handled and overcome.

FOLLOW UP

In many cases, those who will make a buying decision are busy and may be difficult to reconnect with. Too often, sales are lost because a sales representative fails to follow up after the initial call with additional information requested or needed by the customer. The best salespeople establish timelines for follow-up steps in the initial sales call.

PROSPECT CONTINUALLY

It is not uncommon to have peaks and valleys in a selling cycle. For example, the best times for selling holiday parties may be late summer and early fall when such events are being planned. Prospecting for holiday parties, however, should be a year-round effort, as salespersons identify those companies and organizations that will be holding holiday parties in the coming year or have held them in the past.

KEEP IN TOUCH

As noted, the personal selling process is an ongoing one. The best sales performers find ways to keep their establishments' names in their customer's mind to prevent competitors from taking away their business. Some activities designed to do this include the development of email lists with monthly or quarterly updates, holiday card lists, newsletters, or invitations to come to the establishment for customer appreciation activities, which are those activities designed to thank customers for their business.

Personal Selling by Staff

Personal selling on the part of service staff takes the form of suggestive selling and upselling. Upselling is a personal selling strategy where the server provides guests opportunities to purchase related or higher-priced products that the guest wants, but often for the purpose of making a larger sale. A common example of upselling happens when a QSR employee asks a guest who has just purchased a hamburger, "Do you want fries with that?" Suggestive selling and upselling can be powerful personal selling strategies that significantly impact an operation's total sales. In a restaurant or foodservice operation, suggestive selling should maximize guest satisfaction and increase the average check, resulting in increased profitability. The success of suggestive selling depends on having the right people with product knowledge, effective communication skills, and appropriate sales training.

Many employees are reluctant to use suggestive selling because they are shy, or they think that suggestive selling makes them too pushy, or they are uncomfortable with selling. All of these reasons for hesitating to use suggestive selling can be handled with proper training. Even so, it is a good practice to hire waitstaff and bartenders who are comfortable with the suggestive selling process.

TRAINING STAFF TO USE SUGGESTIVE SELLING

Managers who train servers to use suggestive selling commonly point out that it will increase the guest's check and, as a result, the server's tip. However, suggestive selling involves a lot more than just selling additional menu items.

The customer service approach encourages more servers to use suggestive selling. In this approach, suggesting an appetizer, side dish, or dessert is used to enhance the guest's dining experience and maximize guest satisfaction. Emphasizing this point is an extremely effective way to encourage staff to engage in suggestive selling and upselling.

A good suggestive selling training program should include the following:

- Enhancing servers' communication skills so they can be effective with customers

- Developing servers' product skills so they can vividly and accurately describe items to customers

- Informing servers about menu items that complement each other so these can be suggested to customers

- Teaching servers the impact that suggestive selling has on the financial position of the establishment

- Teaching servers the impact that suggestive selling has on their own income

Servers who are effective at personal selling consistently engage in specific activities:

- Suggesting add-on items

- Suggesting specific items; for example, "Would you like lemonade on this hot day?" rather than asking, "Would you like something to drink?"

- Suggesting items that servers themselves enjoy

- Suggesting the establishment's best-selling items to increase the probability that the customer will be happy with the order

- Using props such as dessert trays

- Observing customers' behavior to determine whether they want service or a product; for example, at the end of the meal, watching the guest to see if he or she wants the check or dessert

---

Manager's Memo

In addition to taking a customer service approach to encourage suggestive selling, managers can develop incentives and contests such as these:

1. Reward servers who sell the most.

2. Give sellers a commission for selling non-entrée items such as appetizers and desserts.

3. Hold sales contests that reward employees for selling the most of certain menu items.

These programs work well, but managers should recognize there can be challenges when using them. As a result managers must be cautious when implementing incentive programs. It can be difficult to design incentives and contests that are fair to all servers on all shifts. Also, managers must be careful to avoid creating a culture where servers use suggestive selling or upselling only when there is an incentive or other reward given for doing so.

Exhibit 8.7

Managers should make personal selling training for staff a priority and an ongoing effort. To do so, the training can be conducted formally by a manager or a designated trainer (*Exhibit 8.7*). Also, the topic can be an occasional agenda item for staff meetings. Managers can also set aside time at staff meetings to discuss suggestive selling best practices and challenges.Manager's Memo

Evaluating Personal Selling Effectiveness

As with any marketing or sales program, evaluating the effectiveness of the personal selling effort can be challenging. Too often managers and staff responsible for personal selling may give subjective reasons for low sales productivity:

- The economy is bad.
- Business in our segment of the industry is down.
- We don't sell the right items.
- Our prices are too high.
- Our competitors' prices are too low.

While any of these statements may be true, managers must evaluate personal selling programs objectively. In fact, if any of these reasons are true, it only reinforces the need to assess personal selling efforts. Managers evaluating their own or the personal selling efforts of their staff can use three key steps to do so.

STEP 1: ASSESS RESULTS

Managers can keep a log of sales calls made and revenue generated by each person assigned personal selling tasks. Although sales will fluctuate from month to month, an annual or semiannual average can indicate whether performance is above or below standard.

Managers can motivate personal selling staff by offering appropriate incentives or bonuses for exceptional selling results. Sales staff can also be assessed on motivation and effort. Even nonmonetary recognition, such as preferred parking or public praise, can help encourage good performance. However, unless performance is documented properly, it cannot be properly assessed.

STEP 2: ASSESS KNOWLEDGE

The best salespersons know how to sell and what to sell. Managers responsible for evaluating personal selling success should regularly review their own and each staff member's knowledge of available products and services from the perspectives of the customer. Managers selling special events should be able to quickly and accurately answer basic questions customers are likely to ask:

- How many parking spaces are available at your location?
- What is your maximum seating capacity?
- Can I bring my own specialty cake (e.g., birthday, anniversary) to our event?
- What vegetarian meals do you make available?
- What are your delivery or takeout hours?
- What payment forms do you accept?

Answers to questions such as these may be easy for most managers. Every salesperson representing the operation, however, must know the answers to the questions and be able to address them in a knowledgeable and conversational manner. It is a key part of the manager's job to regularly assess the knowledge level of sales staff and to then provide any additional training needed to help them do their jobs well.

Service staff members' knowledge of the operation's menu and those specific items that complement each other well can be readily assessed by formal testing or simply by conversations with them.

STEP 3: ASSESS THE OPERATION

In the final analysis, it is the manager's job to assess his or her own ability to prospect for business, build customers' trust and rapport, assess the needs of prospects, deliver an effective sales presentation, and successfully close the sale. It is also the manager's job to ensure the products and services sold to customers provide excellent value.

BY THE CUSTOMER/ FOR THE CUSTOMER

Managers can effectively sell their products and services using social media networks if they realize that social media primarily provide a listening platform rather than a selling platform. Managers must resist the temptation to think that social networks are a huge audience to be attacked with a marketing message. Social networks succeed only when the communication in them is based on two-way conversation, with each member taking turns as a speaker and listener.

Social media do contain many selling-related features, but it is essential to understand that while salespersons managed the sales process in the past, today the customer is in control. In fact, today's customer usually knows more about, or can easily find out more about, the products and services sold by an establishment than the sales representatives! For sales staff, listening, not telling, is the key to successfully harnessing the power of social networks and increasing sales.

The job of the managers and service staff is to communicate what will be offered to customers. Even excellent sales personnel will experience minimal sales results when an establishment performs poorly and does not meet its customers' expectations or deliver as promised. Just as managers must assess the quality of the personal selling effort, they must also assess the quality of their own operations. Quality products and excellent service help the outside sales effort. Periodic operational reviews that improve operation performance can also help eliminate performance problems related to personal selling.

ON-SITE MERCHANDISING

Merchandising is the term that describes all of the activities retail managers use when selling their products. These activities can include advertising and personal selling; however, when operation managers use the term *merchandising*, they are generally referring to those sales-related activities that take place within their establishments.

Of course, much of the actual selling that occurs in an establishment takes place between customers and service staff. These interactions are always critical. Many additional on-site selling opportunities exist within operations and, when properly executed, these merchandising opportunities can boost sales and leave guests with positive, lasting impressions of their visits.

Marketing experts agree that there are four important components of on-site merchandising programs that managers should consider:

- Products
- Placement
- Packaging
- Pricing

Products

Managers are well aware of the products listed on their menus and the importance of training service staff to sell these items effectively. Chapter 10 is devoted to using the menu as a marketing tool, but many operations sell additional products that are not on the menu. Managers developing an on-site merchandising program must consider and select the specific non-menu items they want to sell.

In some establishments, the number of different products offered for sale is quite limited and may include only items such as candy, gum, mints, and newspapers. In other operations, the number of non-menu items offered for sale is quite large and may include gift certificates and gift cards, items with the operation's logo such as hats or mugs, music, books, souvenirs, and prepackaged food that might bear the name and logo of the establishment.

The selling of items not specifically listed on the menu is a common practice when, for example, a barbeque house offers for sale its own recipe of sauce in bottles or jars. Similarly, a coffee shop might offer its own logoed ground or whole bean coffee for sale in bags or tins, or a family-style establishment might offer guests whole pies or cakes for carryout sale. In each case revenue is enhanced and in many cases, depending on the products' packaging, the name of the operation is taken home with the guest.

Placement

Placement refers to the location of a product's display or the location of the advertising piece used to promote the product. The best placement of promotional materials to a large degree depends on the product being sold and the advertising form used to sell it. For example, by displaying merchandise, retail food, or bakery products near the cash register, managers can encourage impulse buys from their customers as they order or pay their bill. These point-of-purchase (POP) locations exist wherever customers make their buying decisions.

Using table tents on the tables or counters where customers order is another good way to encourage impulse buys of menu items such as appetizers or desserts. Managers must use caution, however, to ensure their placement decisions are consistent with their operation's overall brand image.

For example, a fine-dining restaurant should not display large or overly attention-grabbing signs in elegant dining areas, while a QSR or fast-casual operation may find it perfectly acceptable to do so. In fact, attention-grabbing posters and signs with the operation's logo, tag line, or food photography of special menu items can help stimulate customer appetites, increase sales of the pictured items, and actually assist with the operation's overall branding efforts.

Where possible, the displays of items available for purchase should include the same logos, tag lines, and designs as the rest of an operation's marketing materials. When they do, customers can better recall the establishment in the future because they will have a reinforced image to associate with it.

Managers can also use tabletop displays or POP locations to notify customers of upcoming events, specials, or promotions. Current customers are among those most likely to come back or attend special events, so keeping them informed about upcoming activities at an operation is always a good idea.

Packaging

Packaging is the physical manner in which a product is presented to customers. For restaurant and foodservice establishments, packaging includes the way both menu items and non-menu items are presented to guests who have purchased them. Most consumers judge a product by its packaging

THINK ABOUT IT . . .

Have you ever purchased a souvenir item from an establishment? What did you buy? Why did you buy it? Do you still have it?

Digital signage is one of the newest and most innovative in-house advertising tools available to managers. With digital signage managers can update items and prices at many locations from the comfort of a central office.

Digital menu display boards can now show videos, play music, and even be programmed to change completely when, for example, an establishment wants to stop serving its breakfast menu and begin serving its lunch menu. Digital signage eliminates unnecessary menu reprint costs and the delays that come with standard sign making. As digital software and hardware technology continue to accelerate, watch for even more on-site merchandising efforts that take advantage of digital speed and flexibility.

before they purchase it, so attractive packaging is critical to the process of encouraging first-time buyers to make a purchase. Having attractive packaging does not mean managers can ignore product quality. Poor-quality products packed in expensive containers or even given to customers in beautifully logoed shopping bags are still poor-quality products. In the long run, most consumers will reject these products.

High-quality menu products are essential to repeat sales and the same is true of non-menu items sold in an establishment. Converting first-time buyers into loyal customers is a manager's goal, and effective packaging of high-quality products will aid in the achievement of that goal.

Pricing

For managers, proper pricing is just as important to the sale of non-menu items as it is to menu items. The primary consideration related to pricing non-menu items is customer perceptions of fairness. If an operation's merchandised products are perceived as being fairly priced, the chance of selling is high. If, however, customers perceive prices as overly inflated, two negative outcomes may happen. First, the products will not sell. Second, the inflated pricing may damage the customers' overall perception of the establishment.

To illustrate, a customer has just finished a nice lunch at a moderately priced establishment. Upon paying the bill at the cashier stand, the customer notices freshly baked chocolate chip cookies available for carryout sale. At less than $1 per cookie, the customer is likely to buy one. Even priced between $1 and $3 (depending on the location), the customer may still make the purchase. However, if the cookies were $10 each, the customer would be highly unlikely to make the purchase.

In this scenario, the business actually loses more than just the sale of the cookie. The customer's perception of the establishment is also likely damaged, with the result that an otherwise excellent dining experience was marred by management's improper pricing decision. The best managers ensure that their pricing decisions for both menu and non-menu items are perceived as fair to customers and to their operations.

SUMMARY

1. **Describe how managers establish advertising objectives.**

   Managers identifying their advertising objectives first must learn where their customers are and then decide where they must be moved via advertising. Awareness-related objectives target those customers who are not at all familiar with the operation. Trial-related objectives encourage customers to become first-time users, while usage-related objectives seek to increase frequency of visits.

Brand building–related objectives seek to increase the strength of the establishment's brand in the customer's mind. Finally, traffic building seeks to increase the total number of customers coming to an establishment. Each objective is important and must be continually assessed as managers seek to obtain and retain a strong customer base.

2. **Explain how to develop an advertising schedule.**

An advertising schedule is a calendar that details advertising and other promotional activities on a weekly, monthly, or seasonal basis. It typically includes the name of the activity, when it is to be initiated and completed, and if the manager prefers, its total cost. When carefully developed and monitored, an advertising schedule helps keep managers from "forgetting" important advertising tasks!

3. **State the methods managers use to evaluate advertising effectiveness.**

Managers use objective rather than subjective measures when assessing advertising effectiveness. Objective measures provide concrete data to managers so that they can determine if they have met their advertising goals. When advertising results are carefully measured, managers can choose to increase the use of the best advertising channels and decrease the use of less effective ones. They can also increase or decrease specific budgets and modify their advertising campaigns as needed.

4. **Describe objective measures of personal selling effectiveness.**

Total number of menu items sold, changes in the number of items sold, and changes in reservations made are all examples of objective measures of advertising effectiveness. Additional objective measures include increases in revenue, total revenue, and the number of new customers visiting the operation in a specific time period.

Managers establishing personal selling objectives assess efforts in enhancing awareness, encouraging trial, expanding usage, brand building, and traffic building. They also focus on customer type, targeting those customers who have not been buyers in the past, those who are current buyers but use the services of competitors, and finally, the manager's current customers. When assessing suggestive selling and upselling results, managers measure the impact of their training on staff improvement. In all cases, personal selling objectives for managers and staff should be measurable and time period specific.

5. **Explain the method managers use to evaluate event and suggestive selling effectiveness.**

To assess personal selling effectiveness, managers can use three steps. First, they keep good records of sales calls made and revenue generated by each person assigned personal selling tasks. These records help indicate whether sales performance is above or below standard. Second, they regularly assess each sales and service person's knowledge of available products and services from the perspective of the customer. They then provide additional sales training if needed. Finally, they ensure the products and services sold to customers provide excellent value because even the best sales efforts will not result in additional sales if an establishment performs poorly and does not meet its customers' expectations.

6. **List and describe the components of an effective on-site merchandising program.**

To develop an effective on-premise merchandising program, managers carefully consider products, placement, packaging, and pricing. The products offered for sale must be of high quality and in keeping with the image of the business. Placement of the products or of advertisements related to them should be carefully placed in POP locations or other spaces in the establishment that are in keeping with its brand image. Attractive packaging is one key to encouraging impulse sales and to turn first-time buyers into repeat customers. Finally, prices for menu and non-menu items must be perceived by customers as equitable if products are to sell and guests are to leave the operation with positive perceptions of its fairness in pricing.

APPLICATION EXERCISE

Pick up a copy of a print advertisement developed by a single establishment or a chain restaurant. Carefully review the entire ad.

1. What do you think was the intended message in this advertising piece?

2. Who do you think is the target market for this piece of communication?

3. Do you think the advertisement will be effective? Why or why not?

4. How could the advertisement be improved?

5. How could the operation's managers objectively measure the effectiveness of this advertisement?

REVIEW YOUR LEARNING

Select the best answer for each question.

1. **Which advertising objective is intended to increase customers' first-time usage of an establishment?**

    A. Trial

    B. Awareness

    C. Brand building

    D. Traffic building

2. **What can managers do to best enhance the impact of their entire staff's suggestive selling efforts?**

    A. Modify menus

    B. Provide training

    C. Reduce menu prices

    D. Record individual employee results

3. **What is the purpose of a logo?**

   A. To promote company recognition

   B. To convey pricing information

   C. To describe company features

   D. To explain company benefits

4. **What marketing term describes the total number of an establishment's new and returning customers?**

   A. Traffic

   B. Revenue

   C. Unit sales

   D. Awareness

5. **Which reason best explains why managers should develop advertising schedules?**

   A. Advertising schedules help build staff morale.

   B. Customers know when their favorite ad will run.

   C. Managers can track which advertisements are most effective.

   D. Advertising costs are reduced when the timing of ads is known in advance.

6. **Which is an objective measure of advertising effectiveness?**

   A. Improve business over 12 months.

   B. Improve customer service immediately.

   C. Prepare better food starting next week.

   D. Increase check average 10% in 90 days.

7. **Which is a subjective measure of advertising effectiveness?**

   A. Serve 10 more guests per day.

   B. Improve drink quality at night.

   C. Sell 10 appetizer plates per week.

   D. Double entrée sales within two weeks.

8. **What is a primary disadvantage of event selling activities?**

   A. Their results are difficult to measure.

   B. They prevent direct customer contact.

   C. They cannot be planned in advance.

   D. They can be very time-consuming.

9. **What marketing term describes a salesperson's continual search for customers?**

   A. Objecting

   B. Awareness

   C. Prospecting

   D. Decision making

10. **What component of an establishment's on-site merchandising program would most directly result in a guest's impulse buy?**

    A. Packaging

    B. Placement

    C. Product

    D. Price

9 Sales Promotions, Publicity, and Public Relations

INSIDE THIS CHAPTER

- Introduction to Sales Promotions, Publicity, and Public Relations
- Sales Promotions
- Publicity
- Public Relations
- Frequent Dining (Guest Loyalty) Programs
- Developing Community-Based Marketing Programs
- Implementing Promotions, Publicity, and Public Relations Activities

CHAPTER LEARNING OBJECTIVES

After completing this chapter, you should be able to:

- Explain the difference between sales promotions, publicity, and public relations in the marketing effort.
- Describe the importance of effective external and internal promotion marketing.
- Explain the impact of good media relations on positive and negative publicity.
- State the reasons managers should include public relations as part of the marketing mix.
- Explain the importance of developing an effective guest loyalty program.
- Identify the goals of community-based marketing programs.

KEY TERMS

CASE STUDY

"Tell me again, why would we want to give food away for free?" asked Ike, the kitchen manager of the Austin Bar-B-Que House.

"Because thousands of people will be there," replied Andrea, the operation's manager.

"So you want to give away thousands of servings of our Sixth Street Chili?" asked Ike. He was referring to the establishment's incredibly popular Texas-style chili.

"Not whole servings," explained Andrea, "just a taste. The chamber of commerce event is called Taste of the Town, and it has invited us and any other establishment that wants to participate to have a booth and hand out samples of what we serve. There's a prize offered for best booth, best food, and most creative presentation. Ike, our chili is so good that we'll win for sure! I just know it!"

1. Do you think giving away free samples at the Taste of the Town event will be a good way to build business at Austin Bar-B-Que House?

2. Assuming that thousands of people see Ike, Andrea, and the Austin Bar-B-Que House food booth at the event, is it more important that they participate or that the establishment wins first prize?

INTRODUCTION TO SALES PROMOTIONS, PUBLICITY, AND PUBLIC RELATIONS

Recall from chapter 8 that advertising and personal selling were two important parts of an establishment's marketing efforts. Sales promotions, publicity, and public relations are also important parts.

Sales promotions provide special incentives for customers to patronize an establishment. There are many types of sales promotions, and different tools or materials that can be used in a sales promotion. All are designed to give customers that extra "boost" to get them into an establishment or to purchase certain items. Sales promotions are useful only when customers know about them, so they are often the focus of an establishment's external and internal advertising.

Publicity is information about an establishment that is distributed for free but is not produced by the operation. A newspaper article announcing the opening of a new establishment is one example of free publicity. The main benefit of publicity is that people often find it more believable than advertising. For example, if a customer reads a glowing review of an establishment printed in a local newspaper, that customer might be more likely to go there than if he or she just saw an advertisement for the establishment in the same paper.

Because establishments do not control publicity, managers must recognize that while positive publicity is a great advantage, negative publicity can damage the credibility of an operation. If an operation receives negative publicity such as a bad food review, managers may need to use other tools in the marketing mix such as advertising or public relations to overcome the negative publicity.

Public relations (PR) is the part of an establishment's communication activities that addresses the operation's image in its community. In some cases, that community may consist of only a very small geographic area, whereas in others it may consist of an entire state or even a whole country.

Effective public relations means managing all communications between an organization and the public it serves. Actors and high-profile sports professionals are among those who use public relations to shape the opinions that people have of them. In a similar way, managers can use public relations as one piece of a coordinated effort to shape the opinions people have of their establishment.

Because they are sometimes (but not always) related, some people may think that *publicity* and *public relations* are synonymous terms. They are not. Many PR activities may lead directly to positive publicity (*Exhibit 9.1*). In other cases, however, PR activities are undertaken simply because businesses want

Exhibit 9.1

Giving back to the community can generate good publicity.

to be contributing members of their communities. In fact, one challenge facing managers is knowing whether or not to engage in a PR activity when there is no expectation of significant publicity resulting from the activity.

For example, an operation's continued food contributions to a local homeless shelter may or may not result in sustained positive publicity. In this case, as in many others, the manager's decision to engage in a PR activity that may yield minimal press coverage is one that must be carefully considered.

Exhibit 9.2 identifies the major components of an establishment's total customer communication effort. Managers must become skilled at using each component in the effective marketing of their operation.

Exhibit 9.2

COMPONENTS OF MARKETING COMMUNICATION

Marketing Component	Defining Characteristic
Advertising	Marketing message content is paid for and controlled by the business.
Personal selling	Marketing message is presented face-to-face.
Sales promotions	These are used to give customers an extra incentive to buy.
Publicity	Message content is free, not controlled by the business, and can be positive or negative.
Public relations	It manages the public's perception of a business.

The best operations managers use all of the major marketing components in *Exhibit 9.2* to help increase the number of customers they serve and the amount of food and beverages those customers buy.

SALES PROMOTIONS

Sales promotions are short-term activities designed to encourage the purchase of a specific product or service. In many cases, a well-designed promotion can result in free publicity or in information that can be used in an establishment's PR effort. In most cases, promotions must be advertised to be effective. Managers can choose to advertise their promotions externally, internally, or both. To best implement a sales promotion, there is a process that managers should follow:

1. Identify sales promotion objectives.
2. Develop the sales promotion.
3. Create supporting advertising material.
4. Inform and train staff prior to the promotion's implementation.

5. Advertise externally.

6. Advertise internally.

7. Implement the promotion.

8. Monitor program effectiveness.

9. Take corrective action as needed.

There are a variety of ways managers can make sales promotions an effective part of their marketing plans. One good way to examine how they do it is to consider the objectives they set for their promotions and how the promotions will be marketed externally and internally.

Sales Promotion Objectives

To determine sales promotion objectives, managers evaluate the needs of their target audiences, their brand, and the establishment's financial goals. In the end, a sales promotion must fit the establishment's audience and brand. For example, it might be appropriate for a casual restaurant to develop a Hawaiian Luau night promotion, where the staff decorates the dining room with tropical-themed items and arranges for traditional Hawaiian or beach music to be played during the dinner hour. A fine-dining restaurant, however, would likely find an identical sales promotion inappropriate for its brand image.

Objectives for restaurant and foodservice sales promotions can include the following:

- Build brand awareness.
- Increase short-term revenue (sales) levels.
- Build long-term market share.
- Introduce a new product or menu item.
- Introduce a new service.
- Entice customers away from direct competitors.
- Reward loyal customers.

Because promotions often involve selling selected products at reduced prices within a specific time period, promotions that result only in temporary sales increases are less desirable than those that help build the customer base of an establishment on a longer-term basis.

Although a sales promotion is typically designed to be in effect for only a specific period of time, the best sales promotions help build long-term revenue levels and inspire customer loyalty. They also should include an objective means of measuring their successfulness.

To illustrate, assume a manager creates a sales promotion to introduce a new entrée to the menu. A sales promotion is designed in such a way that if the new entrée is ordered, a second entrée may be ordered at half its regular price. Parties of two or more are the manager's target audience, but single diners receive a coupon, good for use on a return visit, that entitles the single diner to the half-priced entrée. In this example, the manager could apply one or more objective measures to test the success of the promotion:

- Number of promotional items sold
- Increases in total revenue
- Increases or decreases in check average (see chapter 1)
- New guests served during the promotion
- Total guests served during the promotion
- Guests served during a defined time period that follows the conclusion of the promotion
- Number of promotional items sold during a defined time period that follows the conclusion of the promotion

Sales Promotion Strategies

There are a variety of sales promotion strategies managers can use in their marketing efforts. Each approach offers customers a specific incentive, as shown in *Exhibit 9.3*. Each approach has advantages and disadvantages that managers must understand.

Exhibit 9.3

TYPES OF SALES PROMOTIONS

Method	Description	Incentive to the Customer
Special pricing	Limited-time reduced prices implemented through specials, deals, coupons, or other programs	Savings on an item Low-risk opportunity to try a new item
Frequent dining programs	Gives a benefit in exchange for continuing patronage	Rewards for continued patronage (usually free meals)
Premiums	Free or reduced-price merchandise that may or may not show the name and location of the establishment, usually given away or sold for a reduced price with the purchase of a food item	Free or reduced-price merchandise
Special events	One-time or periodic occasions that provide a special incentive for the customer to patronize the establishment	Varies based on event
Samples	Free, small taste of food items	Risk-free opportunity to try a new item
Contests and sweepstakes	Games and other programs that involve the customer and provide a prize	Chance to win a product or service

SPECIAL PRICING

Sales promotions that involve reduced prices for a specific or limited time are one of the most common ways for businesses to promote their products. This method allows customers to try a product at a reduced cost. For restaurant and foodservice establishments, special pricing programs might include a couple of different approaches:

Deals or specials: Short-term price reductions are offered on a certain product for a specific period of time. Restaurant and foodservice deals or specials often consist of a free meal with the purchase of a select entrée. For example, an establishment may offer a free piece of pie with the purchase of a meatloaf dinner.

Coupons: These certificates are designed to entice the customer to try an establishment or an item, usually by offering a discounted price. The function of coupons is to stimulate demand for a particular item or during a particular period. Coupons are also useful for promoting the trial of a new product. Today, electronically delivered coupons of various types are increasingly marketed to guests.

Servers, menu boards, and table tent cards typically communicate deals and specials at the establishment. Outside the operation, these types of promotions may be communicated via signage, advertisements, or publicity (see *Exhibit 9.4* as an example of storefront signage). Coupons are often included in direct-mail advertisements, takeout menus, and flyers, or made available through online couponing sites.

Coupons offer a huge benefit that most other promotions cannot offer as easily: traceability. If an establishment runs an advertisement with a coupon in two newspapers, for example, the manager can put a different

Exhibit 9.4

code on each coupon. As the coupons are redeemed, the manager can see which ad brought in more business. Large, multiunit operations in particular may use **clearinghouses**, which are in-house coupon departments or third-party firms that specialize in processing coupons and providing other marketing assistance to track coupon origins and patterns of use.

The use of special pricing programs may not always be a good choice. The overuse of discounts—deals, specials, and coupons—can sometimes backfire by creating the customer perception that certain items are not worth the full price. In addition, these types of programs may not be consistent with the image a manager wants to portray for his or her establishment. As with any type of marketing effort, carefully consider how the promotion will affect customers' short-term and long-term loyalty and the establishment's bottom line.

A classic case of oversaturating a market with coupons happened in the pizza industry. Various pizzerias in one community started distributing coupons to households on a weekly basis. Since every establishment distributed coupons, it made it harder for any one establishment to stand out in the crowd. To counter this problem, several shops honored their competitors' coupons. This promotion resulted in deep discounts that the establishments had to honor since they had advertised that they would accept any competitor's coupon. Ultimately, this promotion severely cut into profits.

In another example, a seafood restaurant chain offered an all-you-can-eat special that was extremely popular. Unfortunately, the special price offered on the promotion was so low that the restaurant was often out of the featured product, and it lost a significant amount of money on each guest who selected the promotion. The result was unhappy customers and lost profits.

When considering using a promotion that involves special pricing or discounts, compare the promotion's potential costs and benefits. If using coupons, consider the time and costs associated with delivering and processing the actual coupons as part of the operation's expenses. These costs may vary greatly based on the size and type of the operation. Chain restaurants may be able to split the costs of coupons with other members of the chain or the organization managing it.

FREQUENT DINING PROGRAMS

Frequent dining programs or other rewards programs are used to increase customer loyalty and provide an incentive to customers who purchase a specified number of meals or items or visit an establishment a required number of times. These programs are similar to the frequent flyer programs used by airlines.

For example, a customer may receive a free sandwich after purchasing 10 sandwiches over the course of multiple visits. Typically, frequent dining programs differ from deals or specials in that they require repeated visits to receive the reward. Sometimes the programs can have time limits, such as having to purchase 10 sandwiches within one year to receive a free sandwich.

Establishments that use frequent dining programs often distribute cards to track the number of items a customer has purchased. Customers who use these cards often return to the establishments that sponsor them to build up points. This repeat business helps create customer loyalty.

Managers using this sales promotion method must know their costs and need to clearly establish the rules for its implementation. For example, employees must be trained to follow the program rules so that they do not give away food or food credits unless the customer actually purchases the required items or makes the required number of visits. Frequent dining programs are discussed in greater depth later in this chapter.

PREMIUMS

Exhibit 9.5

Another type of promotion involves the use of premiums. Premiums are merchandise offered to customers for free or for a low price as an incentive to purchase a product (*Exhibit 9.5*). For example, during the holiday season, quick-service chains may offer a holiday toy, figurine, or glass for free or at a discounted price with the purchase of a specific meal. Premiums encourage customers to buy more of a particular product or to return more often to an operation, such as to collect a set of glasses.

There are advantages and disadvantages to premiums. If they are popular, they can bring in a large number of customers. However, if customers are buying a product only to get the premium, the promotion will have a short-term effect, and the promotion dollars could have been better spent in other ways.

In addition, premiums can be expensive, depending on how much they cost and how much, if anything, the establishment charges for them. They usually have a limited life span; for example, an establishment may offer premiums related to a sporting event or movie. Be especially careful when purchasing premiums that have a limited life span. Do not purchase more premiums than needed, but be aware that purchasing too few may result in alienating customers who have come in specifically for the premium.

SPECIAL EVENTS

Special events are one-time or periodic occasions that provide a special incentive for customers to patronize an establishment. The most effective special event promotions provide a "hook" to entice customers to make a special visit to an establishment. For example, a manager might plan wine or beer tastings, establishment tours, or other informational events. Other types of special events include special menus related to popular seasonal ingredients, such as seafood or local produce. Other special events can include festivals related to seasonal or other themes, such as Oktoberfest, a jazz festival, or a family day.

Special events can provide a great vehicle for generating publicity. Cosponsoring the event with other organizations will help promote it. However, special events take a lot of planning and require a great deal of organization. For example, if an establishment is going to host an outdoor music festival, the manager will need to coordinate the entertainment, the stage and equipment, and the extra staffing, among other things. Special events also can be expensive, but an assessment of the potential benefits can help determine whether or it's not worth it.

SAMPLES

Another type of promotion, which customers view as risk-free, is the sample. Samples are small amounts of product offered free to customers to give them the chance to try a certain product or dish. For example, bakeries often offer a sample tray of pastries they are trying to promote.

Samples often induce an immediate purchase, allowing the establishment to quickly sell an item. Depending on the portion size of the sample, the product, and its distribution, samples may be costly or provide a poor return on investment. For example, if a seafood establishment offers samples of an expensive item such as lobster, it may risk losing money if the sample sizes are too big. Similarly, if employees are not trained to ensure that customers do not take unfair advantage of a sample offer, a limited number of customers may consume all of the samples.

Finally, to ensure the best return on this type of investment, the sample quality must be as high as anything else being sold in the establishment. Ensuring that samples are fresh is critical for both food safety and quality reasons.

CONTESTS AND SWEEPSTAKES

Contests and sweepstakes provide customers with opportunities to receive a special product or service. Unlike other types of sales promotions, these programs require that customers actively participate. The rewards given to customers may range from a discounted or free food item to an expensive prize, such as a car or cash. Contests and sweepstakes can provide a great reason for businesses to conduct new advertising campaigns. They also provide a good way to collect information for market research.

In a contest, the customer is asked to submit an idea, such as a slogan for a new product, answer a question, or demonstrate a skill. Contests encourage customers to become involved with an organization. However, the time and effort to set up a contest is often costly, and the contest must be examined for its practicality to the organization.

Sweepstakes are games of chance. Usually, they require customers only to submit their name and contact information. A common type of sweepstakes in some establishments is a drawing for a free meal or other incentive. Often, these establishments place a bowl at the entrance and ask customers to drop in their business card for a chance to win a prize.

With any contest or sweepstakes, define the rules very clearly so both customers and employees understand them. In addition, seek legal advice before implementing any contest or sweepstakes program.

As with any part of the marketing mix, sales promotions need to support the establishment's marketing plan, product positioning, and image. Therefore, carefully consider all choices in sales promotion methods and materials.

Implementing Sales Promotions

Once a manager has determined the objectives and strategies for a promotion, it is time to put that promotion into action. Implementing a promotion can be difficult if a manager is not organized. One way to stay organized is to develop a simple checklist that answers the following questions:

- Who is responsible for the overall promotion?
- What are the elements involved in the promotion?
- Who is responsible for marketing the promotion?
- How many staff members are needed to execute the event?
- What materials and supplies are needed for the event or promotion?
- Who is responsible for working with suppliers to obtain the materials and supplies?
- What are the specific deadlines associated with the promotion such as obtaining a mailing list, or printing and sending invitations?
- What are some potential problems, and what are their solutions?

Preplanning helps ensure the success of a promotion. Staff members are an integral part of an establishment's products and service. They should fully understand any promotional plan before it is implemented and, in many cases, can actually help plan it.

Marketing Sales Promotions

After managers have created and planned sales promotions, they must be marketed. In most cases, managers choose external marketing methods, internal methods, or both to communicate their promotional offerings to customers.

EXTERNAL MARKETING OF SALES PROMOTIONS

The external marketing of sales promotions can use traditional communication channels such as newspapers, magazines, and radio or television broadcasts. Less traditional methods are increasingly popular and they include the use of social media sites, advertising on online restaurant and foodservice review sites, email notifications, and the use of specialized cell phone applications designed for customer communication.

In some cases, personal selling may be an effective way to communicate the details of a promotion to a target market. In addition to advertising and personal selling, managers can choose from a large number of external and internal promotional materials to help launch their promotion. Some of these are shown in *Exhibit 9.6*.

RESTAURANT TECHNOLOGY

Tech-savvy managers increasingly turn to modern communication tools like Twitter when advertising their daily or weekly specials. An establishment could, for example, promote a gift certificate offering using Twitter by tweeting "Follow us by 5 p.m. CST to be entered to win a $100 gift certificate." This promotes the establishment and helps gain followers who would be waiting for the next deal or offer.

Twitter also could be used to promote a new establishment or an event. The week before the event, the manager could tweet, "Follow us and direct message me your email address so I can send you the free entry password to our special event!" This is simply another way to help get customers in the door.

Exhibit 9.6

TYPICAL PROMOTIONAL MATERIALS

Promotional Material	Description
Signage	Menu boards, directional signs, and other signs that indicate where an establishment is located or the items served
Flyers	Paper notices that are either randomly distributed or targeted to a specific group to create awareness of a certain promotion or menu item
Trinkets	Token gifts or give-away items, such as pens, key chains, or stationery, that display the establishment's name and location or phone number
Carryout and door hanger menus	Paper menu for customers to use outside the establishment; door hanger menus for hanging on doorknobs or handles
Apparel	Establishment's name or logo on a t-shirt or other garment
Point-of-purchase (POP) materials	Menu boards, video, print pieces, and other display items near the point of purchase—where customers pay for their purchases
Merchandising materials	Table tents and other display items in the establishment

Exhibit 9.7

STEPS IN THE USE OF POP AND POS MATERIALS

STEP 1
Identify goals of POP and POS materials

STEP 2
Produce POP and POS materials

STEP 3
Train staff in use of POP and POS materials

STEP 4
Display POP and POS materials

STEP 5
Evaluate effectiveness of POP and POS materials

STEP 6
Revise and replace materials as needed

INTERNAL MARKETING OF SALES PROMOTIONS

The external marketing of a promotion seeks to get customers in the door. Effective internal marketing is used to get those customers to participate in the promotion. Examples of internal marketing include signs placed in windows or at the entrances to an operation, banners placed in foyer or dining areas, buttons worn by employees, and advertisements printed especially for placement on dining-room tables.

To select, develop, and implement effective internal marketing tools to support a promotion, managers follow specific steps in using internal marketing tools such as point-of-purchase (POP) and point-of-sales (POS) materials. These steps are identified in *Exhibit 9.7*.

Step 1: Identify Goals of POP and POS Materials. In most cases, managers develop a promotion with the goal of influencing a customer's buying decision. The end goal may be, for example, to encourage the customer to try a new menu item, purchase a gift card, or sign up for a frequent dining program. In each case, any POP or POS materials developed must clearly indicate the call to action.

Recall from chapter 7 that the principles of good advertising call for managers to develop ads that focus on the following:

- Attention: Get the customer's attention.
- Interest: Interest the customer in your message.
- Desire: Create a desire for your product or service.
- Action: Prompt the customer to take the desired action.

These same principles apply to the internal marketing materials developed in support of a promotion.

Step 2: Produce POP and POS Materials. Before POP and POS materials can be hung or displayed around the establishment, they must be produced. In some cases, production may involve the use of professional photographers and printing companies. In other cases, production may simply require drawing on a blackboard (or whiteboard) displayed in dining areas or printing flyers using a manager's office computer. In all cases, however, managers must ensure the materials they produce meet six criteria:

- They are produced in sufficient quantity.
- They are easily read.
- They clearly describe the promotion.
- They maintain the establishment's brand image.

- They include the price or terms (if appropriate).

- They include a distinct clear call to action on the part of the customer (e.g., buy, sign up, register, email, etc.).

Step 3: Train Staff in Use of POP and POS Materials. In many instances, an operation's staff is its most effective selling tool. Knowledgeable servers should be able to explain current promotions to guests who are unaware of them. Keeping staff trained and motivated will help ensure the success of a promotion.

Before a promotion takes place, ensure that staff members know the promotion details so they can include it in their suggestive selling efforts (*Exhibit 9.8*). Staff should be trained properly in order to implement the promotion. If the promotion includes a new menu item, also make sure that staff members know the item's ingredients, especially potential allergens, and its nutritional features. In addition, if a promotion might increase the number of guests over a certain period, ensure that staff is scheduled accordingly.

Exhibit 9.8

Step 4: Display POP and POS Materials. Internal promotional materials must be produced in a large enough size and quantity to ensure that they are seen by all customers. There is a wide variety of potential locations for POP and POS materials:

- Entry doors
- Windows
- Foyers
- Host stands
- Hallways

- Restrooms
- Dining-room walls
- Tables, booths, and counters
- Menus
- Cashier areas

Of course, managers displaying promotional materials must avoid a cluttered look. They must balance the need to overcommunicate with customers with the risk that customers will be unaware of the promotion.

Step 5: Evaluate Effectiveness of POP and POS Materials. Managers consulting with their waitstaff will quickly determine if sales of a promotional menu or other item are meeting expectations or if they are falling short. It is always a good idea to assess the POP and POS materials themselves. Perhaps they are not clear. Perhaps they are not exciting enough. Or perhaps they are missing, torn, or dirty. In all cases, managers should complete an assessment of the internal POP and POS marketing materials early in the implementation of the promotion.

Step 6: Revise and Replace Materials as Needed. If an assessment of the internal POP and POS marketing materials indicates a modification is in order, the changes should be addressed immediately. The promotional materials should be revised or replaced. Potential areas of concern regarding promotional materials may be related to several factors:

- Unclear wording
- Spelling or grammatical issues
- Incorrect price

Spelling and grammatical errors on promotional materials are not limited to only restaurant and foodservice menus and signage. Many businesses make these errors. But, having obvious spelling errors in something issued to the public is a significant concern. If there are problems in what customers *are* seeing, they will naturally question how much the establishment is also overlooking behind the scenes.

Monitoring Sales Promotions

The sales promotion has been planned, advertised, and implemented. Now the manager must monitor the promotion to ensure that it is working according to the plan and that any problems are being addressed. The implementation checklist developed during the planning stage will help monitor the early part of the promotion. In addition, managers should constantly track sales, inventory, staffing, and other aspects to make sure the promotion is implemented correctly. They should also determine if the promotion has the forecasted effect on business.

There are three steps every manager should use to monitor a promotion:

- Meet regularly with the promotion team and employees to give and receive updates on the promotion results.
- Regularly communicate with suppliers to update them on the establishment's changing needs and to ensure that they can accommodate these needs.
- Track sales and other relevant measures before, during, and after the promotion.

The sales numbers help managers evaluate the success of the promotion. After the promotion has been implemented and run its course, the evaluation stage allows the operation's management to determine the return on investment. This evaluation is discussed in detail in chapter 11.

PUBLICITY

Unlike advertising, publicity for a restaurant or foodservice operation is free. That is the good news. Unfortunately, because a manager cannot directly control publicity, publicity can be good or bad. Managers, of course, have as a primary objective to generate as much good publicity about their establishments as they can. Managers also want to minimize the amount of bad publicity they receive. In the event that negative publicity does occur, managers want to be able to minimize its negative impact as much as possible.

Some managers wonder how they can obtain good publicity for their operations. It is not as difficult as it may seem. Consider the following examples of simple activities that would likely generate good publicity for an establishment:

- Offering discounts to schoolchildren who receive good grades or who have perfect attendance
- Donating a portion of sales to charity for a given item or certain parts of a given day
- Offering customers a discount when they bring in a donation for charity
- Sponsoring a local children's sports team and offering incentives for winning a game
- Offering a facility as a meeting site or providing the catering for a fundraiser or meeting

THINK ABOUT IT . . .

Did you ever read an article about a restaurant or foodservice establishment identified as the source of a foodborne illness? Or one that was a crime scene? How did this publicity affect your willingness to visit the establishment?

REAL MANAGER

PROMOTIONS, PUBLICITY AND PUBLIC RELATIONS

You can never go wrong issuing a press release for your events. This is a way to obtain free publicity. Always include who, what, where, when, and why as well as photos when sending out press releases, and state why your event is relevant to your market. One of the largest mentions we received was for sumo wrestling in the late 1990s. USA Today ran a photo and a quote from our company for a bar promotion we executed where guests would put on oversized sumo suits and wrestle with one another!

Other types of programs may not generate direct business but can still provide excellent opportunities for publicity. For example, consider the publicity that might be generated if an operation donates food, labor, or equipment to a shelter providing meals to the homeless or to families in distress.

Good publicity usually does not just happen. The best way to ensure good publicity is by first building positive relationships with the local community. Next, managers build good relationships with the media so the establishment's activities can be readily communicated to them.

Media Relations

While a manager may not be able to control the publicity about his or her establishment, that manager can have a positive effect if he or she knows what and how to communicate to the media. Ideally, managers also should develop professional relationships with media representatives. These actions—providing publicity materials to the media and working with media representatives—are known as media relations.

Good media relations can significantly increase the impact of community relations programs. For example, consider a manager who creates a special program to discount meals for people who donate to the local food bank. If the manager promotes this discount on his or her own or with the help of the food bank, it is likely that the only people who will know about the discount will be those in the target markets of the establishment or the food bank. On the other hand, if the manager has good media relations and can generate a story in the local media, he or she could reach many more people—people who will be more likely to notice the manager's good work and respond in a positive way.

Good media relations are important for generating positive publicity, but they are just as important when an establishment experiences negative publicity. The old saying that any publicity, good or bad, is good publicity is often not true in the restaurant and foodservice industry. For instance, any reporting of poor food quality or service can hurt an establishment's image.

The widespread reporting of an outbreak of foodborne illness, violence, or criminal activity in or around an establishment is never good. Mainstream media or online reports about poor management will also turn off customers. Crisis management is the manner in which a business handles a major event that threatens the reputation and survival of a business. In times of crisis, a restaurant or foodservice operation must have good media relations and public relations programs in place.

CHOOSING THE RIGHT COMMUNICATION CHANNELS

Media professionals are always looking for good news stories. Many of them will be interested in developing a good relationship with a local restaurant or foodservice operator. But, as with all of their marketing efforts, managers need to focus their efforts on reaching their target market. When evaluating the potential offered by various media and communication channels, such as particular publications or radio stations, managers must consider several questions:

- Does the communication channel reach a manager's target market or people who can influence their target market? If so, how much of the target market does it reach? In many cases, managers should use the same factors to evaluate a source of publicity as they would for an advertising campaign.

- How likely is it that the communication channel will be interested in the stories the manager could suggest or submit. Is there a story that will be of interest to the media's own audience?

- Has a good relationship already been developed with the key personnel at the media outlet? If not, how easily could these relationships be developed?

- Can the public relations materials available to the manager effectively compete for attention from the decision makers in this communication channel? If not, can the materials be improved to make them more competitive?

These last two points are interrelated. If a manager has a good relationship with a blog editor, for example, that manager's materials are more likely to get the editor's attention. Likewise, if the manager understands what gets the editor's attention in the first place—if the manager sends effective PR materials—the manager is more likely to develop a good working relationship with that editor.

USING EFFECTIVE MEDIA RELATIONS MATERIALS

To directly generate publicity through the media, businesses commonly send out press releases or media kits. A **press release** or **news release** is a brief presentation of promotional information written in a general and timely news format. Well-written press releases present marketing information as news as seen in *Exhibit 9.9*.

If a business prepares well and has a bit of luck, the information in its press releases will be published or read "as is." More often, the information will be incorporated into a story. A press release may be sent by itself or as part of a press kit. A **press kit**, also called a **media kit**, is a packet of information given to media representatives to answer questions they might have about a business or organization. Press kits also may be given to potential customers, employees, or investors. Some establishments provide their press kits in an electronic format through a Web site or on a CD or flash drive.

Exhibit 9.9

SAMPLE PRESS RELEASE

FOR IMMEDIATE RELEASE
Contact:
Pat Park
Three Lands Restaurant
(612) 555-1200
ppark@threelands.com

THREE LANDS RESTAURANT
141 Lincoln Drive, Minneapolis, Minnesota, 55401
Tel. (612) 555-1200 Fax: (612) 555-1239
www.threelands.com

Three Lands Restaurant Raises Funds for Disaster Relief

MINNEAPOLIS (June 11, 2012)—To help people around the world who have recently experienced a major disaster, the Three Lands Restaurant will donate 25 percent of all revenue collected during its weeklong Summer Fling event starting June 18 to the International Red Cross. Three Lands' Summer Fling is an outdoor event featuring special, grilled menu items and live entertainment.

"We are excited that we can help the Red Cross help so many people while providing a special celebration of the season," says Three Lands General Manager Terry Larsen. "Since so many disasters have occurred recently, we are especially glad to support such a worthy organization as the Red Cross."

Supporters who come to Three Lands' Summer Fling can expect to find a special menu featuring juicy, grilled burgers, chicken, and chorizo; locally grown, grilled sweet corn with chili-lime butter; ceviché salade Niçoise with cilantro vinaigrette; and of course, Three Lands' famous tropical drinks and wide selection of imported beers and wine. Chef-owner Javier Diaz also is offering special dessert items, including guava crème brûlée, tropical fruit snow cones, horchata frozen custard, and chocolate tamales.

Each night of the Summer Fling presents a different local band, including the Motion Poets, Slide Huxtable, The Righteous, and Little Big. Saturday and Sunday, the music starts at noon. For a complete schedule, check the restaurant's Web site at www.threelands.com.

Red Cross regional director, Kasia Puntillo, states, "This type of event brings the community together to help others who really need it. We are so grateful for the help and donations of people like Javier and his staff. I hope everyone turns out to support this event."

Founded in 1998 by chef-owner Javier Diaz,
Three Lands Restaurant offers a blend of cuisines from North America, South America, and Europe.
Its award-winning menu has been recognized nationwide for its creativity.

5. **What rewards will be offered?** The rewards programs offered by airlines allow customers to accumulate miles that can be exchanged for free or reduced-price tickets on future flights. The miles may also be used to "purchase" seat upgrades or other items. In a similar manner, restaurant and foodservice managers must determine what award their customers will get in return for their loyal patronage. Some rewards used by restaurant and foodservice operators include the following:

- Free menu items
- Reduced prices on selected items
- Percentage-off discounts such as 5, 10, or 20 percent off
- Preferred reservations
- Preferred seating

Creative managers can use the data in their guest loyalty programs in a variety of ways. Using the information collected in their loyalty program database a manager could, for example, identify customers who always order wine with their dinner and offer them a special wine promotion. He or she could program the system to send a gift certificate for a complimentary appetizer or dessert item to customers after their fifth visit in a year. In a chain operation, the central office might use its customer database to identify all current customers who live within a 10-minute drive of a new establishment being opened to invite them to a special VIP night held prior to the new operation's official opening date.

One challenge in managing a guest rewards program is choosing what incentives to offer. This can be done only when managers know and understand their target markets.

6. **How will the program be evaluated?** If they are to implement a guest loyalty program, managers must be prepared to commit to the program and follow through for the long term. Managers also must commit to putting proper training procedures in place so the establishment's staff can execute the program internally. Number of members, frequency of visits, and dollar amount spent per visit are all good examples of tools managers can use to assess the effectiveness of their guest loyalty programs. Regardless of the criteria selected, managers must carefully monitor their guest loyalty program results and effectiveness and take corrective action to improve the programs when needed.

THINK ABOUT IT . . .

Do you think most people prefer to do business with those they know personally? How does that affect restaurant and foodservice managers who seek to become active in their communities?

marketing plan. Managers should ask themselves a series of questions before becoming involved with a particular organization:

- Do I believe in the cause of the organization or event?
- Do its goals and philosophies align with the image of my establishment?
- Do its members or participants belong to my target market or have influence with my target market?
- What kind of opportunities does it present for publicity in my target market?
- What kind of support can I provide? Will this level of support make enough of a difference to generate good publicity?

If the target market is families, a manager might become involved with school activities or youth sports teams. Or, if the target market is business professionals, the manager might interact with business organizations or charities in his or her market area.

IMPLEMENTING PROMOTIONS, PUBLICITY, AND PUBLIC RELATIONS ACTIVITIES

When implementing promotions, publicity, or PR-related activities, managers follow a series of effective planning and implementation actions. Although the focus of the different activities may be different, the actions required to implement them are similar. During the implementation of these programs, managers should do the following:

1. **Sequence the activity or event:** Regardless of the promotion, publicity activity, or PR-related event, managers must carefully choose the timing that is best. This is especially true with promotional events tied to holidays or seasons. Also, careful examination of an operation's historical sales records may yield information about those times when it is best to seek additional revenue by increasing customer awareness of an operation.

2. **Inform and prepare key staff members:** When an activity involves the actions of staff (for example, cooks who must learn to make new menu items, or staff who will engage in suggestive selling of new items), the staff members must be well informed and, in many cases, well trained. When they are, it increases the chances that the promotion or activity will be successful.

3. **Launch the activity or event:** After an activity has been well planned and staff is prepared, managers initiate their plans. In this critical time managers, should be available as much as possible to address staff concerns as they occur and to observe the success of the activity.

4. **Monitor effectiveness:** When possible, managers should use objective measures to assess the impact of their promotion, publicity, or PR efforts. In some cases, such as when assessing the impact on an

operation's image of a food donation to a local charity, such an objective measure may be difficult to identify. In other cases (for example, the number sold of a newly developed and promoted menu item) the number sold or other objective measure will be easy to identify. In all cases, however, it is the manager's job to assess the quality and the success of his or her promotion, publicity, and PR activities.

5. **Take corrective action as needed:** In most cases, a successful promotion helps provide information about how to improve the next promotion. Similarly, successful publicity activities or PR campaigns may provide information for future improvement in these areas. When modifications of activities would help improve upcoming or yet to be planned activities, these should be noted by managers and be applied to future events.

Properly used, sales promotions, publicity, and public relations are all very effective marketing tools. Managers can use these tools, as well as advertising and personal selling, to communicate directly with their target markets. When they do so in a creative way, their customers will come, and then come back, time after time.

SUMMARY

1. **Explain the difference between sales promotions, publicity, and public relations in the marketing effort.**

   Sales promotions are targeted activities designed to entice customers to buy. Promotions are most often communicated to customers by external and internal advertising. Publicity is information about an establishment that is spread by the media. Publicity is free, but a manager cannot control the message. As a result, publicity may be good or bad. It can be influenced by developing good relationships with media representatives. Public relations are those manager-controlled activities designed to place a business in a positive light in the eyes of its target market. One effective way for an operation to do that is to become actively involved in the local community.

2. **Describe the importance of effective external and internal promotion marketing.**

   If a promotion is to have its intended effect, customers must know about it. To ensure that guests know about the promotions they offer, managers typically use external communication channels such as newspapers, magazines, radio, and TV. External signage can also be used. When customers arrive at an operation, managers rely on internal selling tools such as POP and POS posters and interior signage to encourage customers to take advantage of the promotion. Unless it is advertised effectively, even the best sales promotion will fail simply because customers did not know about it.

3. **Explain the impact of good media relations on positive and negative publicity.**

   Publicity does not cost an establishment anything directly. As a result, good publicity is a real plus. Negative publicity, however, is also possible. When that happens, it is helpful to have good relationships with those in the media who can allow managers the opportunity to tell "their side of the story." Good media relations may cost very little money, but they do involve a commitment of the manager's time. Investing in strong relationships with media representatives allows good publicity to be distributed more often and more widely. It also allows negative publicity to be minimized.

4. **State the reasons managers should include public relations as part of the marketing mix.**

Public relations programs can achieve several marketing objectives. They can build name recognition by focusing on memorable information about an establishment. They can build credibility because, unlike paid advertising, their message is generally considered to be more credible because customers generally trust news reports more fully than they trust advertising messages.

Public relations efforts are also cost-effective because they create name recognition. They can encourage customer trials without incurring the expense of paid advertising. Advertising, personal selling, and promotions can be expensive. Publicity is free, but without newsworthy activities it can be difficult to attract the attention of the news media. PR activities give media representatives something of interest to report to their readers or viewers.

5. **Explain the importance of developing an effective guest loyalty program.**

Like many industries, the restaurant and foodservice industry is very competitive. The best managers want to develop and keep loyal customers. To do so, these managers can create formal customer loyalty programs. Also known as "rewards" programs, these programs offer an establishment's best customers "special" treatment. The airline, hotel, and casino industries all have experienced great success in developing guest rewards programs. Those in the restaurant and foodservice industry can and should do the same to recognize and reward their best customers.

6. **Identify the goals of community-based marketing programs.**

Community-based marketing programs help an establishment create a positive image within its local market area. They help build an operation's credibility by demonstrating good citizenship. Managers who are active in their communities also build strong relationships with other community leaders. These relationships then help build the operation's business.

Managers also find that community-based activities help them build excellent relationships with other professionals. Most important, participating in community-based activities helps generate positive publicity. It casts operations and their managers in a very positive light.

APPLICATION EXERCISE

Assume you are the manager of an establishment that has just hired a new chef.

1. Create a one-page press release announcing the hiring. Make sure your press release is carefully reviewed for grammatical and spelling errors. Include the date on the press release as well as these items:

   - An attention-grabbing headline
   - The name of your establishment
   - A description of your operation and its menu offerings
   - The establishment's location
   - The name of the new chef
   - An interesting or memorable attribute of the new chef

   - A brief "quote" from the chef explaining why he or she was pleased to have been selected
   - When the chef will start
   - How the chef's hiring will directly benefit your customers
   - Whom the press should contact for further information

2. List three PR activities in which you would be willing to volunteer some of the new chef's paid time to enhance local awareness of your operation.

3. How would you objectively measure the success of your publicity and PR efforts?

4. How could you subjectively measure the success of your publicity and PR efforts?

REVIEW YOUR LEARNING

Select the best answer for each question.

1. **What is the main purpose of a frequent dining program?**
   A. To build brand awareness
   B. To sell products that are slow moving
   C. To provide incentives for guests to return
   D. To encourage nonusers to try an establishment

2. **Which is an example of a promotional premium?**
   A. Holiday glassware
   B. A $2 off coupon
   C. Early bird dinner special
   D. Frequent dining programs

3. **When should managers train staff in use of POP and POS promotional materials?**
   A. When the results of the promotion are being evaluated
   B. After the materials have been displayed
   C. Before the promotion begins
   D. During the promotion

4. **Where would managers display POP materials describing a current sales promotion?**
   A. In a newspaper advertisement
   B. On their customers' tables
   C. On a printed coupon
   D. In a press release

5. **What primary advantage does advertising have over publicity?**
   A. Advertising messages can be controlled by a manager.
   B. Advertising messages generate more customer trust.
   C. Advertising does not need to be scheduled.
   D. Advertising costs less than publicity.

6. An establishment recently received bad publicity because a fight broke out on the sidewalk in front of its location. What action represents a positive way that the manager can minimize the damage of this bad publicity?

   A. Start a social media campaign noting competitors' inferior food quality.

   B. Issue a press release highlighting the establishment's new safety measures.

   C. Reduce food and drink prices for students with a college ID.

   D. Refuse to address the story and hope that it goes away.

7. What is the tool used by reporters to create stories about an establishment?

   A. Media kit

   B. POP display

   C. Special event

   D. Merchandise premium

8. Which is an example of a public service activity that could be undertaken by an establishment?

   A. Offering senior citizen discounts before the dinner rush hour

   B. Offering "Buy One Get One Free" dinners once a month

   C. Contributing unused food to a food bank

   D. Attending a meeting of the city council

9. What is a manager's final consideration in the development of an effective customer rewards program?

   A. Program evaluation

   B. Registration of members

   C. Tracking of member purchases

   D. Determination of appropriate rewards

10. Which characteristic is the strongest reason to form a partnership with a particular community group?

    A. Its members are well-known celebrities.

    B. Its members are friends with the owners.

    C. Its members are wealthy business owners.

    D. Its members are in the establishment's target market.

FIELD PROJECT

Visit a restaurant or foodservice operation running a current promotion. When you arrive at the establishment, take notes on the promotion in order to answer the questions that follow.

1. What is the promotion's call to action (i.e., what are customers encouraged to buy)?

2. How long will the promotion be in effect?

3. Who is the promotion's target market?

4. What appears to be the goal of the promotion? How do you know?

5. By what means were you made aware of the promotion before your visit?

6. What external signage was developed for the promotion?

7. What POP materials were developed for the promotion?

8. What POS materials were developed for the promotion?

9. What merchandising premiums are associated with the promotion?

10. How did the staff members help enforce the promotion?

11. Did the promotion appear to be effective? By what measure?

12. What steps might be taken to improve the quality of the promotion?

10

Menu Marketing

CHAPTER LEARNING OBJECTIVES

After completing this chapter, you should be able to:

- Summarize the key factors that influence customers' restaurant or foodservice menu selections.

- Explain the impact of customer psychology on menu development.

- Outline the principles of effective menu layout and design.

- Describe the process managers use when deciding if a new item should be added to a menu.

- Explain how to design a professional beverage menu.

KEY TERMS

CASE STUDY

"Table 6 says 'Our compliments to the Chef,'" exclaimed Rachel, a server at Walker's Stockyard Steakhouse. Rachel smiled as she entered the kitchen carrying plates from the dining room.

"What did they order?" called out Jack, the Stockyard's chef and kitchen manager.

"Well, they asked me what I would recommend, and I told them my favorite is the Chopped Steak with Red Wine and Rosemary Reduction Sauce. That's what they both ordered, and they told me it was fantastic. I knew it would be," replied Rachel, "and they left me a big tip!"

Jack knew the sauce for the chopped steak was one of his best. The item was easy to make, and the establishment made an above-average profit on each one it sold. But it was listed last of nine items on the steak portion of the menu and it did not sell as often as many of the other steak choices. Jack also knew that when customers bought it, they always raved about it, and many came back just to order that same item again.

1. What do you think would happen if more customers ordered the Chopped Steak with Red Wine and Rosemary Reduction Sauce?

2. If you were the manager of this operation, what changes to the menu would you make to help promote the sales of this unique item?

Exhibit 10.1

FACTORS INFLUENCING GUESTS' FOOD SELECTIONS

An effective marketing plan will get customers in an establishment's door. However, the menu is actually an operation's most effective sales and marketing tool. Customers select menu items for a variety of reasons. Planning an effective menu requires managers to consider these reasons in order to meet the diverse needs of customers.

To understand the importance of the menu, consider this question: Why is a customer willing to pay $9.95 for a hamburger served on a plate in one establishment, when in another the same hamburger is sold wrapped in paper for $2.99 (*Exhibit 10.1*)? When customers look at a menu, they are driven by many considerations in choosing their items. While hunger is sometimes the main reason driving purchases, it is usually not the only force behind customers' decisions.

Marketing managers know that promotional and marketing efforts impact what guests buy. Carefully designed menus, table tent cards, server suggestions, and various types of point-of-purchase (POP) and point-of-sales (POS) merchandising pieces all influence customers.

Menus are important to the success of restaurant and foodservice operations. Therefore, there are several concepts managers should know about using the menu as a marketing tool:

- Know the key factors that influence customers' menu selections.
- Understand food menu design.
- Understand beverage menu design.

Guests order specific menu items for a variety of reasons. Taste, portion size, and presentation are among these reasons. Managers must, however, understand that price and personal health also contribute to menu selection.

Price

The menu prices very often affect what customers select. As a result, the prices printed on a menu have a profound impact on an operation's overall sales and profitability. The placement of the prices on the menu affects purchase decisions. It is recommended that prices be listed directly at the end of the description of the item (as shown on the right-hand side of *Exhibit 10.2*), rather than before the item or next to the item name (as demonstrated on the left-hand side of *Exhibit 10.2*). If price is the first thing a customer sees, then price becomes emphasized in the selection decision. Note that the use of dots connecting the menu item to the price can also invite customers to look at price first.

THINK ABOUT IT . . .

Think about your own menu item selections. What factors do you consider when ordering from a menu? Do you think other establishment guests consider those same factors?

Personal Health

The number of customers with health-based dietary needs has steadily increased in recent years. Meeting these needs could very well help an operation remain competitive. These special needs include several distinct categories:

- Diets that address specific nutritional concerns
- Vegetarian diets
- Organic diets
- Religious diets
- Diets for people allergic to various kinds of food items or ingredients

NUTRITIONAL CONCERNS

Customers today are concerned with nutrition and the nutritional components of food items. Some customers consciously select items based on levels of carbohydrates, proteins, fats, sugars, cholesterol, sodium (salt), calories, or other nutritional characteristics. Some customers may have particular dietary needs because of a medical condition that requires them to be careful in menu item selection.

Exhibit 10.2

PLACEMENT OF MENU PRICE

All managers must ensure that the nutritional content and health claims on their menus are truthful. For example, if menus indicate the number of grams of fat or the milligrams of cholesterol or sodium in selected menu items, these amounts should be as accurate as possible. For some operations, this information may be affected by local or federal laws.

Terms such as *free* as in *fat free*, *low* such as in *low fat*, and *lean* such as in *lean beef* have specific legal or commonly understood meanings, so managers must use those terms carefully and accurately. The health and well-being of guests concerned about nutrition are too important to take lightly. It is not appropriate and may be unlawful to willfully misstate dietary claims in menu descriptions.

It is also important to recognize that customers are just as likely to order an item that is contrary to good nutritional advice because they are celebrating a special occasion or because they are rewarding themselves in some way. Managers need to take into account both of these types of customers: those who are following a special diet of some kind and those who want to indulge occasionally.

Manager's Memo

Menu labeling legislation is a current topic in many jurisdictions. Public concerns typically address the need for a menu to inform and educate consumers about the food items that are available or to require that accurate information be provided.

Many of these concerns typically relate to nutritional issues and the need to make nutritional information available to consumers. This information can address the following details for each menu item:

- Total number of calories
- Total number of grams of saturated fat and trans fat
- Total number of carbohydrates
- Total amount (milligrams) of sodium

For information about the current and pending menu labeling legislation in the United States, check out the Web site of the National Restaurant Association at *www.restaurant.org*. Once on the site, type "menu labeling legislation" into the site's search box.

VEGETARIAN DIETS

Consumers choose to eat vegetarian diets for many reasons, including religious beliefs, concern for the environment, economics, health considerations, animal welfare factors, and ethical considerations related to world hunger. A vegetarian is a person who consumes no meat, fish, or poultry products. All vegetarians avoid eating meat. However, some vegetarians also avoid other animal-based products. As a result, vegetarians fall into several classifications:

- **Vegans:** Vegetarians who eat no food of animal origin, including milk, cheese, and honey, are referred to as vegans.
- **Lacto-vegetarians:** Lacto-vegetarians consume dairy products in addition to their vegetarian diets.
- **Ovo-vegetarians:** These vegetarians add eggs to their vegetarian diets.
- **Lacto-ovo-vegetarians:** Lacto-ovo-vegetarians add both dairy products and eggs to their vegetarian diets.

It is important that managers understand the basic types of vegetarian diets. If a server states, "One of our guests is a lacto-vegetarian; what can we serve him?" the manager must be able to answer accurately.

ORGANIC DIETS

Another trend toward healthier eating includes the interest in and use of organic food. **Organic food** is defined by the USDA as those food items grown by farmers who emphasize the use of renewable resources and the conservation of soil and water to enhance the environmental quality for future generations. Organic meat, poultry, eggs, and dairy products come from animals that are given no antibiotics or growth hormones. Organic food is produced without using most conventional pesticides, petroleum-based fertilizers, or sewage sludge–based fertilizers, bioengineering, or ionizing radiation. Before a product can be labeled "organic," a government-approved certifier inspects the farm where the food item is grown to make sure the farming is following all the rules necessary to meet USDA organic standards. Food that is labeled "organic" according to the USDA may be advertised as such on the menu.

RELIGIOUS DIETARY RESTRICTIONS

Followers of certain branches of religions observe strict dietary rules. Kosher and halal diets are two common examples.

Kosher food is food prepared according to Jewish dietary laws. Ingredients including pork, rabbit, catfish, and any shellfish cannot be part of a kosher meal. Further, meat and dairy products cannot be paired or consumed together. Some restaurant and foodservice operations offer complete kosher meals, whereas others offer kosher food alternatives.

The word *halal* is Arabic, and it means lawful or permitted. Halal food items are those that are lawful or permitted under Muslim dietary laws. While most food items are considered halal, there are exceptions:

- Swine or pork and its by-products
- Animals improperly slaughtered or dead before slaughtering
- Alcoholic drinks and intoxicants
- Carnivores (meat-eating animals), birds of prey, and certain other animals
- Food contaminated with any of the previously listed products
- Some food items that contain gelatin, enzymes, emulsifiers, and flavoring ingredients if their origin is not known

As with serving kosher items, managers wishing to offer halal food items must ensure their menu items do, in fact, meet specific requirements. Managers not familiar with kosher or halal food items are well advised to consult with an expert to ensure that their menu items meet these requirements.

FOOD ALLERGIES

Food allergies occur when the body mistakes an ingredient in food—usually a protein—as harmful and creates a defense system (antibodies) to fight it. There is no known cure, and the only way to prevent an allergic reaction is to avoid the food that causes it.

When a person eats a food to which he or she is allergic, reactions can begin quickly and include swelling of the lips, tongue, and throat; difficulty breathing; hives; abdominal cramps; vomiting; and diarrhea. Symptoms can range from mild to severe, and reactions can occur within a few minutes to up to two hours after eating the offending food.

When persons with food allergies dine away from home, they rely on service staff to provide accurate ingredient information about the operation's menu items so they can make informed selection decisions. Inaccurate or incomplete information puts these customers at risk for an allergic reaction, can end their dining experience, and may require ambulance transport to the hospital.

Education, cooperation, and teamwork are keys to safely serving a customer with food allergies. Although an individual could be allergic to any food, eight food items account for 90 percent of all food-allergic reactions:

- Peanuts
- Fish
- Shellfish
- Milk
- Tree nuts
- Soy
- Eggs
- Wheat

OPEN FOR BUSINESS

WHAT'S THE FOOTPRINT?

In addition to health and perceived safety issues, many guests who prefer organic food are concerned about the environment and are willing to pay higher prices for organically grown food. These guests choose organic food, in part, because they feel they are grown in ways that minimize the use of chemicals such as some pesticides, fungicides, and herbicides.

While some restaurant and foodservice operations plan their entire menu around the use of organic food, many of which are locally grown, other operations provide increasing numbers of organic food choices to appeal to guests with this concern and to demonstrate the operation's interest in the environment.

Peanuts are the leading cause of severe allergic reactions in the United States, followed by shellfish, fish, tree nuts, and eggs. Some reports suggest that fish and shellfish are likely to be the leading cause of food allergy in adults. For some people, just a trace amount of the food can cause an allergic reaction.

Allergic reactions can occur in some persons when they consume very small and even invisible amounts of a problem food. This can happen when one food item comes in contact with another food item and their proteins mix. The contact may be direct, such as consuming milk that is an ingredient in a food. It can also be indirect and involve hands or utensils; for example, when a measuring tool is used for milk and then not washed before measuring an ingredient in a meal prepared for a customer with a milk allergy. Therefore, precautions must be taken to avoid cross-contact with food.

DESIGNING MENUS TO ACCOMMODATE DIETS

Managers who wish to design menus that assist health-conscious guests can do so in several ways:

1. **Place specific items in a separate section of the menu:** Some operations may use sections labeled "Heart-Healthy," "Lite Selections," or a similar heading to help guests find menu items that may be of special interest. It is important to note that the term "Heart-Healthy" is copyrighted by the American Heart Association, which has established restrictions for its use.

2. **Use a visual indicator to call out special items:** Some operations include special menu items with other items on the menu. In this case, managers mark the items with a color or symbol that suggests a special feature. For instance, a vegetable symbol might indicate vegetarian entrées.

3. **Make a general statement:** Some operations include a general statement on the menu such as "We recognize the nutritional and allergen concerns of our guests, and we can prepare some of our items to meet your unique needs. Please discuss your preferences with your server."

Exhibit 10.3

DESIGNING THE FOOD MENU

Some managers may think that a properly developed and designed menu is important for commercial operations, but less so for noncommercial ones. They reason that if a hotel or restaurant or foodservice establishment does not offer guests what the guests want, guests will select other dining alternatives. This is, of course, true. However, it can be just as true in noncommercial settings. For example, if workers in a hospital setting or office cafeteria (*Exhibit 10.3*) are not given attractive menu options, they may elect not to eat there, or even to bring their own lunch from home!

All restaurant and foodservice managers should understand the relationship of good menu design to effective marketing. This includes the psychology of menu layout and design principles and the steps managers should take when considering modifications of their current menus.

Relationship of Menu Design to Marketing

To begin planning a menu, managers must consider a variety of external factors that affect menu development. A menu for an establishment must be planned with an understanding of the marketing environment in which that establishment operates. There are several important environmental aspects to consider:

- Target market
- Competition
- Consumer trends

TARGET MARKET

An important first step in designing a menu is to identify the customers that the operation and its menu are designed to serve. The target market or target customers are guests with similar characteristics and similar demands of the marketplace. This group is most often identified using customer demographic information.

A large part of an establishment's success rests on its management's ability to target a large customer group. The particular characteristics of such a group are important when researching the target market. Factors to be considered include how often customers dine out, the price they are willing to pay, the ambience and type of service they want, the types of food they enjoy, and their proximity to the restaurant or foodservice operation.

COMPETITION

Another important factor to consider is the existence of other establishments competing for similar customers. Once competitors are identified, it is important to research their menu items and selling prices (see *Exhibit 10.4*).

If they are successful, managers will have a good idea of their target market's menu item preferences and pricing expectations. A manager might find it useful to provide similar offerings as his or her competitor. However, to capture some of this target market, the manager must consider how the menu he or she is planning will serve these customers better.

Exhibit 10.4

Example of two establishments vying for the same customers.

One way to attract customers is to offer a unique or signature menu item (see chapter 2). The signature item should be something that suits the character of the operation and comfortably fits with the rest of the menu. Another way to attract customers is to provide menu items similar to those offered by the competition, while setting and meeting higher standards for preparation, presentation, and service.

When examining the competition's menu, pricing is also important (see chapter 6). Remember that one of the reasons customers belong to a specified target market is the price they are willing to pay for the perceived value of the food and service they receive. To be competitive, prices on the planned menu should be similar to those of the competition.

CONSUMER TRENDS

Consumer trends affect the market environment for which a menu is planned. A desire for healthier eating is a long-term trend. Some diets are considered short-lived fads, but others are trends. For example, some consumers once considered low-fat and low-carb diets to be healthy, but both concepts are not as popular now as they used to be. A trend grows and may level off, but its related level of sales is held for a long period of time. As discussed in chapter 1, a fad grows rapidly but then peaks and declines quickly. It is important to distinguish between a fad and a trend because changing a menu may involve several things:

Exhibit 10.5

- Assessing the target customers' interest in the trend
- Investing in equipment not currently owned to properly prepare new items
- Testing and modifying recipes
- Retraining cooks to prepare new food items
- Redesigning the menu itself

Mistakenly treating a fad as a long-term trend could result in changes that have to be changed back when the fad is over. Every food trend must be assessed carefully prior to making a menu change.

For example, a long-term trend that appears to be sustaining interest is the popularity of Asian cuisine (*Exhibit 10.5*). This is actually a subcategory of the healthy eating trend because Asian fare is seen as very healthy. Adding Asian food items to a menu, however, should be done only after careful consideration since it has a large impact on the menu and its delivery. This is because Asian food preparation requires very different equipment and skills than those used in most Western operations. Sometimes adding a new type of food like Asian food does not fit the menu, the establishment's décor, or its brand image. Moreover, even though the popularity of Asian fare may be a long-term trend, the establishment's specific target market may not be interested in it.

Another consumer trend is that of families eating out due to increased numbers of working parents. This trend affects menus in three ways:

- Need for children's items, portions, prices, and menus
- Need for changes or additions to the décor or furnishings such as high chairs, booster seats, and other child-oriented items
- Need for menu items or full meals that can be heated and consumed at home

Managers should follow food trends carefully to ensure they are meeting their target customers' changing menu preferences and needs.

Menu Pricing Psychology

Recall from chapter 6 that managers can use a variety of different techniques when calculating menu prices. From a menu marketing perspective, managers generally choose from three different approaches when arriving at their final menu prices:

- Low-end value pricing
- Midrange value pricing
- Upscale value pricing

LOW-END VALUE PRICING

Value pricing—pricing products and services based on their worth in usefulness or importance to the buyer—is prevalent in the quick-service restaurant (QSR) segment of the industry. In the QSR market, prices tend to be under $10.00, and the most common ending digit for the price is "9," as in $2.99. This is because people tend to round the price down to the nearest dollar, or at least dime. So a $2.99 price is mentally thought of either as "above $2.00" or as "about $2.90."

The QSR market is highly competitive and the price-to-value perception is very important. Because of rising costs of ingredients, utilities, and labor, prices may have to be raised. Customers perceive breaking the dollar barrier as a large increase. If a menu item that was previously considered "above $2.00" is re-priced to "above $3.00," the higher perceived price may lead to a reduction in sales for that item.

If the price increase is necessary, it may be better to increase the price substantially than to increase it slightly. For example, $2.99 should be raised to $3.29 rather than $3.09. In the eyes of the customer, both prices are "above $3.00," but the profit to the operation is increased if the higher price is used.

Be aware of the overall range of pricing on a menu. Another expectation of customers in the QSR segment is that there is not a wide variation in price between the most and least expensive items.

MIDRANGE VALUE PRICING

Prices in the midrange market that includes the fast-casual and casual segments tend to end in "5" as often as in "9," such as $7.95 instead of $7.99. Customers typically perceive both of these prices as "above $7.00 and less than $8.00."

The challenge for managers in this pricing range becomes what to do if a price increase is necessary. If the items available on a menu are unique or differentiated in some way from the competition, then an increase in prices is not as harmful to sales. The recommendation in the market-driven case is for a manager to hold off increasing a price increase until his or her competitors have been forced to raise their prices on similar items. At that time the manager should increase the operation's own price substantially. This strategy may help recover profits lost before the price was raised.

UPSCALE VALUE PRICING

Prices for the upscale or fine-dining markets tend to end in 0, as in $17.00. Many operations elect to leave off the dollar sign, the decimal point, and the zeros, and list the menu price as "17" (for 17 dollars) at the end of the description of the product. This type of operation is also likely to offer a signature dish: one that is so unique or differentiated that there is no comparison price. In this style of establishment, price is considered part of the dining experience. When thinking about price, the customers consider the service, the quality of food, and the ambience. The perception of value in this situation is very different from those in other segments, although customers of all types have an expectation of value for the price.

Menu Layout and Design Principles

Menu planners must consider basic information before designing the menus for their operations. There are several commonly used types of menus:

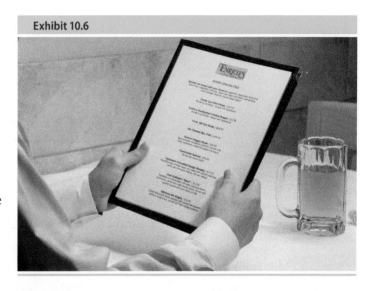

Exhibit 10.6

- **À la carte menu:** These menus have different prices for each menu item. The customer's charge is based on the prices of the items ordered (*Exhibit 10.6*).

- **Table d'hôte menu:** These menus offer an entire meal at a set price. Examples include banquet and buffet menus. Some establishments also set a price for an entire meal with a specified number of courses.

- Cyclical (cycle) menu: These menus are planned for a specified time period and then repeated. For example, a cafeteria may offer a 28-day menu that is repeated every four weeks.

- Du jour menu: A du jour menu changes daily. Many establishments offer daily specials in addition to their regular menu items.

Managers must consider menu length as they develop their menus. This is because the menu must inform customers about all available items. The focus on length reemphasizes the importance of carefully considering the target market's preferences as menus are planned.

Longer menus require more time for customer review and raise the possibility of more questions. More review and more questions slow the ordering process. While customers should be allowed the time they wish to dine, menus designed to sell recognize that table turns allow more customers to be served and additional revenues to be generated. Table turn refers to the number of times a dining-room table is occupied during a meal period.

When designing their menus, managers must realize that design tactics are important. There are several considerations that experienced menu designers follow:

- The menu must be attractive and present a good first impression. Managers should ask themselves if they are proud of their menu. Does it represent the establishment to customers in the most favorable way?

- The menu should not be cluttered; as a rule of thumb, approximately one-half of the space on a menu page should be blank.

- The print size used should be large enough to be read easily, with special consideration given to diners in all age groups.

- All words must be spelled correctly, with no hard-to-understand foreign terms.

- Menu item descriptions, not item selling prices, should be the focus of the reader's attention.

- Menus should be durable and easy to keep clean unless they are single-use menus.

SIZE AND SHAPE

The size and shape of the menu are important considerations. The size should be such that the customer can handle the menu easily. Customers frequently sit down to read the menu and then discuss its contents with other members of their party. Doing this is difficult if the menu is too large. If the establishment serves breakfast, lunch, and dinner, and the menu becomes too large, a separate menu for each meal will reduce the problem.

The most common menu shape is a single-fold menu: one that is hinged in the center like a book. Menus also could be a single page or a trifold in which the right and left panels fold over or meet in the center (see *Exhibit 10.7*).

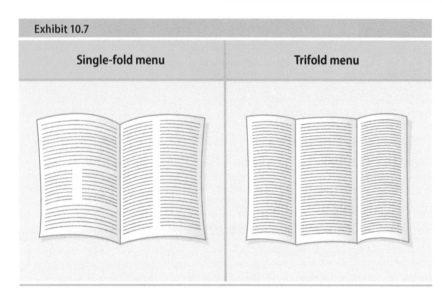

Exhibit 10.7

| Single-fold menu | Trifold menu |

MENU LAYOUT

Modern menus are important merchandising tools that emphasize specific items to encourage customers to select them. Menus must be thoughtfully developed to effectively communicate with customers and influence sales.

Menus that promote specific items use space wisely to describe menu items. Unique items need more space for description. Do not name an item like "Chef Randy's Garden Soup" unless it is described in detail. Otherwise, servers will require more time to explain the soup to customers. Simple ways to promote desired menu items include putting them in a box or using shading or a different font style. In some restaurant and foodservice industry segments, colored print or color photos of selected menu items are other strategies used by menu developers.

Menu layout relates to where items are placed on the menu. Normally, menu item classifications influence the layout. If appetizer, soup or salad, and entrée classifications have been identified, the layout must include space for these classifications.

Some menu designers place categories on the menu in the sequence of service. For example, appetizers are listed before soups and salads, which are listed before entrées. However, menus have prime real estate areas—those areas most frequently viewed by customers. These areas should contain the items that planners most want to sell. *Exhibit 10.8* shows prime real estate areas for some common menus.

TYPE SELECTION

Once managers have determined what categories of food items to offer, headings should be used to indicate these categories on the menu. The headings should be in at least 18-point type. Type size is the size of a letter or character, and is measured in "points," which are a unit of print measurement. There are 72 points per inch, so a 72-point letter would be 1 inch high.

The names of menu items are best printed in at least 12-point type whereas descriptions should be no less than 10-point type (see *Exhibit 10.9*). If the establishment's décor is such that it is quite dimly lit, the type sizes should be larger. Managers should also have available a large-print version of the menu for guests who are visually impaired. The use of too small a type size can result in numerous complaints from guests.

Additionally, the use of uppercase and lowercase letters adds to readability. Menu category headings can be done in all uppercase letters, as can the item names. If the item names are in a foreign language, do not use all uppercase letters because they may be difficult to interpret. The use of uppercase and lowercase letters in descriptions of the menu items also adds interest. In all cases, however, the type size used in the preparation of a menu should be easy for guests to read.

COLOR

The use of color on the menu can either contribute to readability or hinder it. Strong contrast should exist between the background paper and the printed copy. Black ink on white or very light cream-colored paper offers a good contrast and is easy to read. The use of other colors may support the brand identity, but they should be selected carefully.

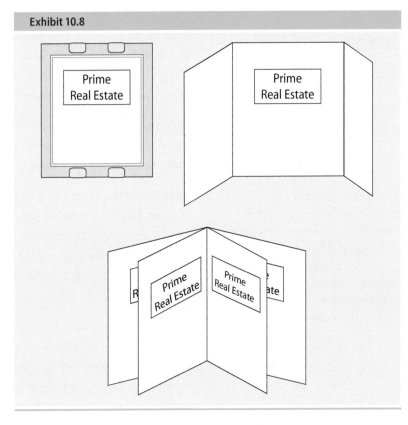

Exhibit 10.8

Prime Real Estate

Prime Real Estate

Prime Real Estate

Prime Real Estate

Exhibit 10.9

Examples of Type Sizes

10 point Helvetica

12 point Helvetica

18 point Helvetica

24 point Helvetica

Manager's Memo

Good menu planners avoid menu design errors. They know all menus must be easy to read and easy to understand. As a result, they design high-quality menus that help sell an operation's most popular and profitable items. They also ensure that the menu descriptions accurately represent the items that will be served. They know that good menu design allows customers to easily choose the items they want and to then get exactly what the operation has promised them.

WHITE SPACE

Consideration must also be given to the amount of space on a menu that is not used for menu copy. In fact, some experts indicate that approximately 50 percent of the menu should be blank space, which is also known as white space, even if the background is not white.

An empty margin around the edge of the paper provides white space. The space between menu items and within the description of each menu item contributes white space and is important to readability.

Leading is the term used to describe the vertical spacing between lines of type. Leading varies from 1 to 5 points in height. One-point leading would leave very little space between lines of type in the description, while 5-point leading would leave a larger amount of space between lines of type. Using 3-point leading is a good choice in most menu applications.

MENU ITEM DESCRIPTIONS

The terminology used on a menu is important for several reasons. Good menu item descriptions help sell menu items. In the past, menu writers used exaggeration or superlative words to describe menu items, such as "mounds of roast beef" or "the biggest salad in town" to sell the menu items. This often led to disgruntled customers, when what they actually received did not meet their expectations.

This issue prompted the National Restaurant Association in 1984 to issue truth-in-menu guidelines (also called accuracy-in-menu) designed to ensure that what was described on the menu matched what was actually served. The guidelines include five categories:

- Descriptions of quantity
- Accuracy in the use of quality indicators
- Use of brand names
- Product identification
- Product points of origin

Descriptions should be truthful and accurate. If a particular brand of barbecue sauce is used in the preparation of an item, then indicate that on the menu with a trademark sign, but always use that barbecue sauce. If the menu indicates that butter is served on certain vegetables, then it would be inaccurate for the cook to put margarine on those vegetables. If Idaho potatoes are listed, the potatoes must have been grown in Idaho. In other words, describing menu items one way and serving them in another contradicts the truth-in-menu guidelines, whether the error occurs in purchasing or production.

Descriptions are best if they use food-related words. Methods of preparation, such as grilled or char-grilled, can be used, but the item must then actually be grilled over an open flame (*Exhibit 10.10*). A recipe description should include a list of most, if not all, main ingredients used in the preparation of a dish.

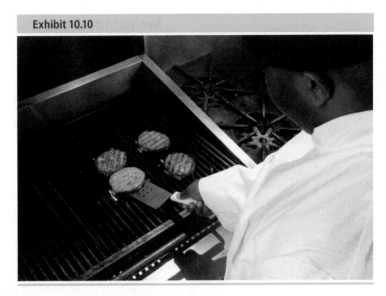

Exhibit 10.10

Describing the flavor components in an imaginative way can sell an item, but managers should also make clear to customers what is included in the preparation of the item. Be sure to list common allergens so people with allergies can avoid the item. Long descriptions take up space and may confuse the customer. A good menu item description is typically 25 words or less.

Remember that menu item descriptions answer potential questions of menu readers. For example, what should customers know about Seafood Fettuccine? Many customers may know that fettuccine is a pasta. However, what type of seafood and sauce is used in preparation? Customers may become annoyed if they must ask their server, and servers will have less time to provide the quality of service that other customers deserve.

Menu planners must consider these issues when writing menu descriptions:

- Write plainly. Avoid technical culinary terms and foreign words unless they are also described in plain English. For example, write *dumplings* instead of *quenelles* and *shredded vegetable garnish* instead of *chiffonade*, or use the foreign term followed by its English language description.

- Define menu items carefully and correctly. For example, New England clam chowder (white) is not the same as Manhattan clam chowder (red).

- Spell all words correctly, such as *portobello* mushrooms, *vinaigrette* dressing, and *au jus* (with natural juices).

- Write carefully. For example, only the last description is correct in the following list:

  - A salmon fillet served with a baked potato ladled with our special sauce

  - A salmon fillet ladled with our special sauce and baked potato

  - A salmon fillet ladled with our special sauce and served with a baked potato

- Review the description. All menu descriptions should be carefully reviewed by someone with a solid command of writing and editing skills.

Menu Modifications

After a menu has been in use for a while, the decision to change it might be made. There are several questions to be answered when making changes:

- Should a menu item be dropped?
- Does the new menu item have sales potential?
- Will the new item fit with the established menu in terms of production, price point, and brand?

Managers considering the addition of a new menu item should carefully go through a series of steps that will help them make good menu modification decisions.

STEP 1: ESTABLISH GOALS FOR THE NEW ITEM

The menu modification process includes the identification and selection of new items to be placed on the menu. This process must consider the target market—those customers whom the restaurant or foodservice operation intends to serve.

Managers considering the addition of a menu item must first address the question of whether the item will simply be added to the existing menu or if it will replace a currently listed item. This decision requires managers to consider the overall size of their menu. Is it to be a large, extensive menu or a more limited menu? Many managers try to maintain a balance between the two. The advantage of a limited menu is the savings in the amount of equipment, inventory, and storage space needed. A limited menu also requires less skilled labor and preparation time because production is simpler. In general, it is easier to control costs and quality with a limited menu. On the other hand, limited menus may make it more difficult to attract a large customer base.

Generally, a more extensive menu can attract a greater number of customers and can encourage regular customers to return because of the larger variety of choices available. An extensive menu, however, may require larger inventory, more storage, more highly skilled labor, more preparation time, more equipment, and a larger production space. In other cases, however, managers in some operations have very large menus but tend to use the same ingredients in a variety of different dishes to keep the size of their inventories down. An example would be a menu with 10 different kinds of burgers created with minor variations of accompaniments that are also used on chicken dishes or appetizers.

A second key consideration in adding a new menu item is whether it can be priced at a level high enough to produce the desired target profit margin. Every operation incurs costs in the production of its menu items. Every operation also has competition affecting the prices that it can charge. Some

Manager's Memo

In many cases a restaurant or foodservice operation's menu is not determined by the manager. This is the case, for example, when a single restaurant is part of a large group or chain of restaurants, each of which must offer the same menu items. Restaurant and foodservice professionals planning menus in central locations and for large numbers of units typically seek input from individual unit operators. Even when menus are planned centrally, however, the menu developers use the same good planning principles used by individual owners and managers who are free to choose their own menu items.

items can be produced and sold in such a way that enough profit is realized. That is not always the case. Even though a new menu item may be right for an operation and liked by customers, it might not be able to be produced at a cost low enough or sold at a price high enough to provide value for the customer and make a profit for the operation.

Menu size and cost are always two key issues to be addressed when considering menu additions. Additional measurable menu-related goals may be identified:

- Number of estimated sales of the new item
- Percentage of guests selecting the new item
- Impact on check average of including the new item
- Impact on total revenue of including the new item
- Number of first-time guests served due to the addition of the new item

Results from testing the proposed item can then be compared to the measurable goals initially set for it.

STEP 2: DETERMINE POSSIBLE NEW MENU ITEMS

If the decision is made to consider the addition of a new menu item, management turns its attention to the specific questions that must be addressed prior to brainstorming all of the possible new menu items. These questions typically address a variety of issues:

- Time of day and the items commonly served at that time
- Cuts of meat, fish, and poultry available within the establishment's cost limitations
- Equipment and other capabilities of the kitchen
- Skills and motivations of the cooking and serving staff
- Preparation techniques available for use
- Variety of the menu items in regard to color, texture, and flavor
- Nutritional value of the menu items
- Food tastes and interests of customers as determined by market research or experience
- Reputation and brand of the establishment
- Desires of the customers for speed and convenience versus atmosphere and luxury

Managers can use these questions to select viable alternatives from the list generated in the menu item brainstorming session.

STEP 3: ESTABLISH A FORMAL TESTING SYSTEM

Experienced managers know that simply making a new menu item that is tasted and then liked by the chef or manager is not a good way to determine if the item should actually be placed on the menu. A proposed menu addition should "pass" a formal test before becoming a potential menu addition.

It is the job of the manager to determine the factors used in the test. While taste would certainly be one important concern, there will be others. For example, consideration may have to be given to the available capacity of the kitchen production station that will be responsible for producing the new item. If the kitchen staff is already overloaded at the sauté station, for instance, adding a new sautéed item to the menu will have a negative impact on production. Or, if the new item requires more production resources, all other work may have to slow down to accommodate it.

Similarly, a major change in the menu offerings may require the purchase and installation of a new piece of equipment to prepare the item. In addition to the budget impact of the new equipment purchase, it may be a challenge finding the new equipment an appropriate place in the production line.

Many pieces of cooking equipment need electricity, gas, water, or drainpipe connections; some require several connections. A hood to remove smoke and odors from a new piece of equipment may be necessary. The addition of a menu item may quite literally rearrange the whole kitchen!

The criteria managers use to establish a "passing" score will vary based on the menu item under evaluation. To determine the passing score managers can choose from a variety of menu item characteristics:

• Appearance	• Ease of preparation
• Taste	• Preparation time
• Smell	• Cost
• Popularity	• Proposed selling price

Each of the characteristics selected can be assessed and an appropriate score (for example, on a scale from 1 to 10) can be assigned to each characteristic by each menu item evaluator. The menu item's achieved score on each criterion can then be summed to identify the items that scored the highest. Whatever the criteria used, managers should know of them ahead of time and then apply them to each menu alternative being evaluated.

STEP 4: IDENTIFY, TEST, AND REFINE ALTERNATIVES

After new menu addition alternatives have been identified, they must be tested and refined. If the proposed item can be produced within the operation efficiently, is within cost parameters, and fits the brand, then it should be evaluated for sales potential.

An important first step in this process is to have the staff try each new item. In most cases, if servers like it, they will be enthusiastic in selling it. Service personnel will also need to be trained to identify, describe, and answer customer questions about the new menu item if it is to be effectively sold.

If the cooks like it and can produce it efficiently, they will prepare it to the best of their ability. If the menu items are too difficult to produce, cooks may become frustrated or less motivated to perform their duties well.

STEP 5: CONDUCT CONSUMER FIELD TESTS

After the production staff and waitstaff have refined an item's preparation and service, it is ready to be served to guests. Many managers suggest promoting sales of the new item by listing it on a POP table tent card or POS promotional display. Also, they have servers actively sell it by suggesting it to their customers. Managers can also provide servers with an incentive to sell the new item during a test period of a predetermined length.

STEP 6: EVALUATE TEST RESULTS

After the test item has been sold, formally assess guests' reactions to it. Ask for customer comments either verbally or through a feedback card. Or, carefully examine and then record the average amount of the item remaining on guests' plates returned to the kitchen.

In most cases, the new item should be tested on customers more than once. Different customers have different likes and dislikes. Many experts suggest that if 60 percent or more of the customers say they like the item and would order it again, it can be considered a good potential addition to the menu.

STEP 7: CHOOSE A COURSE OF ACTION

The final decision to include or exclude a menu item often depends on more than customer tastes and preferences. It may also depend on whether the item can be priced to meet the targeted profit margin and price point category the establishment uses. Successfully executing a menu also must take into account operating efficiency and staff capability.

Each goal established for the item in step 1 of the process should be carefully assessed prior to making a final determination. If the item meets the identified goals, it should be added. If it does not, it should be rejected in favor of a stronger alternative.

DESIGNING THE BEVERAGE MENU

Offering alcoholic beverages to customers is an integral part of the dining experience at many establishments. Many customers regard it as an enjoyable accompaniment to their food. If it is in keeping with the character of the establishment, pairing items from the food and alcoholic beverage menus that complement each other can enhance customers' dining experiences.

Offering alcoholic beverage service also plays a very important role in the profitability of an operation. It comes as no surprise, then, that managers want to create beverage menus that effectively market alcoholic beverages to their guests.

The types of alcoholic beverages served in a particular operation depend on the type of liquor license issued to the establishment, the customers' expectations, the types of food offered, the brand image, and the establishment's costs. Most states separate liquor licenses into different categories:

- Beer only
- Beer and wine
- Beer, wine, and spirits

An important role of the beverage menu is to make customers aware that the establishment serves alcoholic beverages. The alcoholic beverages offered and the look of the beverage menu should support the theme of the establishment or type of food offered.

Alcoholic beverages may be included on the food menu if they are few in number. Sometimes they are listed on a separate page; in other instances, they are listed in a separate section. It is recommended that space on the food menu be used to offer house-specialty alcoholic beverages that are profitable.

An alcoholic beverage–only menu can be used if the establishment wants to merchandise a larger selection of alcoholic beverages, in which case it is recommended that the most profitable house specialties are featured and positioned prominently. If the wine inventory is very small, a few featured bottles of wine might make up a display in the dining room or occupy a set-off block on the food menu. If there is a more extensive wine inventory, a separate wine list, a special menu that includes only wines and their prices, is a good way to merchandise wines. Some operations with extensive wine selections also use a sommelier (the French term for the wine steward or the person responsible for wine in an establishment) to suggest and serve wines to guests.

In designing a wine list (see *Exhibit 10.11*), some decisions have to be made about the wines that will be offered. Those decisions are made within the context of the brand image of the establishment, the type of dining being offered, the customers' expectations, and the types of food appearing on the menu.

Another decision concerns whether wines will be offered and priced by the glass, the bottle, or some combination of both (see *Exhibit 10.12*). Once these decisions have been made, the design of the wine list can begin.

There is no single correct way to prepare a wine list; instead, there are a variety of ways. There are even model wine lists available to managers from a variety of sources. A manager's wine distributor can be helpful in making suggestions about the design of a wine list. The final decision about its format, however, should be based on what managers wish to emphasize and the level of information desired by guests. In most cases, wine lists will include all or some of the following information:

- Grape variety

- Vintner or producer

- Geographic origin

- Vintage (year bottled)

- Price

- Description of the wine's characteristics

- Description of broad food categories that go well with the wine (e.g., beef, poultry, or fish)

- Description of particular dishes or specific food preparations the wine complements

Managers designing wine, beer, and spirits menus or including beverage item descriptions on their regular menus should follow the same basic principles used in food menus. All beverage menus should meet these criteria:

- It is clean and easily readable.

- It is consistent with the operation's image and brand.

- It lists individual drink or bottle prices in an easy to understand manner.

- It is accurate and truthful.

- It uses prime real estate effectively.

Exhibit 10.11

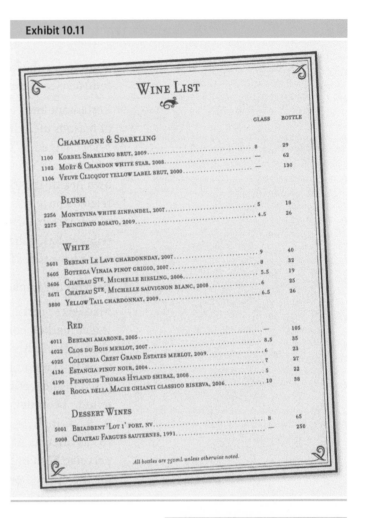

		GLASS	BOTTLE
CHAMPAGNE & SPARKLING			
1100	KORBEL SPARKLING BRUT, 2009	8	29
1102	MOËT & CHANDON WHITE STAR, 2008	—	62
1106	VEUVE CLICQUOT YELLOW LABEL BRUT, 2000	—	130
BLUSH			
2256	MONTEVINA WHITE ZINFANDEL, 2007	5	18
2275	PRINCIPATO ROSATO, 2009	4.5	26
WHITE			
3601	BERTANI LE LAVE CHARDONNDAY, 2007	9	40
3605	BOTTEGA VINAIA PINOT GRIGIO, 2007	8	32
3606	CHATEAU STE. MICHELLE RIESLING, 2006	5.5	19
3671	CHATEAU STE. MICHELLE SAUVIGNON BLANC, 2008	6	25
3800	YELLOW TAIL CHARDONNAY, 2009	6.5	26
RED			
4011	BERTANI AMARONE, 2005	—	105
4022	CLOS DU BOIS MERLOT, 2007	8.5	35
4025	COLUMBIA CREST GRAND ESTATES MERLOT, 2009	6	23
4136	ESTANCIA PINOT NOIR, 2004	7	27
4190	PENFOLDS THOMAS HYLAND SHIRAZ, 2008	5	22
4802	ROCCA DELLA MACIE CHIANTI CLASSICO RISERVA, 2006	10	38
DESSERT WINES			
5001	BRIADBENT 'LOT 1' PORT, NV	8	65
5008	CHATEAU FARGUES SAUTERNES, 1991	—	250

All bottles are 750mL unless otherwise noted.

Exhibit 10.12

Increasing numbers of establishments offer quality wines by the glass and by the bottle to optimize wine sales and their guests' dining experiences.

SUMMARY

1. **Summarize the key factors that influence customers' restaurant or foodservice menu selections.**

   Restaurant and foodservice guests order their menu selections for a variety of reasons including taste, portion size, and method of preparation. The price charged by the establishment will also have a big impact on a guest's willingness to buy a specific item. Finally, many customers consider their own health-related concerns before choosing a specific menu item. Health-related concerns may be about the levels of fat, sodium, or the total number of calories in a dish. Some customers observe vegetarian, organic, or religion-based diets that affect menu choice. Still other guests may avoid items because of food allergies.

2. **Explain the impact of customer psychology on menu development.**

   Managers creating menus must consider three external factors: target market, competition, and consumer trends. Managers generally choose from three different psychological approaches when arriving at their final menu prices. These are low-end value pricing, midrange value pricing, and upscale value pricing. In low-end value pricing, menu prices tend to be under $10.00, and the most common ending digit for the price is "9," as in $2.99. In midrange pricing, menu item prices tend to end in "5" as often as in "9," such as $7.95 instead of $7.99. Customers typically perceive both of these prices as "above $7.00 and less than $8.00." Prices for the upscale or fine-dining markets tend to end in 0, as in $17.00. Many managers leave off the dollar sign, the decimal point, and the zeros, and list the menu price as "17" (for 17 dollars) at the end of the description of the product.

3. **Outline the principles of effective menu layout and design.**

   Managers know that the menus themselves must be attractive and reflect favorably on the operation. Menus should be uncluttered and be easy to read. Approximately one-half of the space on a menu page should be blank (white space). Menus should be durable and easy to clean unless they have been designed for one-time use.

   The menu should be written in a way that is grammatically correct and all words should be spelled properly. There should be no hard-to-understand terms. Finally, the menu should emphasize descriptions of the menu items to be sold rather than the prices charged.

4. **Describe the process managers use when deciding if a new item should be added to a menu.**

When managers determine that it is time to consider an addition to their existing menus, they go through a series of steps designed to help ensure the new item's success. The first step is to establish revenue, unit sales, or other goals for the item. Alternative menu items are then assessed and a formal testing system is put in place. Managers test and refine their chosen alternatives, a process that includes serving the item to customers. Based on customer feedback and their own assessments of the item's ability to achieve its goals, managers then make the decision to add, or not to add, the new item to the existing menu.

5. **Explain how to design a professional beverage menu.**

To a large degree, managers designing wine, beer, and spirits menus follow the same basic principles used in food menus. Like food menus, beverage menus should be clean and easy to read. The look of the menus should be consistent with the operation's image and brand. Beverage menus should list individual drink or bottle prices in a clear manner, and use effective layout principles to optimize sales. While beverage menus such as wine lists may be brief or very detailed, these menus, like all beverage menus, should always be truthful and accurate.

APPLICATION EXERCISE

You plan the menu for your establishment, which is busy and profitable. However, you have received several comment cards in the last month from regulars asking you to offer a few healthier menu items. You have decided to look at two menu offerings to determine how they might be changed to meet your customers' changing preferences.

1. Describe three changes you could make to each menu offering to increase its appeal to health-conscious customers.

a. Southern Fried Chicken: One-half chicken, deep-fried and served with whipped potatoes, creamy gravy, and southern-style green beans with bacon and onions

b. Lasagna: Made with Italian sausage, four kinds of cheese, and egg noodles, and served with freshly baked white bread and Caesar salad

2. How would the changes you recommend affect the prices you will charge for these modified menu items?

3. How would the changes you recommend affect the manner in which you would market these items?

REVIEW YOUR LEARNING

Select the best answer for each question.

1. **Which types of food are considered kosher?**
   A. Food prepared according to Jewish dietary laws
   B. Food low in sodium and dietary cholesterol
   C. Food prepared for lacto-vegetarians
   D. Food items that are low in cost

2. **The concerns of which group are of most importance when designing an establishment's menu?**
   A. The establishment's owners
   B. The establishment's managers
   C. The establishment's employees
   D. The establishment's target market

3. **What is the greatest danger in modifying an establishment's operation and menu to include a fad food?**
   A. Guest satisfaction will decline.
   B. Employees must learn new skills.
   C. Managers must calculate a new menu price for the added item.
   D. Costs incurred will be wasted when interest in the menu item fades.

4. **When using a value-pricing approach, in which restaurant or foodservice market segment would there be the smallest variation between an operation's highest- and lowest-priced menu items?**
   A. QSR
   B. Casual
   C. Fast casual
   D. Fine dining

5. **Which restaurant or foodservice operation would be most likely to use a cyclical menu?**
   A. Sandwich shop
   B. College cafeteria
   C. Upscale steakhouse
   D. Carryout pizza parlor

6. **What is the minimum type point size recommended for easy reading of items listed on a menu?**
   A. 10
   B. 12
   C. 36
   D. 72

7. **How much of a menu should be blank space?**
   A. 10%
   B. 35%
   C. 50%
   D. 75%

8. **A proposed new menu item is popular with customers. What is a reason for a manager deciding against putting this new item on the menu?**
   A. Its cost of production is too low.
   B. Its selling price would be too high.
   C. Its preparation time would be too short.
   D. Its cost of production cannot be accurately determined.

9. **How can managers best optimize the sale of wines and their guests' dining experiences?**
   A. Offer only wines by the glass.
   B. Offer only wines by the bottle.
   C. Offer wines by the glass and bottle.
   D. Offer midpriced wines by the bottle and high-priced wines by the glass.

10. **What term, when used on wine lists, identifies the year in which a wine is bottled?**
    A. Varietal
    B. Vintage
    C. Variety
    D. Vintner

FIELD PROJECT

Obtain a menu from each of three operations that offer similar menu items. Suggestions include QSR operations serving similar food (e.g., burgers, chicken, or subs), campus dining outlets, pizza parlors, or steakhouses.

Choose five menu items offered by each operation and address the following questions for each of the items you have chosen for evaluation.

1. Which operation does the best job of describing the menu item? Why?
2. Which operation charges least for the menu item?
3. Which operation charges most for the menu item?
4. Which operation will likely sell this item to the largest number of its customers? Why?
5. Which operation does the best job of producing its menu? Why?

11 | Evaluating the Marketing Effort

INSIDE THIS CHAPTER

- Evaluating the Marketing Effort
- Evaluating the Impact of Marketing on Guest Purchases
- Assessing Product Quality
- Assessing Service Quality
- Measuring Marketing Returns on Investment (ROIs)

CHAPTER LEARNING OBJECTIVES

After completing this chapter, you should be able to:

- Identify the areas managers assess when evaluating their marketing efforts.

- List the tools managers use to evaluate the impact of marketing on guest purchases.

- Describe the main methods managers use to assess product quality.

- Describe the key areas managers evaluate when assessing service quality.

- Explain the importance of assessing marketing-related return on investment (ROI).

KEY TERMS

hard data, p. 287

menu mix, p. 272

mise en place, p. 281

payback period, p. 287

payback ratio, p. 287

return on investment (ROI), p. 286

sales dollar percentage, p. 273

sales volume, p. 272

sales volume percentage, p. 273

secondary sales, p. 271

secret shopper, p. 281

soft data, p. 288

total contribution margin, p. 276

variance, p. 267

CASE STUDY

"You know, this is really hard," exclaims Peggy, the manager at the Wagon Wheel Family restaurant. "And it's frustrating!"

"What's hard and frustrating?" asks Casey, the assistant manager.

Casey and Peggy are in Peggy's office working on the marketing plan that will be put in place next year at the Wagon Wheel.

"Creating the marketing budget for next year is frustrating," Peggy explains. "We spent a ton of money for advertising and promotions last year."

"I know, but business is good. We spent a ton of money on food and labor, too. So what's the problem?"

"Well, that's the whole thing," says Peggy, "I know we need food and our staff, but I actually suspect half our marketing budget might just be wasted."

"And so?" asks Casey.

"And so . . . that's the problem," interrupts Peggy, "I don't think I know which half!"

1. Why is it important that Peggy know which of her advertising-related costs actually contribute to the success of the establishment?

2. What will likely happen if Peggy cannot develop an effective way to assess whether each of her marketing-related expenses is good for business?

EVALUATING THE MARKETING EFFORT

An effective marketing plan is management's best attempt at planning how to attract customers from its target market, how to please those customers with products and services, and how to deliver these products and services in a consistent and profitable way. At the end of every marketing plan or element within it, managers should examine the extent to which they achieved their goals so they can benefit from their mistakes and successes. Managers must evaluate their marketing efforts.

First, they must assess the overall success of their marketing plans. External and internal marketing factors contribute to the success of the plan. Managers look at these factors to understand why things worked out the way they did. They also determine what they may want to do differently in the future.

After evaluating their plans, they evaluate the key elements of their operations. This evaluation helps them identify areas that may need improvement to support their marketing plans. After they have carefully evaluated their operations, they will know how successful their past marketing investments were and where best to invest in the future.

Evaluation of both the plan and the operation should begin as soon as the deadline date for the marketing plan or activity has passed. Managers consider a variety of issues when assessing whether their marketing-related goals were achieved:

- What helped achieve the goal?
- Were there any internal factors (elements managers could control and improve) such as the following that contributed to the success:
    - Knowledgeable staff
    - Great-tasting products at the right price
    - New menu items
    - Excellent service
- Were there any external factors (elements outside the operation and that the manager could not control) such as these that contributed to the success:
    - Good economy
    - Successful local events
    - Results of local elections
    - Improved or resolved national situations
    - Increased interest in sporting events
    - Increased interest in community-related activities
    - Holidays, celebrations, or seasonal factors

Managers must consider additional points if it is determined that a marketing goal was not met. First, they need to find out the primary reason why the goal was not met. They must determine if there were any internal or external factors that contributed to not meeting the goal. *Exhibit 11.1* provides some examples of the types of internal and external factors that may occur.

Exhibit 11.1

FACTORS THAT CAN CAUSE A FAILURE TO REACH MARKETING GOALS

Internal Factors	External Factors
Improper food preparation, especially for a new, unfamiliar menu item	Depressed economy
Excessive delay between food preparation and serving	Major local layoff
Unmotivated staff	Negative publicity not caused by the operation like a widely reported health or food supply scare
Wrong products served	Severe weather such as heat wave, rainstorm, or slippery roads
Products priced incorrectly	
Poor customer service	Natural disasters such as hurricanes or floods
Ineffective promotional strategy or implementation	Threats to public safety including terrorism or a crime wave
Shortage or absence of supplies	
Faulty or out-of-service equipment	

Once the marketing evaluation phase is completed, it is important for managers to use the information they have obtained to identify how to improve the success of their businesses. For example, if an operation fell short of its goal of increasing the amount spent per guest, the manager will need to determine the cause, and then decide what can be done about it.

To illustrate, assume that after the evaluation of a specific menu item promotion, a manager realized that the staff did not sell as many of the menu items as planned. There may be many reasons why the operation did not meet its sales goals:

- The servers had never tried any of the menu items, and felt uncomfortable trying to sell items with which they were unfamiliar. One way to improve this situation would be a two-phase training program for the servers. The first phase is to have them work with the chef when

Exhibit 11.2

deciding which items are being promoted and having the servers taste each product so they become familiar with them. The second phase is to work with the servers on selling techniques that will increase sales of the products (*Exhibit 11.2*).

- The menu items were not prepared, held, plated, and served at the desired quality level. In this case, the solution might be improved training of the kitchen staff that includes a description of the menu items, their preparation, their shelf life, the labor requirements for their preparation, and the look of the plate presentations.

- The menu items were not explained clearly. As a result, customers ended up believing that they contained unpopular ingredients or allergens. In this case, more nutritional information might be provided on the menu or on table tents.

- The length of the promotion was not understood by staff or customers. As a result, food items were not available when customers thought they should be. The solution would be to improve communication of the promotion, so staff and customers clearly understand the beginning and ending dates of the promotion.

- The manager did not correctly estimate how difficult the promoted items were to prepare, how long they took to prepare, or how many employees were required to create them. This caused excessive delay between the items being ordered and served. In this case, the manager must improve his or her forecasting skills and, in the future, involve more people in the planning process so that estimates will be more accurate.

There are many reasons why marketing efforts can go wrong, and many reasons why they can go right. Managers should evaluate what has happened in their own operations. They need to determine how to fix the things that went wrong, or how to repeat the things that went right. That is how they can improve their marketing skills and their operational profitability.

Typically, any shortfalls or variation from a manager's marketing plan will be due to both uncontrollable external factors and controllable internal factors. Managers must take note of the uncontrollable external elements that helped or hindered their marketing plans so they can correctly incorporate them into the next plan. This is an opportunity to learn from experience. Likewise, they must determine what improvements are needed in the areas they can control so they can improve them as needed.

As has been mentioned previously, establishing marketing goals and standards are very important for increasing the profitability of a restaurant or foodservice establishment. Evaluating goals to see what worked and what did not will help make an operation more efficient and profitable. Proper evaluation helps managers minimize the chances of repeating the same mistake over and over again. Evaluating successes will also enable them to target their resources toward those marketing-related areas that can grow their businesses and make them even stronger.

Managers must always invest in marketing their businesses to get them started and to make them grow. The question is *not* whether or not to invest. Instead, there are questions surrounding how much to invest, in what areas to invest, and what benefits will be gained from the investment. The answers to these questions allow managers to better design the next marketing and operations plans.

To start, many managers break their assessments into several categories. Begin the marketing evaluation process by assessing each of the key marketing areas:

- Personal selling
- Advertising
- Publicity
- Public relations
- Promotions (external and internal)

Personal Selling

Recall from chapter 9 that personal selling can be one of a manager's most effective marketing tools. Some managers have difficulty developing an effective assessment program for the personal sales effort because of the nature of the activity. For example, in a very weak market, even a highly qualified manager may have difficulty selling special events. Similarly, service employees may have difficulty achieving suggestive selling goals. On the other hand, in a very strong market even managers and staff who are minimally qualified may achieve significant sales levels.

Results such as total sales volume generated and sales leads converted to sales are important criteria for assessing the selling effort. However, the number of personal selling activities undertaken can be just as important. Managers can

REAL MANAGER

EVALUATING THE MARKETING EFFORT

When I first started Patrick Henry Creative Promotions, Inc., one of my earliest successful promotions was for Bobby McGee's Restaurants. It had 18 locations and was looking for a promotion that would drive the beverage business. At the time, Corona Beer was extremely popular so I thought a promotion tied to Corona would drive beverage sales.

I implemented "The Corona Club" on Thursday nights at all locations. Customers could purchase a Corona for $0.87 (the year was 1987) from 6:00 p.m. until 10:00 p.m. Little did I realize just how popular Corona was, and in the first few weeks, locations were experiencing lines out the door. The Honolulu location actually sold more than 40 cases in one night. Bobby McGee's became the place to be on Thursdays. The promotion was over a three-month period and not only did it draw a great crowd, but we found out that wine and liquor sales increased simply from the increase in guests. The guests were ordering more items than Corona and overall beverage sales increased by 20%.

We noticed shortly after our successful Corona Club night that other venues implemented the same promotion, which we felt was a great compliment for what we had created at Bobby McGee's.

compare the number of planned activities in the marketing plan to the number of activities actually completed. *Exhibit 11.3* is an example of a tool managers might use to make assessments of this type.

Exhibit 11.3			
PERSONAL SELLING GOALS VERSUS ACTUAL ACTIVITIES			
Sales Staff Member *Lars Hulstadt*			
Personal Selling Activity	**Goal per Marketing Plan**	**Actual Completed Activity**	**Manager Comments**
Monthly personal phone calls to prospects	20 per month	18	
Monthly in-person sales calls to prospects	10 per month	2	Review steps in making sales call appointments and follow up.
Monthly personal phone calls to members of frequent dining programs	20 per month	22	
Attendance at chamber of commerce monthly meeting	12 per year	11	
Attendance at local restaurant association chapter monthly meeting	12 per year	12	
Service on local "Mayor's Task Force for Tourism"	Yes	Yes	

In this example, the sales staff member seeking to expand selling opportunities is achieving relatively good results in all areas except in-person sales calls. This is so despite the fact that Lars is attending many community-wide meetings like chamber of commerce and restaurant association meetings that would likely result in in-person sales opportunities.

In this case, the manager should review with Lars the steps required to set sales appointments and follow up on in-person sales opportunities. The manager's feedback, which includes comments and opinions about the situation, may help Lars overcome problems in this area. This review also affords Lars the chance to provide feedback to the manager. This feedback may result in changes to Lars's personal selling goals in the next year's marketing plan.

Advertising

Recall from chapter 8 that effective managers set measurable objectives for their advertising programs. They also use practical tools to measure the results. For example, the objective of a radio ad might be to increase sales by 5 percent over the previous monthly average. This objective is measurable, unlike a more subjective one that seeks to simply increase business. Objective measurements give managers the information necessary to determine whether they have achieved their advertising goals.

Note that most managers do not have the budgets, expertise, or time to conduct detailed analysis of their advertising efforts. Instead, their measurement tools are practical ones that are easily applied, such as customer counts or number of menu items sold. Therefore, managers assessing advertising efforts should take the following steps to determine whether their advertising program is positively affecting the operation's financial goals:

1. Review specific and measurable advertising objectives included in the marketing plan.

2. Apply appropriate measurement tools such as the following:

   • Number of items sold

   • Changes in number of items sold

   • Changes in reservations made

   • Increases in revenue

   • Total revenue

   • New customers

3. Assess any differences between planned and actual results.

When assessing advertising effectiveness, managers may wish to evaluate changes in the actual amount of sales achieved or the number of customers served. In other cases, they may be more interested in the percentage differences between planned results and actual results in these same areas.

Variances, which are the differences between planned results and actual results, are easy to calculate. Managers use this formula:

Actual results − Planned results = Variance

These variances can be positive (favorable) or negative (unfavorable). To illustrate, consider an example where the manager had planned for $11,000 in sales, but achieved only $10,000 during the stated time period. In this case, the variance would be unfavorable:

$$\$10,000 - \$11,000 = -\$1,000$$

In this example, there is a negative (unfavorable) revenue variance because the manager estimated that the establishment would generate more revenue than it actually did. Some managers use parentheses to express a negative variance. For example, they would write ($1,000) rather than −$1,000 when expressing a negative variance of $1,000.

Note how the formula works when calculating a favorable variance. Assume that the same manager had planned for $10,000 in revenue, but actually achieved $11,000 during that time period:

$$\$11,000 - \$10,000 = \$1,000$$

In this example, there is a positive (favorable) revenue difference because the actual amount of revenue generated was greater than the amount planned.

Managers sometimes talk about variances in dollar figures. At other times, they may discuss variances in terms of a percentage difference. Variances can be calculated as a percentage difference using the following equation:

(Actual results − Planned results) ÷ Planned results = % variance

In this example:

$$(\$11,000 - \$10,000) \div \$10,000 = \% \text{ variance}$$

Or

$$\$1,000 \div \$10,000 = 0.1$$

By multiplying the resulting number by 100, managers can convert to another, but identical percentage form.

$$0.1 \times 100 = 10\%$$

To further illustrate, consider that a manager had planned for 9,500 customers in a given week, but actually serviced 10,450 customers in that time period. The percentage variance for this example is calculated as follows:

$$(\$10,450 - \$9,500) \div \$9,500 = 10\% \text{ variance}$$

In this example, the restaurant or foodservice operation generated a 10 percent positive (favorable) difference in weekly customer count because the actual weekly count was 10 percent greater than planned.

Exhibit 11.4 is one example of a tool managers might use to assess the effectiveness of planned advertising activities. Sample ad activities and their assessments are included for illustration purposes.

Remember that the goal of any advertising program assessment is to demonstrate the direct impact of advertising on sales and profitability. Managers can then duplicate successful efforts and modify less successful programs in the future.

MANAGER'S MATH

Stephanie created an advertising campaign designed to increase her weekly customer counts by 10 percent over last year's weekly customer counts. She carefully maintained records of her customer counts last year, her forecast for this year, and her actual results in the following table.

Last Year's Actual Customer Count	Planned Results (Forecast) Customer Count	This Year's Actual Customer Count	% Variance (Compared to Last Year)
573	630	641	

1. What is the difference in the number of customers Stephanie served per week this year compared to last year?

2. What is the percentage difference in the number of customers Stephanie served per week this year compared to last year?

3. Assume all of the changes in customer counts could be directly attributed to the ad campaign Stephanie initiated last year. Did Stephanie achieve the goal she had established for this advertising effort?

(Answers: 1. 68; 2. 11.8%; 3. Yes)

Exhibit 11.4

MARKETING PLAN ADVERTISEMENT ASSESSMENT

For Year 2012

Planned Advertising Activity	Goal	Actual Results	Variance	Manager Comments
Activity #1: Run newspaper coupon ad introducing new Mahi Mahi Taco dinner.	Redeem 100 coupons per week	Redeemed 115 coupons per week	15% favorable	Very good ad campaign. Duplicate it in the future.
Activity #2: Promote adult Halloween costume party advertised via six 30-second radio ad spots.	200 attendees	75 attendees	−62.5% unfavorable	Minimal attendance. Consider increasing external marketing efforts, using alternative advertising sources, or eliminating this activity next year.
Activity #3:				
Activity #4:				
Activity #5:				
Activity #6:				

Publicity

Recall from chapter 9 that unlike advertising, publicity is free but a manager cannot directly control its content. As a result, publicity can be good or bad. Managers, of course, want to generate as much good publicity about their establishments as possible. Managers also want to minimize the amount of bad publicity they receive. In the event that negative publicity does occur, managers want to be able to minimize its negative impact to the greatest degree possible.

To assess the effectiveness of their publicity-related efforts, managers can do the following:

- Count the number of publicity-generating events sponsored by the operation during the period covered in the marketing plan

- Count the number of publicity-generating events the operation participated in during the period covered in the marketing plan

- Count the number of times the operation is mentioned positively in the press typically followed by the operation's target market

- Count the number of times the operation is mentioned negatively in the press typically followed by the operation's target market

- Assess the amount of effort devoted to establishing and maintaining good relationships with local media representatives

Public Relations

Publicity is free, but without newsworthy activities, an operation will be unlikely to attract the attention of the news media. Public relations activities are those that can help initiate positive publicity. Effective public relations efforts can have the following impacts on a business:

1. Build name recognition by undertaking activities that result in favorable mentions in the media

2. Enhance trustworthiness by having those in the media deliver positive comments about the operation, because readers trust news outlets more than paid advertising

3. Lower advertising costs because public relations activities can be undertaken at a lower price than paid advertising

Managers can also assess the effectiveness of any PR campaigns called for in the marketing plan. If the campaign was effective, it will have met the goals established for it in the operation's plan. If it has not been effective, it will not likely have met those goals.

Promotions

Recall that sales promotions are short-term activities designed to encourage the purchase of a specific product or service. As with the other marketing areas discussed previously, managers should have clear and measurable objectives for their promotions. An example might be a statement such as this one:

> By December 31, we will increase our revenues from pasta dishes by $48,000, which would be a 20 percent increase over the prior year.

With a measurable objective, a manager can use the variance formula previously introduced to determine the difference between the actual performance and the goal. Remember that the purpose of such an analysis is to identify those promotions that did or did not help an establishment achieve its goal.

In most cases, managers undertake both external and internal promotional activities. External activities include announcing promotions (short-term activities designed to encourage the purchase of a specific product or service) through advertising or publicity. Internal activities include on-site suggestive selling efforts and the development of point-of-purchase (POP) and point-of-sales (POS) materials that help stimulate customers' impulse buying. Upon completion of any promotion, managers can evaluate its effectiveness, using several measures:

- **Sales of the promotional item:** The actual sales of the promotional item should be assessed to determine if they met previously established goals.

- **Amount sold after the promotion:** If it is established that sales continue to climb after the promotion, then people may be buying the item for its quality and not only because of the promotion.

- **Increased or decreased sales for other menu items during the same period:** This is called secondary sales. When a person dines at an establishment because of the promotion and then buys another item, such as a glass of wine or an appetizer, a secondary sale has occurred.

- **Number of new customers attained during the promotion:** This requires tracking the number of new customers who dined because of a promotion. A significant number of new customers can help sales if these customers develop into long-term, repeat customers.

- **Which server sold the most promotional menu items?** This information can be useful when evaluating individual server performance. It is also helpful in determining if any additional training in suggestive selling (see chapter 10) needs to be conducted for servers who did not sell as much.

Once the results are known, they must be shared. Communicating the results of a promotion's success to an establishment's service and kitchen employees is important for a variety of reasons:

- Generating good feelings among staff members about their hard work
- Building teamwork and morale
- Encouraging ideas on how to improve performance
- Fostering good communication between front- and back-of-the-house employees

EVALUATING THE IMPACT OF MARKETING ON GUEST PURCHASES

In most cases, the ultimate goal of marketing is simply to increase the sales achieved by an establishment. Essentially, this can be done in one of four ways. A successful marketing plan allows managers to do one or all of the following:

- Serve more guests
- Serve more to *each* guest
- Serve more guests *and* serve more to *each* guest
- Make more profit from each guest sale

RESTAURANT TECHNOLOGY

Today's modern POS systems make it easy for managers to evaluate how many guests they have served, when they serve them, and what the guests are buying.

Comprehensive POS systems allow managers to monitor inventory levels, streamline ordering and receiving processes, enhance the profitability of their operations with customizable reporting and analysis tools, compare operational results against established standards or budgets, create waitlists, manage reservations, and even implement gift card and loyalty programs for guests.

With the computing power now available to managers, assessing sales levels and check averages by day part, day, week, and month is extremely easy. In fact, most POS systems offer managers a wide number of choices in the ways the systems can report data on how many guests are served and what those guests are buying.

Considered in this way, managers want to know what their guests are buying, how much each guest spends, and the profits resulting from each sale. To assess these three factors, managers evaluate their menu mix, check average, and contribution margin. All of these evaluations, described in the following text, are tools that managers can use to measure the impact of marketing activities on the purchases that are made by their guests.

Menu Mix

Menu mix refers to all of the servings of a menu item that are sold compared to the total sale of all competing menu items. *Exhibit 11.5* shows an example of the menu mix that could result from a day an establishment offered five entrée choices and served 152 guests. In *Exhibit 11.5*, **sales volume** refers to the number of times a menu item sells in a specific time period, such as for a day, a week, or a month.

Exhibit 11.5

ONE-DAY MENU MIX EVALUATION

Entrée	Sales Volume
Skewered Shrimp with Fried Rice	37
Pork Medallions with Sweet Potatoes	25
Rib-Eye Steak with Onion Rings	42
Herbed Chicken and Stuffing	29
Planked Salmon with Asparagus	19
Total	**152**

The data for *Exhibit 11.5* can be obtained from an operation's POS system or computed by hand from the orders written on guest checks. In either case, managers can use the information in *Exhibit 11.5* to create a sales ranking for the items, as shown in *Exhibit 11.6*.

Exhibit 11.6

ONE-DAY MENU MIX EVALUATION WITH ITEM RANKING

Entrée	Sales Volume	Sales Volume Rank
Skewered Shrimp with Fried Rice	37	2
Pork Medallions with Sweet Potatoes	25	4
Rib-Eye Steak with Onion Rings	42	1
Herbed Chicken and Stuffing	29	3
Planked Salmon with Asparagus	19	5
Total	**152**	

From *Exhibit 11.6* it is easy to see that Rib-Eye Steak with Onion Rings was this operation's best-selling item (number 1 rank) and Planked Salmon with Asparagus had the lowest sales volume (number 5 rank).

While some managers simply want to identify their best-selling items, other managers prefer to know the percentage of guests who selected each item, or the sales volume percentage. They can calculate that percentage using this formula:

Item sales volume ÷ Total sales volume = Sales volume percentage

For example, calculating the sales volume percentage of Rib-Eye Steak with Onion Rings would look like this:

42 ÷ 152 = 27.6%

Using this approach, managers can know even more about their menu mix. For example, as *Exhibit 11.7* demonstrates, whereas Rib-Eye Steak with Onion Rings is still the best-selling item at 27.6 percent of total sales, Skewered Shrimp with Fried Rice sells almost as well with 24.3 percent of total sales. When taken together, these two items account for 51.9 percent of the operation's total sales on that day.

Exhibit 11.7

ONE-DAY MENU MIX EVALUATION WITH SALES VOLUME PERCENTAGE

ENTRÉE	SALES VOLUME	SALES VOLUME %
Skewered Shrimp with Fried Rice	37	24.3%
Pork Medallions with Sweet Potatoes	25	16.4
Rib-Eye Steak with Onion Rings	42	27.6
Herbed Chicken and Stuffing	29	19.1
Planked Salmon with Asparagus	19	12.5
Total	152	100.0%

Some managers prefer to carefully examine the sales dollar percentage for each of the menu items they sell. The sales dollar percentage is the percentage of sales a menu item accounts for, expressed in dollars rather than volume. Managers seeking to make this analysis use a two-step process:

Step 1: Calculate the individual item sales using this formula:

Sales volume × Menu price = Item sales

Step 2: Calculate the sales dollar percentage for each item using this formula:

Individual item sales ÷ Total item sales = Sales dollar percentage

OPEN FOR BUSINESS

MANAGER'S MATH

A manager is evaluating her menu. Part of her evaluation includes the calculation of each menu item's sales dollar percentage. Create a chart like this one, then address the questions that follow.

MENU MIX EVALUATION: SALES DOLLAR PERCENTAGE

Entrée	Sales Volume	Menu Price	Item Sales	Sales Dollar %
Roasted Garlic Chicken	358	$11.95		
Loin of Pork with Port Wine Reduction	215	14.95		
8-Ounce Seared Sirloin	412	13.95		
Crab-Stuffed Tilapia in Cream Sauce	287	11.95		
12-Ounce Seared Sirloin	135	18.95		
Total				**100.0%**

1. What is the total number of entrées sold in this period?
2. What is the total dollar amount of sales achieved in this period?
3. Which menu item contributed the most sales dollars in this period?
4. Which menu item contributed the least sales dollars in this period?
5. What menu item–related recommendations would you have for this manager?

(Answers: 1. 1,407 total entrées; 2. $19,227.65; 3. 8-Ounce Seared Sirloin; 4. 12-Ounce Seared Sirloin)

For the Rib-Eye example, assume that the establishment sold $627.90 worth of Rib-Eye dinners and $2,173.15 total for all items. The sales dollar percentage would be calculated as follows:

$$\$627.90 \div \$2,173.15 = 28.9\%$$

Exhibit 11.8 shows the sales dollar percentage analysis for the five-item menu used in this example.

The value of using the more detailed sales dollar percentage approach can be shown by comparing the results for Pork Medallions with Sweet Potatoes presented in *Exhibit 11.6*, with the results in *Exhibit 11.8*. In *Exhibit 11.6*, the pork dish is the fourth most popular. However, *Exhibit 11.8* shows it to be third in the sales dollars contributed to the operation.

Managers can use the types of analysis shown in *Exhibits 11.5* through *11.8* to make pre- and post-marketing activity analysis as they assess the impact of specific marketing efforts on their operation's overall menu mix. These are some of the tools that can be used to answer the question "How well did our marketing activities work?"

Exhibit 11.8

ONE-DAY MENU MIX EVALUATION WITH SALES DOLLAR PERCENTAGE

Entrée	Sales Volume	Menu Price	Item Sales	Sales Dollar %
Skewered Shrimp with Fried Rice	37	$12.95	$479.15	22.0%
Pork Medallions with Sweet Potatoes	25	15.50	387.50	17.8
Rib-Eye Steak with Onion Rings	42	14.95	627.90	28.9
Herbed Chicken and Stuffing	29	12.95	375.55	17.3
Planked Salmon with Asparagus	19	15.95	303.05	13.9
Total	152		$2,173.15	100.0%

Check Average

Recall from chapter 1 that check average is the average amount spent by each guest visiting an establishment. The calculation is as follows:

Total revenue ÷ Number of guests served = Check average

In many cases, the purpose of a sales promotion is to increase an operation's check average. This is typically the case, for example, when promotions are focused goals such as these:

- Increasing appetizer sales
- Upselling guests to larger entrée portion sizes
- Increasing dessert sales
- Increasing after-dinner drink sales

Managers can use a modified version of the variance formula introduced earlier in this chapter to calculate the percentage change in check average that occurs after a sales promotion. Applied to check average that formula looks like this:

(Post-promotion check average − Pre-promotion check average) ÷ Pre-promotion check average = Percentage change in check average

To illustrate, assume a manager's operation had a check average of $18.00. The manager initiates an effective promotion designed to increase dessert sales. At the conclusion of the promotion, the manager again calculates the operation's check average and finds it to be $19.50. Using the percentage change in check average formula, the results would be as follows:

($19.50 − $18.00) ÷ $18.00 = 8.33%

In this example, an 8.33 percent increase in check average occurred during the dessert promotion.

Contribution Margin

Recall from chapter 6 that contribution margin (CM), or gross profit, is what is left over after the food cost of a menu item is subtracted from the menu selling price. Menu items are often evaluated based on CM: the contribution of the items to the total profitability of an operation.

To make this determination, the manager needs to know two crucial pieces of information: the food cost for the preparation of each menu item and the menu item selling price. Then the food cost of the menu item is subtracted from the menu selling price using this formula:

Item selling price − Item food cost = CM (or gross profit)

The remainder (difference) in the formula is the item's CM or gross profit. The CM for a sample menu is presented in *Exhibit 11.9*.

Exhibit 11.9			
ONE-DAY MENU MIX EVALUATION WITH CM			
Entrée	**Menu Price**	**Food Cost**	**CM (Gross Profit)**
Skewered Shrimp with Fried Rice	$12.95	$4.51	$ 8.44
Pork Medallions with Sweet Potatoes	15.50	5.71	9.79
Rib-Eye Steak with Onion Rings	14.95	5.38	9.57
Herbed Chicken and Stuffing	12.95	3.37	9.58
Planked Salmon with Asparagus	15.95	5.90	10.05

In this example, the sale of the Planked Salmon contributes the highest CM. Each sale of the Skewered Shrimp contributes the least.

Most managers also assess the total contribution margin for each menu item. Total contribution margin for an item is determined by multiplying the contribution margin for each menu item by the number sold of that item. This information provides a picture of the items that are contributing the most to profit and to the payment of expenses. The total contribution margins for the sample menu are shown in *Exhibit 11.10*.

Exhibit 11.10			
ONE-DAY MENU MIX EVALUATION WITH TOTAL CM			
Entrée	**Item CM (Gross Profit)**	**Sales Volume**	**Total CM (Gross Profit)**
Skewered Shrimp with Fried Rice	$ 8.44	37	$ 312.28
Pork Medallions with Sweet Potatoes	9.79	25	244.75
Rib-Eye Steak with Onion Rings	9.57	42	401.94
Herbed Chicken and Stuffing	9.58	29	277.82
Planked Salmon with Asparagus	$10.05	19	190.95
Total		**152**	**$1,427.74**

The analysis of the total contribution for each item changes the apparent profitability of the individual menu items. In this example, the Rib-Eye Steak with Onion Rings contributes the most money to the overall gross profit. When examining the initial analysis in *Exhibit 11.9*, it appeared as though the Planked Salmon with Asparagus contributed the most to gross profit and the Skewered Shrimp with Fried Rice the least. Now it appears that the Skewered Shrimp contributes the second-highest amount to gross profit based on overall sales. This analysis illustrates why menu items need to be analyzed using more than one method, or a combination of methods, in order to make sound decisions about their pre- and post-promotion impact on profitability.

ASSESSING PRODUCT QUALITY

Managers must evaluate how items sell. They must also evaluate other aspects of the operation. Each aspect affects the marketing plan, and an effective marketing plan draws customers to an establishment. However, those customers must receive quality products and service if they are to return. All marketing activities are similar in that they promise customers they will receive good value for their dining-out dollars. Establishments must keep these promises. It is the job of the manager to ensure they do. For that reason, the careful assessment of the operation's products and services is an important part of marketing plan evaluation.

To evaluate product quality, managers gain insight from two important sources. The first of these is customer feedback. The second is an internal assessment of product quality that managers undertake on their own.

Customer Feedback

Customer feedback is the industry term used to describe the variety of thoughts and opinions about an operation that customers express to the operation's owners, managers, and staff (*Exhibit 11.11*). Customer feedback may be positive. A guest expressing great satisfaction with his or her meal is an example of positive feedback. Feedback can also be negative. A customer complaining about the quality of the food is negative feedback.

It would be wonderful if 100 percent of the customer feedback was positive, but that is not very realistic. Even well-trained preparation and service staff make mistakes that can lead to customer dissatisfaction. Also be aware that some customers may provide negative feedback even when products and services have been delivered in accordance with quality standards established by management. Regardless, managers should carefully monitor the positive and negative feedback received from their customers.

Managers can monitor customer satisfaction by assessing feedback received from three important sources:

- Direct comments
- Customer surveys
- Social media sites

DIRECT COMMENTS

Feedback in the form of direct comments from customers can be either positive or negative. These voluntary comments result when customers are extremely pleased or displeased with the purchases

Many guests use social media Web sites to help them choose a restaurant or foodservice establishment. On these sites, real customers post real comments about their dining experiences.

When real customers post comments on social media Web sites, the comments may reflect positively or negatively on an establishment. Some comments from satisfied customers will no doubt be glowing, while comments from less happy customers may be highly critical. Because that is true, managers should continually monitor the most popular of these sites so they can gain insight and information useful in improving their products and services.

Exhibit 11.11

THINK ABOUT IT . . .

Consider the jobs you have held. How did you feel when a customer complained to you about a product or service quality–related issue that you knew was not justified? What did you do?

KEEPING IT SAFE

Cleanliness and sanitation are two areas every customer assesses when he or she visits a restaurant or foodservice operation. Customers consider these issues when deciding whether they will or will not return in the future. An effective marketing and advertising effort may generate first-time customers, but if an operation is perceived as dirty, those customers will not likely return. Because that is true, managers can actually view the food safety–related aspects of their operations as marketing efforts. An emphasis on cleanliness and sanitation not only helps make an operation a safe place in which to work, it is a key factor in creating repeat business.

they make. In addition to unsolicited comments, managers and servers can solicit direct comments from customers with a sincerely asked question similar to "How was everything today?" Positive feedback to this question will likely include such comments as: "Our compliments to the Chef!," "Best food I ever ate!," and "That was outstanding!"

Managers welcome positive customer feedback as do kitchen workers and service staff. Many managers keep a customer comment log to record when, and about what items, such comments are received. A regular review of the log can provide valuable information to managers seeking to determine which menu items are the most popular and which promotions were the most successful.

Of course, some customers will not provide positive feedback. Negative feedback in response to the same question of "How was everything?" can include such comments as: "I didn't really like it," "It was overcooked [or undercooked]," or "I don't think we'll come back."

Comments of this type should also be recorded in the customer's feedback log. Negative feedback can also provide valuable information as long as the log is reviewed by managers on a regular basis. If the comments consistently indicate a problem with an employee or an operating procedure, the manager should address and correct the situation immediately. This may be done by offering additional training to the employee or by modifying and improving the operational procedure.

In most cases, more negative than positive feedback will be relayed to managers (see *Exhibit 11.12*). Despite the tendency of customers to make negative comments more often than positive ones, managers should take negative comments seriously. These comments should be investigated and a proper response should be promptly delivered to the guest. Negative comments that are consistent or follow a pattern may indicate a serious product quality problem that should be immediately addressed by management.

Exhibit 11.12	
VOLUNTARY COMMENTS	
Customer Opinion of Product or Service	**Likelihood of Voluntary Comments**
Outstanding	Sometimes
Excellent Very Good Average	Rarely
Poor Awful Bad	Often

Voluntary feedback has a bias toward the negative.

CUSTOMER SURVEYS

The answers to formal customer surveys or comment cards serve as a second source of customer feedback. *Exhibit 11.13* is an example of a menu item quality and variety survey. Such surveys can be placed directly on tables or delivered to guests when their checks are presented to them. Increasingly, managers deliver guest surveys to email addresses voluntarily supplied by their customers.

Exhibit 11.13

SAMPLE MENU-ITEM QUALITY AND VARIETY SURVEY

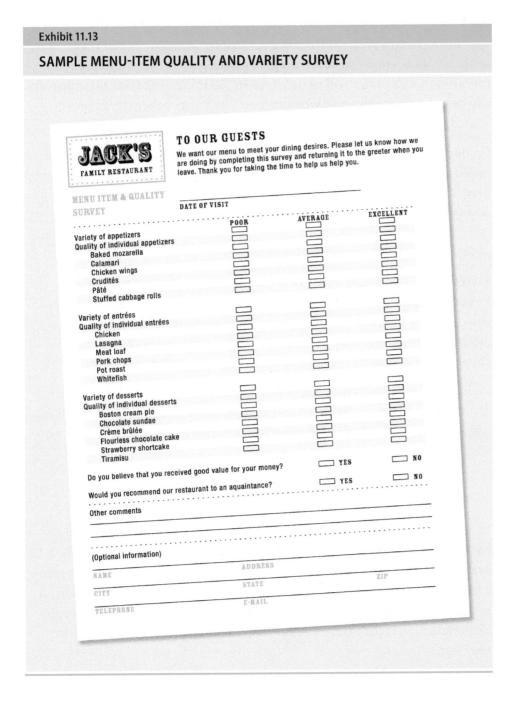

RESTAURANT TECHNOLOGY

Today's mobile society ensures that most consumers are never far from email access. Smart phones, laptops, notebooks, and desktop computers are all means by which customers check email, and managers can deliver guest surveys or comment cards.

Guest survey specialists recommend that managers follow these steps to maximize survey response rates via email:

1. Offer an incentive for responding.
2. Assure respondents their comments will not be linked directly to them by name.
3. Express a sincere intent to take action as a result of the survey respondents' opinions.
4. Set a deadline for responding.
5. Follow up by sending a thank-you to all survey respondents.

An advantage of collecting customer comments with a formal survey is the detailed feedback the survey can provide. The survey results can be reviewed individually or summarized by managers into reports that can provide valuable information about how guests view an establishment's products. This is especially important when a company specifically features a product-related feature in its advertising. For example, if a pizza company advertises that its pizzas are "piled high" with toppings, it is important to determine whether customers agree that they are. If customers do not agree, the company would be advertising a feature that customers simply do not agree exists. Knowing product-related information will often give managers insight into which products should be promoted or advertised in the future. It can also supply information to managers about their operations' ability to deliver on service-related promises made in advertising. For example, if a pizza restaurant promises that its pizzas will be delivered in "30 minutes or less," guest surveys can help the company know whether their customers believe that service-related promise is being fulfilled.

Product- and service-related questions provide valuable information. Open-ended questions such as "How did you hear about our operation?" may also be used to gather information about the success of external promotions and advertising efforts in increasing customer counts.

SOCIAL MEDIA SITES

Increasingly, guests voluntarily post their feedback about restaurant and foodservice establishments on blogs and social networking sites. Managers who regularly monitor these sites can gain valuable insight into how their establishment is viewed by past guests. They can also assess how potential customers may view their operations based on the posted comments.

Web-posted comments most often provide very targeted information, such as favorite menu items, most common likes and dislikes, and value received for money spent. This information can play a key role in future marketing and advertising for any operation.

Management Assessment

In addition to customer feedback, managers rely on their own skill and background, as well as the quality assurance systems they have established, to evaluate the quality of products their operation delivers. An operation's menu items, for the most part, are the establishment in the eyes of its customers. A manager's customers are continually evaluating the operation's menu items. This evaluation is the primary reason why customers will return—or why they won't.

PRODUCT QUALITY CONTROLS

As a manager, do not wait for business to fall off before discovering that the quality of the menu items has declined. Evaluating menu items is the responsibility of everyone in the operation—chefs, servers, managers, and owners—and it should be done regularly. Doing so is the only way to ensure that product standards are being met and that each menu item tastes the way it should. The best managers have well-established quality standards for all of their products. However, these product quality standards are of little value unless all employees follow them.

It is the job of the manager to set up and continuously operate a quality inspection system to verify that quality standards have been met in the past and will be met in the future (see *Exhibit 11.14*). A quality inspection system may include several steps:

- Checking each plate as it comes from the kitchen on its way to customers
- Randomly taste-testing menu items, making sure to sample every menu item each month
- Using a "secret shopper" who visits an operation pretending to be a customer, orders and samples a complete meal, and then provides detailed feedback on its taste and appearance as well as the quality of service

PREPARATION PROCESS CONTROLS

A manager's operation might serve great dishes that people love and are willing to pay for, but if the labor costs are too high, the operation could still be in trouble. On a continuing basis, managers must evaluate how difficult it is to prepare each item, how long it takes to prepare each item, and how many employees are required to prepare each item. All these dimensions of food preparation have costs that must be paid for by revenue, and the higher these costs are, the lower the profit. There are two ways to determine these costs, and both have advantages and disadvantages:

1. **Observing preparation in action:** A manager can observe his or her kitchen employees as they prepare actual customer orders and as they do the *mise en place*—preorder preparation work. The advantage of this method is that it allows the manager to see how people actually do things. The disadvantages are that it takes a large amount of time and the rush of meal hours can affect how things are actually done rather than how they should be done.

OPEN FOR BUSINESS

BY THE CUSTOMER/ FOR THE CUSTOMER

There is no denying that restaurant and foodservice customers talk about their experiences online, and with great reach and influence. They tweet, post, blog, chat, and assign ratings about operations and their experiences whether they are good or bad. They also talk about whether or not they will return to the establishment or recommend it to their peers.

Conventional marketing wisdom has held that a dissatisfied customer tells 10 people. But in the new age of social media, that same customer can use social media sites to tell 10 million. This is why it's so critical for managers to ensure they make good on their marketing promises. They do so by consistently providing products and services customers feel deliver real value on each of their visits.

Exhibit 11.14

The taste and appearance of every menu item served must meet the manager's quality standards.

Exhibit 11.15

2. **Running preparation tests:** A manager can run test preparations of menu items during off hours (*Exhibit 11.15*). The advantage of this method is that it allows the manager to determine the ideal preparation time. The disadvantage is that employees will know they are being tested and will make sure they follow all the required procedures, even the ones they might skip in their actual work.

The ideal solution involves using a combination of both methods to ensure excessive costs or poor product quality are not the reasons for failing to achieve the revenue targets and goals previously identified in an operation's marketing plan.

ASSESSING SERVICE QUALITY

Ensuring product quality is one step in reaching the goals established in a marketing plan. Ensuring service quality is just as important. Experienced managers know that, in most cases, the number of service-related customer complaints is greater than the number of product-related complaints. As a result, managers should develop and use service quality surveys similar to those used to assess product quality. *Exhibit 11.16* is an example of such a survey.

Careful analysis of service quality surveys helps managers determine whether service-related improvements or changes are necessary. Managers should pay particular attention to survey questions addressing whether customers feel they receive good value for the money. The answers to these questions can help managers evaluate how customers feel about how the operation's prices compare to the value of the services received. If customers believe that their money is well spent, it means they value the service levels offered.

When analyzing service-related comment cards and surveys, it is important to keep in mind that, just like product quality surveys, it is more common for people to complete them if they have had a poor experience than if they had a good one. If the negative comments are random, it may simply indicate a one-time bad experience. However, managers should still investigate the negative comment and respond properly to the guest. Negative comments that are numerous, consistent, and follow a pattern usually indicate a more serious problem that needs immediate management attention.

While the specific service-related concerns of an establishment will vary based on industry segment such as quick-service restaurant (QSR), fast-casual, casual, or fine-dining operations, all managers should carefully monitor the two most important service-related issues: promptness and cleanliness.

Exhibit 11.16

SAMPLE SERVICE-QUALITY SURVEY

JACK'S
FAMILY RESTAURANT

TO OUR GUESTS
We want your dining experience to be all that you hoped it would be. Please let us know how we are doing in meeting your service needs by completing this survey and returning it to the host when you leave. Thank you.

SERVICE - QUALITY SURVEY

DATE OF VISIT

	POOR	AVERAGE	EXCELLENT
Parking lot convenience	☐	☐	☐
Parking lot cleanliness	☐	☐	☐
Valet service value for price	☐	☐	☐
Friendliness of greeter/host	☐	☐	☐
Coat check service	☐	☐	☐
Décor	☐	☐	☐
Table location	☐	☐	☐
Linens and silverware	☐	☐	☐
Helpfulness of server	☐	☐	☐
Friendliness of server	☐	☐	☐
Accuracy of meal served	☐	☐	☐
Promptness of table service	☐	☐	☐
Cleanliness of restrooms	☐	☐	☐
Cleanliness of restaurant	☐	☐	☐
Quality of private room (if utilized)	☐	☐	☐

Do you believe that you received good value for your money?   ☐ YES   ☐ NO

Is there a particular employee you would like to single out for praise?   ☐ YES   ☐ NO
If yes, please explain.

_____

Would you recommend our restaurant to an aquaintance?   ☐ YES   ☐ NO

Other comments

_____
_____
_____
_____
_____

(Optional information)

NAME _____ ADDRESS _____

CITY _____ STATE _____ ZIP _____

TELEPHONE _____ E-MAIL _____

Promptness and Knowledge

No one likes to waste time, and no one likes to have other people waste his or her time. Promptness is a valued characteristic of good service. However, it is important to recognize that the customer, not the server or manager, defines promptness. What is "prompt" service for one customer might be "rushed" service for another customer and "slow" service for a third. This means that servers must be able to read their customers and determine how quickly they want to be served.

Managers should constantly monitor the promptness of service provided by their service staff. They should look for the same signs that their servers

---

Manager's Memo

Managers observing guest service in their own operations can learn a lot simply by carefully watching customers. Here are some customer service clues that can be easily observed:

1. If the customer is sitting and doing nothing, or looking for the server, the customer wants some service. The customer could want to have something corrected or could be waiting for the serving of the next course.

2. If the customer is finished with the current course and is sitting for a while, the customer probably wants speedier service. A quick question by the server or manager can verify this.

3. If the customer lets the course sit for a while or is not finished with one course when the next course is served, service is too speedy.

RESTAURANT TECHNOLOGY

Critical measures of service promptness vary by industry segment. For example, in the QSR segment, advanced technology video cameras and light sensors that are interfaced to an operation's POS system are used to automatically calculate, record, and report to managers the time (in seconds) that pass between the following intervals:

- Customer arrival in the drive-up lane and customer order placement

- Customer order placement and order delivery

- Customer arrival at the pick-up window and customer departure

Most QSRs have a goal of serving drive-through customers in less than two minutes. Customers often measure that wait time both objectively and subjectively. They may not mind waiting five minutes to be served if they feel that a long line is moving steadily. If only one car is in front of them and it takes the same five minutes to be served, they will likely be dissatisfied with the speed of service.

Exhibit 11.17

should be looking for. Going a step further is even better: Talk to customers about the promptness of service and whether it is meeting their needs. If promptness of service is a problem, two things need to be done:

- Alert the service staff that promptness is important and that the customer sets the standard.

- Train the service staff in detecting the speed of service desired by a customer.

The observation of customers is a subjective measure of promptness. Many managers can also use objective measures of promptness. Commonly used objective measures of promptness include monitoring the time elapsed between several events:

- Customer arrival and seating

- Order placement and order delivery

- Customer arrival and departure

Regardless of the measurement methods used, managers must continually assess the speed at which guests are served if they are to meet their operation's long-term sales objectives.

Professional service staff must understand how kitchens work. Staff members need to know what items are offered, how they are made, and how they taste. For this to happen, they need to communicate with the chef or other kitchen personnel before each shift to review what items are being prepared for that day, what the specials are, and how all these items are prepared. By understanding the products offered, the service staff will be able to answer customers' questions.

Also, it is important that service staff members have credibility in the eyes of customers. One sure way to lose credibility is an inability to describe the menu items. Many customers ask the service staff to recommend an item (*Exhibit 11.17*), which means that staff members should taste a product before recommending it. Good managers ensure that service staff members taste the products and also identify what to look for in products. For example, if a guest cannot eat spicy food, the server must be able to recommend the appropriate menu items. Customers always expect to be served promptly and by friendly, helpful, and knowledgeable staff.

Cleanliness

Maintaining a clean establishment is important not only for the proper handling of food but also for increasing sales. Restaurant and foodservice professionals realize that their customers expect a clean and safe place to eat. Keeping the establishment clean reduces the chances of slips, trips, and falls by employees and customers; it also reduces or prevents outbreaks of foodborne illness. A clean, sanitary environment is very important to customers, and any manager would have a hard time marketing a dirty operation.

Local health departments establish sanitation standards that operations must meet in order to be certified to conduct business. Health departments establish sanitation procedures to ensure guests and employees are safe from problems concerning general safety and food safety.

In turn, managers must establish their own procedures and standards for cleaning. Since there are so many areas to clean in a restaurant or foodservice establishment, managers must be well organized. Many managers develop a cleaning schedule for every part of their operations. These cleaning schedules should indicate several important details:

- What needs to be cleaned
- When it needs to be cleaned
- How it should be cleaned
- Who should do the cleaning

An example of a cleaning schedule is shown in *Exhibit 11.18*.

Exhibit 11.18

ESTABLISHMENT CLEANING SCHEDULE

Item	What	When	Use	Who
Floors	• Wipe up spills	• Immediately	• Cloth mop and bucket, broom and dustpan	Bussers
	• Damp mop	• Once per shift, between rushes	• Mop, bucket, safety signs	
	• Scrub	• Daily, at closing	• Brushes, squeegee, bucket, detergent, safety signs	
	• Strip, reseal	• Every six months	• Check written procedures	
Walls and ceilings	• Wipe up splashes • Wash walls	• As soon as possible • Food-prep and cooking areas: daily • All other areas: first of the month	• Clean cloth, detergent	Dishwashing staff
Worktables	• Clean and sanitize tops • Empty, clean, and sanitize drawers	• Between uses and at the end of the day • Weekly	• See cleaning procedure for each table • See cleaning procedure for table	Prep cooks

Developing a cleaning schedule is not enough. Managers must also monitor the cleaning process while it is taking place and then verify that everything has been cleaned according to maintenance schedule and cleanliness standards. The manager or a designated employee must conduct regular inspections of all the cleaned areas, and these inspections must be part of the cleaning schedule.

MEASURING MARKETING RETURNS ON INVESTMENT (ROIs)

When managers create marketing plans for their operations they set specific and measurable targets or goals such as the number of guests to be served or sales volume levels to be achieved.

Many managers go even further. They estimate the return on investment (ROI) that will be achieved in their marketing expenditures. ROI is a performance measure used to evaluate the quality of an investment. It is also used to compare the efficiency of a number of different investment alternatives.

When plans are made for an operation, managers should set financial goals such as payback period, payback ratio, and return on investment, as shown in *Exhibit 11.19*. For example, if an owner decided to buy a new sign for a business, he or she should identify exactly what benefits it would bring to the operation.

Effective managers can calculate the ROI of different marketing investment options available to them and then choose the ones with the highest projected ROI. By assessing the actual ROI achieved, managers can assess the effectiveness and efficiency of their choices and then take corrective action if necessary. Managers can calculate ROI using hard data or soft data.

Exhibit 11.19

FORMULAS FOR EVALUATING RETURN ON INVESTMENT

Payback period: Length of time it takes for an investment to pay for itself
Dollars invested ÷ Dollars returned per year = Payback period in years

Payback ratio: Ratio of money returned over the life of the investment to the amount of the investment
Lifetime dollars returned ÷ Dollars invested = Payback ratio

Return on investment: Payback ratio expressed as a percentage
Lifetime dollars returned ÷ Dollars invested × 100% = ROI

Hard Data Returns

Hard data are the type that can be readily quantified by numbers or statistics. Examples of hard data include the cost of the investment as well as the measurable dollars that result from that investment. When hard data are available, managers are able to calculate precisely their ROI.

To illustrate, assume a manager was considering purchasing a new digital exterior sign that could be programmed to display the operation's daily specials in an eye-catching way to potential customers driving by her establishment. The sign would cost $15,000 to purchase and install, but it would last for five years. The manager estimates the sign would create $25 of additional profit per day for her operation. Over one year, she would earn an additional $9,125; over the five-year life of the sign, she would earn a total of $45,625. Using the hard data available to her, this manager could assess this potential investment using three different investment quality–related formulas:

- Payback period
- Payback ratio
- Return on investment (ROI)

PAYBACK PERIOD

The payback period is the length of time it takes for an investment to pay for itself. The payback period formula is as follows:

Dollars invested ÷ Dollars returned per year = Payback period in years

In the example of the digital exterior sign, the payback period would be calculated as follows:

$$\$15{,}000 \div \$9{,}125 = 1.64 \text{ years}$$

In this example, the sign would pay for itself in 1.64 years (19 to 20 months).

PAYBACK RATIO

The payback ratio compares the money returned over the life of the investment to the amount of the investment. This is the payback ratio formula:

Lifetime dollars returned ÷ Dollars invested = Payback ratio

In the example of the digital exterior sign, the payback period would be calculated as follows:

$$\$45{,}625 \div \$15{,}000 = 3.04$$

In this example the payback ratio is 3.04, or about $3 returned for each $1 invested.

RETURN ON INVESTMENT (ROI)

Return on investment is the payback ratio expressed as a percentage. The formula for calculating ROI is shown here:

$$\textbf{Lifetime dollars returned} \div \textbf{Dollars invested} \times \textbf{100\%} = \textbf{ROI}$$

In the example of the digital exterior sign, the ROI would be calculated as follows:

$$\textbf{\$45,625} \div \textbf{\$15,000} \times \textbf{100\%} = \textbf{304\%}$$

In this example, the manager would see a 304% return on her investment over the lifetime of the digital sign.

To achieve the estimated return on investment for an item such as the sign, the item needs to provide the actual return estimated for each year of its lifetime, and the item needs to last as long as its expected lifetime. Unfortunately, there are many reasons why this may not happen:

- The yearly returns were overestimated.
- The item cannot be used as originally predicted.
- The item requires repair, which reduces the annual returns.
- The item does not last for the expected lifetime.
- The item is replaced with newer technology before its useful life has been reached.

The manager will have to determine whether he or she has received an adequate return despite these limiting factors.

Soft Data Returns

Soft data are not objective and usually consist of informal comments or opinions. For example, the statement "I think the investment will be a good one for us" is soft data.

For investments in which returns are subjective estimates, such as the return on an upgraded music system, the actual impact of the investment may be very difficult to determine and may be inexact. As a result, the calculations for ROI may not be as useful as they are with investments in which hard data results can be estimated more accurately. In these cases, managers may have to rely on their "gut feeling" or their own subjective evaluations. Nevertheless, some evaluation of investments with subjective elements must be done on occasion so managers can make decisions about whether to make them.

Training Investments

The returns on an investment depend on the actual use of the investment over the number of years that the investment is supposed to bring returns. For example, an investment such as training typically assumes the trained employees actually use the skills and knowledge they have gained for a long period of time. Unfortunately, there are many reasons why this might not happen:

- The supervisor "untrains" the employees back to the old ways.

- The employees leave the operation.

- The employees get too little reward for implementing the training and stop doing it the new way.

It is not enough for managers to do a good job of planning their investments; they also have to monitor and manage them so predicted returns are achieved. This means managers must do regular evaluations of their operations. Additionally, they must remember that when their operations are performing well, they will have a better chance of successfully implementing their marketing plans and, ultimately, generating the profits needed to achieve their ROI goals.

SUMMARY

1. **Identify the areas managers assess when evaluating their marketing efforts.**

   One way to initiate the marketing evaluation process is by assessing each of the key marketing activities. These activities are personal selling, advertising, publicity, public relations, and promotions. Each of these five key marketing areas is likely to be in use to greater or lesser degrees in every restaurant or foodservice operation. By systematically assessing results in each of these important areas managers can gain a better understanding of what worked and what did not work in their marketing plans. This information can then be used to modify and improve future marketing plans and efforts.

2. **List the tools managers use to evaluate the impact of marketing on guest purchases.**

   To properly evaluate their marketing efforts, managers want to determine what their guests are buying, how much each guest spends, and the profits resulting from each guest sale. To assess these factors, managers evaluate their menu mix, check average, and contribution margin.

   Menu mix reveals the popularity of each menu item. Check average measures the amount each guest spends per visit. Contribution margin (CM), or gross profit margin, is the amount remaining after the cost of food is deducted from the selling price of a menu item. Those menu items that contribute the most CM to an operation are its most profitable menu items and should be well marketed.

3. **Describe the main methods managers use to assess product quality.**

   To evaluate product quality, managers use two important information sources. The first of these is customer feedback. This feedback includes all of the thoughts and opinions about an operation that customers express directly to the operation's owners, managers, and staff. Customer feedback may be positive or negative. Feedback can be gathered from direct customer comment, customer surveys, and social media sites. In addition to customer feedback, managers make their own internal assessments of product quality and use that information to refine and improve their operations. The combination of customer feedback and personal inspection lets managers know how well they are doing in ensuring quality and the steps that must be taken to improve their operations.

4. **Describe the key areas managers evaluate when assessing service quality.**

   The specific service-related concerns of establishments vary based on their industry segment; however, all managers should carefully monitor the two most important service-related issues in any operation: promptness and cleanliness. Promptness is speed of service. Service speeds can be too slow or too fast and as a result should be carefully monitored. Maintaining a clean establishment is important not only for the proper handling of food but also for increasing sales. That is true because all customers expect their food to be prepared and served in a clean and safe environment.

5. **Explain the importance of assessing marketing-related return on investment (ROI).**

   Every businessperson must make investments in his or her business. Estimating returns on investment (ROI) prior to making them allows managers to compare the efficiency of a number of different investment alternatives. Assessing the returns on investments already made allows managers to evaluate the wisdom of their investment decisions. Variations of ROI assessment can include the calculation of payback period and payback ratio. Effective managers seek to calculate the ROI of different marketing investment options available to them and then choose the ones with the highest projected ROI.

APPLICATION EXERCISES

Exercise 1
Calculating Sales Dollar Percentage

Sally, the assistant manager of a restaurant, has been asked to do a menu analysis. The manager thinks that there are too many entrées on the luncheon menu and is concerned about the sales percentage of each item. The manager would like to remove at least one item from the luncheon menu in order to streamline kitchen operations. Sally has been given the information shown in the table, gathered from yesterday's records.

Determine the sales dollar percentage of each item. Then decide which item to remove from the menu based on its sales dollar percentage.

Which one should be removed? _____

Entrée	Number Sold	Menu Price	Total Sales Dollars	Sales Dollar %
Fish and Chips	42	$9.95		
Giant Hamburger	51	8.50		
Reuben Sandwich	25	7.75		
House Club Sandwich	27	5.75		
Crab Salad in Pita	21	7.95		
Vegetarian Wrap with Cheese	23	6.95		
TOTAL	**189**			

Exercise 2
Analyzing What Really Happened

You are the manager of Pete's Pizza and Pasta. Recently, you set up an aggressive plan to increase sales and your customer base. You succeeded in increasing return visits by your current customers. However, you fell considerably short at increasing the number of new customers and increasing the average guest check.

Shown below is your business plan for the year and your actual results. Explain why you did not meet your new customer and guest check goals. Then list the areas that you should concentrate on improving for the coming year in order to do better.

Business Plan for Pete's Pizza and Pasta

Overall Objective:

Pete's Pizza and Pasta will increase sales by a minimum of $100,000 over sales of the last fiscal year. We will increase sales by adding new customers, increasing the frequency of visits, and increasing sales per guest check.

New Customers:

We will add 500 customers to our existing customer base of 4,000 over the fiscal year.

Action Plan:

- Develop a referral plan with other businesses in the area.
- Conduct a direct mail campaign.
- Introduce new desserts.
- Add entertainment on weekend nights.
- Advertise quarterly in local papers.

Repeat Customers:

We will have 50 percent of our customers return to our store three times a year, up from two times a year for the previous year. The percent of returning customers also will increase 25 percent from last year.

Action Plan:

- Develop a direct mail list and calendar to communicate with our customers.
- Provide activities every three months to encourage our customers to come back.
- Establish a frequent dining program with a discount on the fourth visit.

Increase the Guest Check:

Increase sales from $11.00 per guest to $13.75. This is a 25 percent increase.

Action Plan:

- Raise prices on every item by 10 percent.
- Suggestive-sell bigger-sized pizzas and drinks.
- Introduce a new dessert tray to customers.

SALES GOALS

New Customers	Last Year's Actual	This Year's Goal
Number of new customers	300	500
Average guest check	$ 11.00	$ 13.75
Sales from new customers (Number × Average check)	3,300.00	6,875.00
If customers return two times a year (2 × Sales)	6,600.00	13,750.00
If customers return three times a year (3 × Sales)		20,625.00
Sales from new customers (actual and goal sales)	6,600.00	20,625.00
Increased sales from new customers (This year's goal − Last year's actual)		14,025.00

Repeat Customers	Last Year's Actual	This Year's Goal
Number of repeat customers	1,000	2,000
Average guest check	$ 11.00	$ 13.75
Sales from repeat customers (Number × Average check)	11,000.00	27,500.00
If customers return two times a year (2 × Sales)	22,000.00	55,000.00
If customers return three times a year (3 × Sales)		82,500.00
Sales from repeat customers (Actual and goal sales)	22,000.00	82,500.00
Increased sales from repeat customers (This year's goal − Last year's actual)		60,500.00

Projections

Overall sales projected (New customer goal + Repeat customer goal): $103,125
Increased sales (New customer increase + Repeat customer increase): $74,525

RESULTS ONE YEAR LATER

Customers	Goal	Actual
Number of new customers	500	300
Number of return visits by new customers	3 times	2 times
Number of repeat customers	2,000	2,000
Number of return visits by repeat customers	3 times	3 times
Average guest check	$13.75	$12.00

Give some reasons why you think Pete's Pizza and Pasta did not meet their new customer and guest check goals. Provide your thoughts as to what areas the restaurant should focus on.

REVIEW YOUR LEARNING

Select the best answer for each question.

1. **Which would result in a positive sales variance?**
   A. Actual sales levels exceed planned sales levels.
   B. Actual sales levels equal planned sales levels.
   C. Planned sales levels exceed actual sales levels.
   D. Planned sales levels were not achieved.

2. **Larry is the manager of Pepper Peak Pizza. Larry forecast that he would serve 8,000 customers this month. Larry actually served 10,000 customers. What was the percentage variance in Larry's customer forecast for this month?**
   A. 2%
   B. 18%
   C. 20%
   D. 25%

3. **Which area of marketing could be partially assessed by counting the number of times the operation is mentioned positively in articles appearing in the local press?**
   A. Personal selling
   B. Advertising
   C. Promotions
   D. Publicity

4. **Which is an example of a secondary sale?**
   A. Customers visiting an establishment for the first time due to a radio ad
   B. Customers booking a wedding dinner during a personal sales call
   C. Customers pairing the daily special with a bottle of wine
   D. Customers purchasing a promotional menu item "to go"

5. **Sharon's establishment offers 15 entrée choices. On a day Sharon served 600 guests, her Cajun Seafood Pasta entrée sold 150 servings. What was the menu mix sales volume percentage for Cajun Seafood Pasta on that day?**
   A. 10%
   B. 15%
   C. 25%
   D. 40%

6. **Theresia's very busy operation served 500 guests on Friday night. Her check average on Friday night was $30. What were Theresia's sales on that Friday night?**
   A. $150
   B. $1,500
   C. $15,000
   D. $150,000

7. **The Herbed Chicken and Stuffing currently sells in Carl's establishment for $12.95. It costs $3.40 to make. Carl wants to raise the price of this dish to $13.95. What will be the contribution margin of the dish if Carl raises the price?**
   A. $8.55
   B. $10.55
   C. $12.55
   D. $13.55

8. Managers can assess service quality using which approach?
   A. Check plates before they leave the kitchen.
   B. Observe food preparation during the dinner rush.
   C. Randomly taste test items as the chef prepares them.
   D. Monitor average time between order placement and delivery.

9. **Latisha wants to purchase a new grill. The grill will cost $8,000. Latisha estimates she will increase profits by $2,000 per year by allowing her chef to expand the number of menu items available. What is the payback period for this proposed investment?**
   A. One year
   B. Two years
   C. Four years
   D. Six years

10. **Which change in an item would cause its actual return on investment to exceed its originally projected ROI?**
    A. The item required extensive repairs after its purchase.
    B. The item's yearly financial return was underestimated.
    C. The item's life span was shorter than originally projected.
    D. The item's installation costs were much higher than expected.

FIELD PROJECT

Advertising or Promotion Evaluation

This project will allow you to focus on the key marketing issues in this guide and to determine how the material presented is used in a real-world situation within a particular operation. You will prepare a detailed explanation of which marketing efforts in the operation you believe are working, as well as what you would suggest for changes or improvements.

The goal of this activity is not for you to directly match what you think the operation's goals should be versus what they actually are, but to further understand that every operation will actively choose what to incorporate into their establishment's promotions based on the market variables present.

The Assignment

Work with a restaurant in your area to gather the information listed below about the establishment:

1. Current menu
2. Information on the local area in which the restaurant is located
3. Advertising piece
4. Information on competition
5. Competitor's advertising piece or promotional item
6. Promotional item/piece
7. Organizational chart
8. Past financial statements (with marketing break outs)
9. Mission statement
10. Operation/employee schedule

There is no set number on the amount of items to include for your evaluation; however, the more information you include, the more thorough your analysis will be. Much of this information may be accessible over the Internet.

Once you have researched the operation, evaluate its advertising piece or promotion in light of the other information you have obtained, and prepare a report containing their evaluations and recommendations.

Here are some things you should include in your report:

1. Brief overview of the restaurant

   - Classification of the restaurant in terms of service and style

   - History of the restaurant (if available)

   - Mission statement (the restaurant's values)

   - Current state of the establishment (look at financial and operations reports)

2. The restaurant's market

   - Demographics

   - Competitors

3. Advertising piece or promotional item

   - What is the intended goal of the promotional item?

   - How would you evaluate it?

   - Does it target the correct market?

   - Suggestions on making it better?

   - Ideas/suggestions for additional pieces?

   - Is the image supported by this piece?

4. Anticipated outcome of the advertising piece or promotional item

   - Do you think this advertising or promotion will be a success?

   - How will this impact sales/revenue?

   - Do you believe this fulfilled the mission of ROI?

   - How will this impact the long-term success of the operation in general?

5. How the piece actually fared

GLOSSARY

Advertising Any form of marketing message that managers pay for and deliver in an identifiable but nonpersonal way.

Advertising campaign A coordinated series of advertisements and promotions used in the same time frame to meet certain objectives.

Advertising schedule A calendar that tracks advertising and other promotional activities on a weekly, monthly, or seasonal basis.

À la carte menu A menu in which each item is priced separately, to provide a range of lower- and higher-priced items.

Alternative revenue source (ARS) A source of money in addition to that raised from loans and personal savings, such as co-branding partnerships or grants.

Baby boomers U.S. citizens born between 1946 and 1964.

Barriers to success (SWOT analysis) Things outside the establishment's control that might cause a weakness.

Benefits The advantages or favorable results obtained from purchasing a feature.

Brand The single term owners and managers use to describe an establishment's distinguishing features.

Brand identifier The name, logo, signage, employee uniforms, décor, pricing, service level, and other characteristics that, when taken together, make one restaurant or foodservice operation different from another.

Brand name The specific brand identifier that contains the words, letters, or symbols used to identify a single establishment or a company consisting of many establishments.

Brand placement The category in which a restaurant or foodservice operation competes.

Brand position statement A concise summary of the brand's values, competencies, company culture, and target market.

Broadcast communication channels Media that are broadcast over the airwaves, including radio and television.

Bundled (price) Two or more products that may be combined, and thus offered for sale at one price that is attractive to customers.

Business cost The price paid to obtain or produce an item required to operate a business.

Business plan A formal statement of business goals, an explanation of how the goals can be achieved, and the detailed steps for reaching the goals.

Capacity (service) The different service-related situations and outcomes that exist when establishments are busy and when they are slow.

Casual restaurants Restaurants that provide table service to guests and serve moderately priced food in an informal atmosphere.

Causal research Research that looks for cause-and-effect relationships.

Cell phone application (app) Short for *cellular phone application*; a computer application that runs on advanced cellular phones.

Chain restaurant A group of restaurants, each of which uses the same brand identifiers.

Check average The average amount spent by each guest visiting an operation.

Clearinghouse An in-house coupon department or third-party firm that specializes in processing coupons and providing other marketing assistance to track coupon origins and patterns of use.

Co-branding When two companies join together to share the expense of marketing the products and services each company offers to its own customers.

Commercial foodservice operation An establishment, such as a restaurant or bar, that is typically open to the general public.

Communication channels The means by which a business talks to its customers.

Community relations Interactions with the people in the local area to create awareness of and trust for a business.

Competitive advantage A characteristic that makes an establishment different from and superior to its competition.

Competitive analysis An analysis that examines other establishments that offer similar products.

Concept statement (business plan) The part of a business plan that details exactly what type of establishment will be created.

Consistency (service) The same level of service every time the guest visits the establishment.

Consumer rationality The tendency of buyers to make their buying decisions based on their belief that the purchase will be of direct benefit to them.

Contacts Participants in a social network.

Contribution margin (CM) What is left over after the food cost of a menu item is subtracted from the menu selling price.

Convenience restaurant A facility at which a customer usually eats because it is very easy for him or her to do so.

Corporation A formal business structure recognized as a legal entity having its own privileges and liabilities separate from that of its owners.

Crisis management The manner in which a business handles a major event that threatens the reputation and survival of the business.

Customer appreciation Activities designed to thank customers for their business.

Customer loyalty A situation where customers make frequent, repeat visits to an operation, proving that marketing efforts are working.

Cyclical (cycle) menu A menu planned for a specified time period and then repeated.

dba An abbreviation that means "doing business as," typically used when a sole proprietor's business is operated under a different name.

Demographic Information including customer's age, gender, race, geographic location, or other personal characteristics.

Descriptive research Research that focuses on revealing details about a market population.

Destination restaurant An establishment that customers visit primarily for the sake of the visit itself.

Direct labor cost The cost for preparing and serving all guest meals in a given period, calculated by multiplying employees' hourly wage by the number of hours worked.

Direct mail Mail sent to the home or workplace of potential customers.

Discretionary income The money left after a person has met all his or her expenses or debts.

Drive-through customers Customers who place and receive their take-away food orders without leaving their cars.

Du jour menu A menu that changes daily.

Economic environment Factors that directly affect the purchasing power and the spending habits of those in a target market.

Entertainment district A collection of restaurants and foodservice establishments, nightclubs, and music venues grouped in one geographic area that attracts a large number of customers.

Event sales Personal selling undertaken by an establishment's managers, also referred to simply as "sales."

Executive summary (business plan) A document that provides readers of a business plan with the highlights of the plan.

Exploratory research Research that focuses on understanding more about a situation and defining it very clearly.

External marketing activities Activities that involve sending messages to guests outside a restaurant or foodservice operation.

External pricing factors Conditions outside an establishment's control when pricing its menu items, such as economic conditions or seasonality of products.

Fad A short-term increase, sometimes quite large, in the popularity of some product or service.

Farm-to-fork The path food follows from those who grow or raise it to those who will prepare and serve it.

Fast-casual restaurants Restaurants that do not provide guests table service, but their food quality, overall service level, and décor is intended to be higher than that typically found in a quick-service restaurant.

Features Characteristics of the actual menu items and services sold to guests.

Financial plan An estimation of the cash needed to open a business or buy an existing business.

Fine-dining restaurants Restaurants that offer guests the highest-quality food and full table service.

Focus group A small-group meeting designed to learn what people think of a new product, service, or idea.

Food allergies When the body mistakes an ingredient in food as harmful and creates a defense system (antibodies) to fight it.

Food cost The expense of the food products used to make the menu items an operation sells.

Food cost percentage The food cost divided by the revenue generated from the sale of the food.

4 Ps of marketing The four key ingredients—product, promotion, place, and price—that managers use to create their own recipes for marketing their operations.

Frequency The average number of times a single viewer is exposed to an ad during a given time period.

Frequent dining program A reward program used to increase customer loyalty and provide an incentive to customers who purchase a specified number of meals or items or visit an establishment a required number of times.

Fringe benefits Costs including labor-related items such as employee health care, vacation and sick leave pay, retirement contributions, or other benefits that may be paid all or in part by the employer to benefit the employees.

Graphics Visual representations that may include photographs, drawings, numbers, symbols, maps, and diagrams.

Gross profit A company's revenue minus its cost of goods sold.

Guest Anyone using an establishment's services.

Guest loyalty program The policies and procedures managers put in place to identify the specific ways an operation will reward its best customers.

Guest profile A marketing tool that helps managers focus on the specific characteristics of guests they hope to attract to their operations.

Halal Food that is lawful or permitted under Muslim dietary laws. Prohibited food items include alcoholic beverages and some meats and meat by-products.

Hard data Data that can be readily quantified by numbers or statistics.

Household All of the people who occupy the same dwelling.

Inseparability (service) The tendency of restaurant and foodservice customers to connect the quality of service provided with the personal characteristics of the employee who provides it.

Intangibility (service) A characteristic that is not able to be seen, touched, or held before or after it is experienced.

Internal marketing activities Activities designed to send messages to guests who are already physically present in an establishment.

Internal pricing factors Factors affecting pricing decisions that management can control, including financial goals, food costs, labor costs, and other operating expenses.

Internet-based communication channels Computer programs that allow for one-way or two-way communication between Internet users.

Junk mail Mail that is routinely seen as a nuisance and that is often discarded without opening.

Kosher Food prepared according to Jewish dietary laws. Ingredients including pork, rabbit, catfish, and any shellfish cannot be part of a kosher meal.

Labor cost The amount paid to all employees for preparing and serving each meal.

Lacto-ovo-vegetarians Vegetarians who add both dairy products and eggs to their vegetarian diets.

Lacto-vegetarians Vegetarians who will consume dairy products in addition to their vegetarian diets.

Leading The vertical spacing between lines of type.

Lifestyle The patterns in which people live and spend time and money.

Market environment The economic, legal, vendor, and competitor conditions faced by a business.

Marketing The formal process of telling and showing potential customers how their needs and wants will be met by a specific operation.

Marketing activities schedule A schedule used to guide marketing efforts that identifies what will be done, when it will be done, and who will do it.

Marketing information system (MkIS) A combination of tools and procedures for collecting, analyzing, and distributing marketing information that is used for developing, implementing, and evaluating marketing activities.

Marketing mix The strategies and tools managers use to effectively market their operations.

Marketing plan A detailed listing of specific activities designed to reach the revenue goals of an operation.

Market positioning How an operation gets its target market to notice its products and services and consider them for future purchase.

Market research A process that seeks to obtain relevant and accurate information about particular groups of people or segments in a market.

Market segment A category of customers based on demographic variables such as age, ethnicity, education, or income level.

Market share The number or value of units sold by a business during a given period, which is expressed as a percentage of the total market size.

Market size The number or value of units sold to an entire market in a given time period (normally a year).

Market trends Long-term increases or decreases in some factor outside an establishment's control.

Mass marketing The process of treating everyone in the market as having the same needs and wants.

Media kit A packet of information given to media representatives to answer questions they might have about a business or organization; also called a **press kit**.

Media relations Providing publicity materials to the media and working with media representatives.

Menu layout The placement of items on the menu, normally by menu item classification.

Menu mix All of the servings of a menu item that are sold compared to the total sale of all competing menu items.

Merchandising All of the activities retail managers use when selling their products.

Mise en place Preorder preparation work in a restaurant or foodservice operation's kitchen.

Needs Emotional or physical requirements that occur when a person is deprived of something, such as food.

News release A brief presentation of promotional information written in a general and timely news format; also called a **press release**.

Noncommercial foodservice operation An operation not typically open to the general public whose goal is to provide cost-effective meals for a specially targeted audience; also commonly referred to as a nonprofit or institutional foodservice.

Objection A reason given by a potential customer that could justify a decision not to buy.

Objective measure A measure that can be used to evaluate real changes in data.

Organic food Food items grown by farmers that emphasize the use of renewable resources and the conservation of soil and water to enhance the environmental quality for future generations.

Other operating costs Expenses that are not related to food or labor.

Ovo-vegetarians Vegetarians who add eggs to their vegetarian diets.

Packaging The physical manner in which a product is presented to customers.

Partnership A business structure consisting of two or more owners who agree to share in the profits and losses of a business.

Partnership agreement A contract that details the rights and responsibilities of each co-owner of a business.

Payback period The length of time it takes for an investment to pay for itself.

Payback ratio A ratio that compares the money returned over the life of the investment to the amount of the investment.

Peer group A social group consisting of people who are equal in such respects as their interests, age, education, or socioeconomic status.

Personal selling The presentation of a marketing message delivered by one or more employees of a business for the purpose of making a sale.

Place The location of the operation or the way the product is delivered.

Placement The location of a product's display or the location of the advertising piece used to promote the product.

Point of purchase (POP) Display of products in locations where customers make their buying decisions, such as near the cash register.

Point-of-sale (POS) system A system that records an operation's sales, product usage, and other important information on a daily, by shift, hourly, or other basis.

PR campaign A series of targeted activities, promotions, and advertisements designed to raise awareness or enhance the image of an establishment.

Premium Merchandise offered to customers for free or for a low price as an incentive to purchase a product.

Press kit A packet of information given to media representatives to answer questions they might have about a business or organization; also called a **media kit**.

Press release A brief presentation of promotional information written in a general and timely news format; also called a **news release**.

Price What a customer gives up to obtain a product from an operation.

Price point The position, or point, an establishment's prices hold on a scale of lower- to higher-priced menu offerings.

Pricing strategy A rule that guides the price-setting effort, also known as pricing objectives.

Primary information Data that are carefully collected to address a specific business need.

Prime costs Food costs plus labor costs.

Prime real estate (menu) Areas on a menu most frequently viewed by customers.

Prix fixe menu A menu that consists of predetermined items presented as a multicourse meal at a set price.

Product The product or feature sold by an operation to a customer.

Profit formula Revenue − Expense = Profit.

Profit-oriented pricing A strategy in which target profits, which can be a particular dollar amount or a percentage of revenue, drive prices.

Pro forma A detailed estimate of the income, expenses, and profits achieved by a business over a specific time period.

Promotion The means of communication between an operation and a customer.

Prospecting Trying to find new customers.

Psychographic Characteristics of a customer that relate to that customer's personality, values, attitudes, interests, or lifestyle.

Publicity Information about an establishment that is distributed for free but is not produced by the establishment.

Public relations (PR) The part of an establishment's communication activities that addresses the operation's image in its community.

Public service Activities undertaken by a business for the good of a community or for members of society at large.

Quick-service restaurants (QSRs) Restaurants characterized by their limited menus, fast service, and modest prices.

Reach The estimated number of unduplicated audience members that tune in to a particular channel or program at least once during a reported time period.

Return on investment (ROI) The **payback ratio** expressed as a percentage. The formula for calculating ROI is: Lifetime dollars returned ÷ Dollars invested × 100% = ROI.

Revenue The sales achieved by an operation in a specified time period.

Sales dollar percentage The percentage of sales a menu item accounts for, expressed in dollars rather than volume.

Sales-oriented pricing A strategy whose goal is to maximize sales volume, or total revenue, rather than profit.

Sales promotion A short-term activity designed to encourage the purchase of a specific product or service.

Sales volume The number of times a menu item sells in a specific time period, such as a day, a week, or a month.

Sales volume percentage The percentage of guests who selected each menu item.

Sample The people who represent a target market. Also, a small amount of product offered free to customers to try.

Sample size The number of sample units to be researched.

Sample unit The smallest element being researched, such as a business, family, or individual.

Secondary sales Sales that occur when a person orders a promotional item and then buys another item at the same time, such as a drink or an appetizer.

Secret shopper A person who visits an operation pretending to be a customer, orders a meal, and then provides feedback on its taste and appearance, and quality of service.

Service Actions or benefits provided to buyers of a product.

Service industry Companies that primarily earn revenue by providing products and intangible services such as food, lodging, or transportation.

Shareholder An individual or group that owns one or more portions (shares) of a corporation.

Signature item A menu item that customers associate with a single restaurant or chain of restaurants.

Snail mail The traditional form of mailing in print format.

Social media networks Networks consisting of individuals who stay electronically connected for reasons such as friendship or shared knowledge.

Socioeconomic status The financial position of a consumer or group of consumers relative to other consumers.

Soft data Data that are not objective and usually consist of informal comments or opinions; for example, statements such as "I think this is a good investment."

Sole proprietorship An operating business structure in which one individual owns, and frequently operates, the business.

Sommelier A service staff member who assists customers in selecting wines to go with their menu choices.

Spam Unsolicited email or other forms of communication.

Special event A one-time or periodic occasion that provides a special incentive for customers to patronize an establishment.

Spot (broadcast) Typically a 15- or 30-second broadcast time period on either radio or television that occasionally may run up to 60 seconds.

Standardized recipe A recipe that gives a known quality and quantity at a known cost.

Start-up funds The amount of money an owner currently has on hand, as well as the total amount needed to start the business.

Status quo pricing A strategy whose goal is to maintain an establishment's competitive position relative to the other operations in its market.

Strategic business segment A specific revenue-generating source.

Strategic marketing activities Activities that address an operation's basic business objectives.

Subjective measure A measure that has no common standard; different evaluators can come to different conclusions about the same performance change, such as saying that "business has picked up."

Suggestive selling Personal selling undertaken by service staff that takes the form of making recommendations or suggestions to guests about items the guests might be interested in buying.

Sweepstakes Games of chance that usually require customers only to submit their name and contact information.

SWOT analysis A process that identifies an operation's strengths and weaknesses and examines its opportunities and threats.

Table d'hôte menu A menu that offers an entire meal at a set price.

Table turn The number of times a dining-room table is occupied during a meal period.

Tactical marketing activities Activities that focus on how things are done.

Tag line A three- to seven-word phrase that accompanies a logo, which is easily remembered by customers.

Targeted marketing Marketing that treats people as different from each other and makes a focused appeal to the distinct portion of potential customers that make up an establishment's target market.

Target market Potential customers whose specific needs and wants the organization will seek to meet.

Target profit The amount of profit an owner hopes to achieve.

Total contribution margin A number determined by multiplying the contribution margin for each menu item by the number sold of that item.

Trademark A brand identifier that has been given special legal status so that only its owners can decide when and how it may be used.

Traffic The total number of customers served by a business.

Trial The purchase and use of a product or service for the first time by a particular customer.

Type size The size of a letter or character, measured in "points," which are a unit of print measurement—72 points equal 1 inch.

Upselling A personal selling strategy where the server provides guests opportunities to purchase related or higher-priced products that the guest wants, but often for the purpose of making a larger sale.

Usage The number of times a particular customer frequents a business in a specific time period.

Value pricing Pricing products and services based on their worth in usefulness or importance to the buyer.

Value statement A concise description of the value an operation's targeted customers will experience when they purchase its products and services.

Variance The difference between planned results and actual results.

Vegans Vegetarians who eat no food items of animal origin, including milk, eggs, and honey.

Vegetarian A person who consumes no meat, fish, or poultry products.

Vendors The people or organizations that sell the goods and services an establishment needs to operate.

Wants Desires that are shaped by a person's culture and personality.

White space Blank space on a menu with no text on it.

Wine list A special menu that includes only wines and their prices.

Wireless communication channels Computer-based and non-computer-based systems that deliver information via public airwaves, including Web sites, email, social media, and cell phone applications.

INDEX

NOTES

NOTES

NOTES

NOTES

NOTES